ENDANGERED CHILDREN

Neonaticide, Infanticide, and Filicide

PACIFIC INSTITUTE SERIES ON FORENSIC PSYCHOLOGY
Edited by Harold Hall

With the support of Pacific Institute for the Study of Conflict and Aggression, Kamuela, Hawaii

Titles in this Series

Understanding and Preventing Violence: The Psychology of Human Destructiveness
Leighton C. Whitaker

Detecting Malingering and Deception: Forensic Distortion Analysis (FEA), Second Edition
Harold Hall and Joseph Poirer

ENDANGERED CHILDREN

Neonaticide, Infanticide,
and Filicide

Lita Linzer Schwartz
Natalie K. Isser

CRC Press

Boca Raton   London   New York   Washington, D.C.

BP

Library of Congress Cataloging-in-Publication Data

Schwartz, Lita Linzer.
    Endangered children : neonaticide, infanticide, filicide / Lita Linzer Schwartz, Natalie K. Isser.
        p. cm. — (Pacific Institute series on forensic psychology)
    Includes bibliographical references and index.
    ISBN 0-8493-1309-0
    1. Infanticide. 2. Filicide. 3. Abusive parents — Psychology. I. Isser, Natalie. II. Title. III. Series.

HV6537 .S28 2000
364.15′23—dc21
                                                        00-028948
                                                           CIP

No claim to original U.S. Government works
International Standard Book Number 0-8493-1309-0
Library of Congress Card Number 00-028948
Printed in the United States of America 1 2 3 4 5 6 7 8 9 0
Printed on acid-free paper

6/16/04

Preface

Are Children Expendable?

Drought is one of Mother Nature's means of population control. Tens of thousands can die from one outbreak of plague or one flood. Countries and cultures often control population growth by war, with thousands killed or starved to death on each side. Those societies whose economies cannot support a growing population enact population-limiting laws or simply practice wholesale neonaticide when families grow too large or the newborn is the "wrong" gender (i.e., female), for all cultures' moral codes are constituted within the exigencies of survival. A case can be made that while infanticide is abhorred, it is routine in societies lacking the resources to feed all their children (Posner, 1998). Scheper-Hughes (1989) noted that in the "impoverished Third World today — women have had to give birth and to nurture children under ecological conditions and social arrangements hostile to child survival, as well as to their own well-being" (p. 14). Under these adverse conditions, women either purposely neglect or allow weak and infirm infants to die as part of their policies to ensure the well-being and survival of the rest of their families.

Although we are more aware today, as the 20th century ends, of instances of child-killing, this crime is not a modern phenomenon. Despite universal reprobation, neonaticide and infanticide have been practiced on every continent and by people on every level of cultural complexity, from hunters and gatherers to those in "higher" civilizations, including our own ancestors and contemporaries. "Rather than being the exception, it has been the rule" (Williamson, 1978, p. 61). People are horrified when parents kill their children, and the media focus a great deal of attention on such crimes. It is likely that we are more aware of such occurrences today simply because modern communications carry these news items farther and faster than in the past. This may also provoke "copycat" cases as less mentally stable or less capable parents see killing their children as a solution to their problems, whatever those may be.

Today, most societies deplore child homicide, and many debate the right to abortion. Population problems, though, exist now as they have in the past.

In a sense, those individuals who commit neonaticide, infanticide, or filicide are also practicing population control, but after the fact of birth instead of before conception. These individuals and their acts against their children are our subjects of study. Child-killing within the family can be divided into three categories by the age of the victim: neonaticide, infanticide, or filicide. The murderer in these cases is usually one of the child's parents; occasionally it is someone acting *in loco parentis.*

To begin with, we must provide a context for the crime by looking at the roles of neonaticide, infanticide, and filicide in history. To do this, we will discuss these crimes as they occurred in biblical and ancient times and up to our modern era. Apart from historical research, we know that these crimes were also the core of much literature, from *Medea* (Euripides, 431 B.C./1938) to the contemporary novel, e.g., *The Angel of Darkness* (Carr, 1991), and were certainly evident in many folk and fairy tales still read to children. These crimes also often have a cultural endorsement that we in the U.S., and in most Westernized cultures, do not quite comprehend.

We will focus on neonaticide which is not a culturally supported matter, but rather an individual one, and we will also keep this crime distinct from infanticide and filicide as they occur under different circumstances. An abundance of questions arise from each of these crimes. These questions lead inevitably to discussion of the politics and semiotics involved in contraception, abortion, and sex education.

Depending upon the circumstances of the individual case and, to a lesser extent, the community in which the neonaticide occurs, how much media attention is given to the specific case? What is the effect of media focus on the crime and its perpetrator(s)? Does media publicity affect the penalty to be paid by the murdering parent(s)?

In some cases, the mother of an abandoned neonate may not be found, as often happens in large cities. How does she live with herself afterward, even if she is not punished by the courts? If she is found, should she be regarded as legally insane at the time of the crime or as guilty of manslaughter or first or second degree murder? To what extent should her age and/or circumstances be considered in weighing both the charge and, assuming she confesses or is found guilty, the penalty? Is imprisonment the appropriate penalty? These questions lead to examining the crime from the perspective of therapeutic jurisprudence. If the baby's father was involved in the neonaticide, does that change the legal perspective? If he was not involved, should he be permitted to escape any penalty for his role in the pregnancy which led to the crime? The law varies from community to community, as well as state to state and nation to nation, and has changed over the centuries. Awareness of these variations is necessary to the construction of any new policies.

Many of these same questions arise in cases of infanticide and filicide, with other issues added to the list. In an era when births are shown in almost complete detail in soap operas or "family" television shows, there seems to be little excuse for anyone to be uninformed about infantile crying and bodily functions. What psychological factors operate to repress such knowledge in the minds of those who kill infants for crying too long or too often? When social welfare agencies exist in virtually every community in the U.S., why are some parents so overwhelmed by child care that they murder a child rather than seek outside help? In cases where the parents separate, why does one parent kill the child(ren) rather than provide child support or permit the other to have visitation or shared custody? Why are children the victims of their parent's inabilities to cope with life?

The issues of sex education, contraception, abortion, and even euthanasia are related to some of the proposals to cope with these dilemmas, but they are fraught with sharp political nuances and insuperable divisions of opinion and passion. The chapters to follow will try to treat these questions with objectivity. They will also not only provide sociobiological, historical, and literary perspectives on neonaticide, infanticide, and filicide, but seek to answer the many psychological questions that arise from these crimes. In short, we will examine the mothers' backgrounds and motives; the role, if any, of mental illness; the response of the legal system in terms of charges and penalties; and future directions of preventive measures.

The Authors

Lita Linzer Schwartz, Ph.D., is a graduate of Vassar College, Temple University, and Bryn Mawr College, and is Distinguished Professor Emerita of The Pennsylvania State University's Abington College (née Ogontz Campus). A licensed psychologist in Pennsylvania, she also holds a Diplomate in Forensic Psychology from the American Board of Professional Psychology. She has received three awards from Penn State: "Outstanding Teacher" from the College of Education Alumni (1981–1982), Christian R. and Mary F. Lindback Award for Distinguished Teaching from the University (1982), and "Career Achievement" award from the College of Education (1992).

Dr. Schwartz is a Fellow of the American Psychological Association, Pennsylvania Psychological Association, and American Academy of Forensic Psychology. She is a member of the International Council of Psychologists, Academy of Family Mediators, Association of Family and Conciliation Courts, and the Professional Academy of Custody Evaluators. She has also served on the editorial boards of several professional journals.

In addition to teaching, she is actively involved in a number of writing projects on topics as varied as adoptive and surrogate parenting, cults and sects, media violence and its impact, gifted children, and female artists and photographers. For relaxation, she is an active photographer.

Natalie Isser, Ph.D., is a graduate of the University of Pennsylvania, and is Professor Emerita of The Pennsylvania State University's Abington College.

She is a member of the American Historical Association, The Western Society for the Study of French History, and the Delaware Valley Association of Modern European Historians. In addition to the books and articles co-authored with Dr. Schwartz, she has written on French anti-Semitism, human rights, and French public opinion and diplomacy during the Second Empire.

She teaches part time and has continued research on a variety of topics such as American melodrama, movies, and history; and the social and cultural roots of American populism.

Endangered Children is the third book co-authored by this interdisciplinary team. They have also co-authored more than ten articles and conference presentations, in addition to developing and co-teaching a course in "Cultural Pluralism." Their book, *The American School and the Melting Pot,* was named an "Outstanding Academic Book, 1986–1987" by *Choice,* publication of the American Library Association.

Acknowledgments

We are very appreciative of the interest and effort provided by the Pennsylvania State University's Abington College Library staff, especially Jeannette Ullrich and Binh Le, who guided us through innumerable computer mazes and found the "unfindable" sources when we could not. We are also appreciative of Steve Isser's input with respect to legal sources.

Natalie K. Isser
Lita Linzer Schwartz

Table of Contents

Children: An Endangered Species Throughout History

1

This chapter and Chapter 2 emphasize the historical, cultural, literary, and sociobiological connections of neonaticide, infanticide, and filicide. Including these aspects provides a context for understanding not only these homicidal acts, but why our horror at them is affected to a greater or lesser degree. This background also reveals attitudes toward women which permeate societies and indeed is taught to little children in fairy tales which feature wicked figures (wolves, ogres, and others) who kill children, as well as wicked stepmothers who abuse them.

Those who are familiar with the Bible of Western religions are also familiar with the story of Moses, the infant who was abandoned in a basket which floated on the Nile. They are aware that first-born children were slain when Moses, long since rescued and grown to manhood, sought to lead his people out of Egypt, although it was not the parents who killed them. The implication is that this Divine act was in the cause of a greater good — convincing Pharoah to release the Hebrews from slavery. This biblical tale has been replicated in the New Testament and in other religions, indicating the universality of the religious themes which often employ the metaphor of abandonment or murder of the first-born male.

It will quickly become apparent from the historical and cultural surveys that poverty, whether of the individual or of the society, plays a significant role in whether or not children are allowed to live. When it comes to literature, however, emotions dominate the motives — anger, jealousy, shame, revenge — and these tend to reflect the era and culture in which they were written. Literature is also the vehicle by which the artist explains gender, power, and moral relationships between individuals and society.

Resnick (1970) was the first to define neonaticide as the killing of an infant at or within hours of his birth, while infanticide was the murder of a child up to 1 year of age, and filicide, the murder of a son or daughter older than 1 year. These crimes were regarded as unnatural acts because women, especially, were supposed to love and nurture children. These unnatural acts were ranked in the past with witchcraft, heresy, parricide, sodomy, and murder — acts that challenged the established order and stability of society as well as the social order of the family. At all times and in all places, child homicide was also a constant reminder of the fragility of the prevailing moral order.

In the past, the killing of newborn infants occurred for a variety of reasons: sacrifice, primitive birth control, eugenics, shame, and fear of punishment for adultery or illegitimacy. Jimmerson (1990), for example, wrote of classical Chinese texts from as early as 2000 B.C., recalling cases of infanticide and infant abandonment. References to direct infanticide can be found in later texts. Jimmerson gave the example of the Legalist philosopher Han Fei, who, writing in the third century B.C., noted: "Moreover, parents' attitude to children is such that when they bear a son they congratulate each other, but when they bear a daughter they kill her. Both come from the parents' love, but they congratulate each other when it is a boy and kill it if it is a girl because they are considering their later convenience and calculating their long-term interests" (Jimmerson, 1990, p. 49). Other evidence shows that the practice continued in China: the Han dynasty's (206 B.C. to 220 A.D.) cases included punishment for infanticidal parents. Beginning in the 12th century, the government began to set up foundling homes for abandoned children, first in Fujian province, where female infanticide was particularly prevalent, and later in other central southern provinces (Jimmerman, 1990).

Culture and primitive superstitions also played a large role, with common customs and perspectives that transcended time and society, indicating a persistent thread of behavior and values. These cultural similarities are still prevalent today.

Gender and Child Homicide

Gender relationships have also played a very large role in the analysis of child homicides. Women were and are more often the victims of crime, abuse, battering, and rape, and women, alone, can bear children. Thus women in illicit relationships, whether actively participating or seduced or raped, were forced to bear the stigma of the relationships if they became pregnant. They bore it alone if the men involved did not wish to acknowledge their responsibilities. The women also had to endure the abortions or the burdens of unwanted children. Child homicide was and is the most prevalent violent crime of women, while men commit 87.5% of all homicides and most of the violent felonies (Minturn and Stashak, 1982).

Throughout history, prosecutions of and convictions for neonaticides and infanticides have been, on the whole, more merciful than those of other kinds of homicides. Most contemporary societies have also refused to punish neonaticides as they do other homicides. Customs and laws often treat child murderers in a selective and targeted manner. For example, it has been alleged that fathers are generally punished more severely than mothers (Resnick, 1970). This might be because gender stereotypes and cultural images of women produce responses which affect public sympathy and attitudes when women kill their offspring. (The truth of Resnick's allegation will be discussed in Chapter 5.) Women have been perceived either as the "mother," virginal and pure, or as Eve, the wanton temptress. The word "mother" brought to mind the symbol of the warm nurturer, and if reality failed this expectation, a cultural disappointment was evoked, frequently abetted by individual experience. Our cultural assumptions were that mothers are self-sacrificing, compassionate, caring, and above all, loving. We have often confused the notion of "good mother" with that of the "good woman" (Neal, 1995). Hence, one of the commonly held assumptions was that women were not criminals and that any illegal activities on their part was, therefore, pathological. Mothers who killed their infants, which is unnatural, were considered to be either "mad" or evil sociopaths ("bad") (Wilczynski, 1991). Women, when tried for crimes, were too often judged not just on the basis of their legal infractions "but also for their compliance or variance with stereotypically female behavior" (Wilczynski, 1991, p. 72). If the female had not conformed to assumed gender characteristics, she was perceived as "bad." This was especially true in cases of neonaticide and infanticide because these crimes contradicted the concepts of motherhood and femininity which involved nurturing, unselfishness, and above all the projection of the child's role in the family (Knelman, 1998).

Stereotypes affected the way in which we characterized and punished women. This often led to confused and ambiguous laws. Either the accused were good women who were victims, or unnatural and wicked. Since women *could not* kill their children if they were normal, there must have been mitigating circumstances such as mental aberrations. The arguments based on mental disturbance were frequently used to create sympathy and leniency for mothers, and were based on the belief that reproduction and lactation produced emotional disturbance. "This concept could appear to legitimate the notion that women are inherently unstable because of their biology, which, of course, had implications for the integration of women into spheres outside the domestic" (Lansdowne, 1990, p. 41). This behavioral pattern seems to have been derived from a combination of sympathy for the defendants, based on an awareness of the social environment which was so unfriendly to women, and on the difficulty of distinguishing between murder and natural infant mortality. All peoples, however, even those that practiced child sacrifice and exposure, as we shall demonstrate, abhorred child homicide.

The Literary Legacy

Infanticide came to possess enormous symbolic significance as evidenced in mythology and its treatment in other literature. The myths are the reflection and creation of cultures. They are, as in the *Medea* story and fairy tales, reconstituted and reordered at different times and places in order to help us grasp the essential values of our cultures. Often they are integrated into the popular culture and become the arbiters of taste and an integral part of the political dialogue. Literature, art, and popular culture, with their symbols, analogies, and sometimes simplifications, enable us to grasp some of the moral ambiguities inherent in all discussion of child homicide.

The problems of child homicide involve not only the crime itself, but also the social and economic environments that spawn the despair and insensitivity which make such acts possible. The codes of the communities which involve shame or disgrace, or punishment for transgressing sexual behavior dicta, also push young women to commit such evil acts. Psychological and sociological analysis, to be discussed later, can help to understand these factors which shape the way we regard and treat those who commit child homicide both in practice and law. However, it is the literature, stories, and popular tales which also provide rich insights.

Legacies of Ancient Cultures

In ancient Greece, exposure of newborns was not only permitted, but in some cases, especially in Sparta, enforced by law. Weak or deformed infants were destroyed either because of their imperfections or for fear that they would become a ward of and cost to the state. Plato called for eradication of babies "begotten by inferior parents," while Aristotle felt exposure was the best method of controlling overpopulation (Langer, 1974). Hellenist Greece's sex ratios favoring males indicated that exposure remained the choice of family and sex selection (Pomeroy, 1993).

The Romans continued this practice. Under the doctrine of Pater Potestas, only the father could choose to put his child to death (Lagaipa, 1990; Mays, 1993). The mother could not expose the baby without his authorization, but divorced fathers who denied paternity, and fathers of illegitimate infants had no rights (Lee, 1994).

Both Greek mythology and literature refer to this common method of birth control. Many of the infants exposed in the Greek stories — Zeus, Poseidon, Hephaistus, Asclepius, and Oedipus — were the products of illicit relationships between the gods and mortal women (Bennett, 1922). The founders of Rome, Romulus and Remus, were raised by wolves. Although the Greeks did abandon newborns as their best form of birth control, they nevertheless loved their children and, indeed, chose exposure or abandonment in the hope that some childless couples might adopt and save the children — another common thread in the myths.

Unlike the classical world, Judaism, developed in the Middle East, renounced any form of neonaticide and condemned all practices that smacked of child sacrifice or exposure. The Old Testament stories firmly negated any form of child homicide. These traditions were incorporated into Christian doctrines and firmly embedded into the Canon Law of the Catholic, and later the Protestant churches. During the Middle Ages, infanticide was firmly denounced, although it was difficult to detect as children died from overlaying, neglect, or disease (Langer, 1974). When detected, the church issued harsh penalties (horrible deaths) if the child was unbaptized or illegitimate. In contrast, married women who killed their children were treated more leniently — generally a public humiliation with public penances for a number of years (Kellum, 1973). Child homicide was regarded with severity, although infant mortality was very high. Literature and fairy tales thus contain matter-of-fact stories of child abuse and neglect. Yet even these myths and tales reveal a consistent horror of child murder in the ancient world.

Mythologies

Mythologies of all cultures contain tales of gods, goddesses, and heroes, of great deeds, wars, and catastrophes which reveal much of the morality and values of the cultures that created them. Ancient myths were also part of the religious and moral traditions, and contained a variety of metaphors to describe an incomprehensible and often inimical environment. They frequently elucidated an ideal of communal behavior and moral truths for individuals. Graves (1988) claimed that the study of myths should begin with archaeology, history, and religion other than psychology, and these old stories do indeed by their analogies reveal much early history. Dundes stressed the importance of folklore as "an autobiographical ethnography of a people, which makes implicit worldview principles and themes … explicit" (Bendix and Zumwalt, 1995, p. 20).

Fairy Tales

Fairy tales illustrate the poverty and difficulties of peasant life in pre-industrial societies — worlds of stepmothers, orphans, excruciating toil, life at a bare subsistence level, and overt unrepressed emotions. Peasant life was brutish, short, and mean, and fairy tales illustrated this well. *Hansel and Gretel* and "le petit poucet" were representative of the abandonment of children in hard times. Other forms of infanticide and child abuse occurred frequently in these stories. Parents turned their children out to become beggars; often they sold their offspring to the devil; or the parents ran away, abandoning their children (Darnton, 1985).

Mothers in these fairy tales often adhered to the stereotypical image of the mother described earlier, and it is the stepmothers who were cruel in the tales of *Snow White, Cinderella,* and *Hansel and Gretel.* In other cultures of the Middle East, Africa, and India, the myths often speak of the "Great Earth Mother Goddesses," goddesses of fertility and procreation, some of whom are also responsible for death. "The good mother and the evil mother of European folk tales were often seen to coexist in one unpredictable goddess of birth and death in mythologies throughout much of the world" (Amighi, 1990, p. 132).

Child Homicide in Literature and Opera

One of the most notable plays in the Western literary canon is Sophocles' *Oedipus,* in which the father, Laius, exposed his infant son because of a fateful prophecy on Mount Citharon. Laius wounded his son's ankles to justify his abandonment, but the infant was rescued by a shepherd. Oedipus lived to fulfill his awful destiny despite his father's attempt at filicide.

However, it is the story of *Medea,* based on ancient mythology and recreated by Euripides, which permeates our culture and symbolizes the inherent weakness of all societies.

Medea

Euripides' play has been performed on stage with regularity. It vividly uses the act of filicide to engage our emotions with the destiny of Medea and rivets the audience's outrage upon her crimes. It is a complicated emotional portrait which gains our sympathy even as it moves us to horror and anger at the protagonist's final act of revenge. Medea was a witch, a feminist, and a powerful woman. She was a woman obsessed by love who betrayed her father and killed her brother to help her lover, Jason, obtain the Golden Fleece. In return, he pledged marriage, protection, and love. She left her home to go to a strange land — Corinth — where she was regarded as an outsider and a barbarian. She was plagued by feelings of guilt, loneliness, rejection, and passionate love, all of which are recognized and pitied by the chorus in the opening scenes. Her husband, despite his debt to Medea, abandoned her for another woman — Creon's daughter, the princess of Corinth. Betrayed, she sought to avenge her honor. Medea vowed revenge and used her occult powers to kill Princess Glauce and Creon, and then wreaked final vengeance on Jason by killing their sons. In committing these unspeakable murders, Medea overstepped the bounds of revenge and honor, and was abandoned by the chorus.

Euripides' drama is especially effective because both Medea and Jason are archetypes — she, the overly passionate and erotic female who turns to violence, and he, the callous husband who, with sophist rationalization, can dismiss his wife and children and assume that, as long as he supports them, he is justified (Ashe, 1992). So important is this story that contemporary writers have characterized infanticide and filicide as, "the Medea syndrome" (Crouch, 1987). Indeed, much of the legal and psychiatric literature used Euripides' *Medea* as the paradigm of child homicide (Ashe, 1992; Reid, 1997).

The drama was based on earlier Greek myths which the audience of ancient times recognized and knew very well. In one older version Medea was partially a victim as Creon avenged Medea's murder of his daughter by killing 13 of Medea's 14 children and placed their bodies on display in the Agora, or marketplace (Graves, 1988). The Corinthians felt that this story was a stain on their reputation and, according to legend, commissioned Euripides to write a play where he absolved Creon of child homicide, made Medea the "barbarian" as the perpetrator of filicide, and heightened the dramatic effect by reducing the number of children slain to two (Graves, 1988). Other versions of the original myth involved the gods — Zeus, Hera, Aphrodite, and Eros.

Another explanation for the change and revision of the original myth by Euripides was laid to political events. Athens, the so-called center of Greek civilization, had repressed a rebellion against her domination by the Island of Melus and committed innumerable atrocities unworthy of a humane people. Euripides wanted his play to expose the fragility of civilization and its moral code (Hornblower, 1983). Since theater was, for the Athenians, their "school," he used the characters of Medea and Jason to reveal the qualities of intermingled good and evil, reason and emotion. He used the heinous crime of filicide as a metaphor for the inhumanity of the Athenians, but carefully kept the analogy more palatable to the Greeks by making Medea a sorceress and barbarian (Barlow, 1989; Vasillopulos, 1994).

The play still strikes a resonant chord within us. The relationships are familiar in their primitive emotions of obsession and erotic love. What gives the play such power is that Medea is not all evil. While she is not lovable, she is a powerful voice for women's rights, although that voice is muted by her terrible crime. It is the complexity of the characters and meanings of the filicide, honor, and duty that still command our interest.

Faust

One of the other legends that revealed the same ambiguity about neonaticide was that of Dr. Faustus. This legend, a part of folklore and literature, was the tale of men who sold their souls to the devil in return for riches, pleasure, youth, knowledge, or power. The fable permeated both popular and literate culture, and, like the Medea syndrome, the cliché, "Faustian bargain," has become part of our language. The legend arose from the tales of a real person, Dr. Johannes Faust, who was born in Knittlingen and died about 1540. He was probably a travelling doctor and con-artist who sold "magical" potions and cures. His notoriety led Luther to denounce him as the "Devil's brother-in-law" and Melanchton to characterize him as full of devils (Brenton, 1996). The story was so good that it gradually became a part of early German legends and, in 1587, appeared in a collection by J. Spies (Grim, 1988). It was so well-liked that it became a part of popular culture and frequently was performed as part of puppet shows and plays at local fairs. A variety of widely distributed pamphlets and prints also circulated the story.

The reoccurrences of neonaticide received renewed attention in the literature of the 18th century, especially in Germany in the 1760s to 1780s (Werner, 1917/1966). Both horror and sympathy for these unnatural crimes, based upon a sense of the callousness of seducers and rigidity of the law, pervaded the general literature. That was probably the reason that Goethe, the German poet and dramatist, included this theme in his work.

Goethe reconstituted the old legend into a powerful story that captured men's inner fears of aging, death, and the search for knowledge. *His* Faust made a pact with the devil to regain his youth and happiness. Part one of Goethe's long poem rested on the debates between Faust and Mephistopheles, in which Faust was regaled with song and wine in various funmaking establishments and had an illicit relationship with a young girl named Gretchen (a/k/a Marguerite). In the course of this ugly seduction, her brother was killed trying to defend her honor and her mother died from a poisoned draught under mysterious circumstances, possibly at Gretchen's hand. She bore an illegitimate child, and in her maddened and grief-stricken condition she committed neonaticide. She was captured and condemned to death for the double murders. On the eve of her execution, Faust commanded Mephistopheles to help him rescue her. They came to rescue Gretchen/Marguerite riding on the backs of magic horses, but she was frightened by Mephistopheles and prayed to God. She paid the full penalty of decapitation. However, God was merciful because she had repented of her sins, and her soul eluded Mephistopheles, as did Faust, who also repented and was saved. Goethe added the sordid story of Gretchen to the plot of the original legends, but hers is the minor story (Goethe, 1808/1950).

In this tale, the neonaticide was not the center of the metaphor, but rather Gretchen suffered for failure to avoid temptation and her lapse of moral scruples even though she was perceived as a victim of Faust and his evil companion's seduction. The story reflected, as our study will also show, the concept that women who kill babies are unnatural and must suffer from some form of dementia. Goethe also revealed the shame and humiliation that would befall her in the anger and contempt her brother expressed to her (Piers, 1978). She was punished by death for two murders. This was made more acceptable to readers because she had been suspected in the death of her mother.

The Faust story, as adapted by Goethe, appealed to an avant–garde culture, but its attraction was also felt by opera composers and their librettists. The two best known are the operas by Berlioz and Gounod. The *Damnation of Faust* by Berlioz was truer to the Goethe poem than Gounod's libretto. In the Berlioz drama, Faust was placed in Hungary, and the seduction of Marguerite occurred through the magic of Mephistopheles. Marguerite was condemned, but Mephistopheles made a pact with Faust — in return for his soul, the girl was delivered. She repented her sins and was saved.

The love story in Berlioz's opera was minor and only significant in explaining Faust's damnation. In contrast, the Gounod opera libretto revealed, in its story line, the problems of shame and abandonment which often led young women to deny their pregnancies and commit murder. This version focused on the love story between Faust and the young woman and was meant to appeal to a wider, more popular audience than the one by Berlioz.

"Popular culture in much of Europe allowed a degree of sexual contact during courtship and bridal pregnancy was common" (Wrightson, 1982, p. 7). If the girl or woman was abandoned or misled, however, the disapprobation became disproportionate to the dilemma and the young woman became a victim. Gounod's opera, while based on the Faust legend, placed the love story in this latter context. After Faust made his pact with the devil, he saw Marguerite and set out to woo her. She was a young and foolish woman led astray by the blandishments of the more sophisticated Faust (beautifully shown in the famous "Jewel Song") and was lured into an illicit relationship. Her brother, Valentine, tried to defend her honor, but was killed by Faust who, with Mephistopheles, was forced to flee. Subsequently, Marguerite had her baby, but in her shame lost her mind and committed neonaticide. She was condemned to die and was executed, despite Faust's attempts to save her.

Jenufa

A modern variation of this latter theme was powerfully portrayed in the opera, *Jenufa,* by Leon Janacek, first performed in 1916. In his libretto, based on a story by Gabriella Preissova, the heroine Jenufa is in love with young Steva and has an affair with him. He then abandons her in favor of the mayor's daughter. Jenufa has a child, but her former suitor, Laca, is unwilling to assume the care of his rival's child. Jenufa's stepmother, fearing that Laca's proposal is Jenufa's last chance for marriage, secretly kills the baby but assures

Jenufa that it died of natural causes. Jenufa agrees to marry Laca, but, on the day of her wedding, the baby's body is found and the stepmother confesses to the murder. She is arrested and, although there is widespread revulsion at her crime, Jenufa forgives her because the motive had been to make her happy. The opera ends with Jenufa and Laca gaining maturity, their love enhanced through suffering (Kobbé, 1919/1987).*

The power of the music and the story is augmented by the libretto which uses the theme of infanticide to illustrate the complexity and diversity of human motives and emotions. Moreover, by maintaining feminine stereotypes, the librettist keeps the heroine's purity fresh by making her the loving mother, and even the stepmother who commits the unspeakable crime out of love for her stepchild. The ambiguity of moral behavior in this opera again illustrates problems of mitigating circumstances which are so often cited in cases of child homicide, as will be seen in the coming chapters.

An Historical Note

During the Middle Ages, and even up to early periods in modern times, there was great credulity. Belief in witchcraft was widespread. Sometimes the midwife or wet nurse would be accused of witchcraft, or women accused of neonaticide or infanticide would claim that they were possessed by the devil. More common than actual murder was the abandonment of infants. The living newborn was left in a public place, sometimes on the steps of a church or convent in the hope that the child would be cared for by others.

If in the past it was difficult to discern a viable living infant, the law often used the legal fiction of concealment to either punish mothers who could not be detected as having murdered their infants, or to mitigate the sentences of mothers who were convicted of so doing. "From its inception as a sex-specific crime in 1623, infanticide has been concerned with theories about women. The initial object of the law was to punish single women for becoming pregnant and for refusing to live with their sin. Thus the crime was created to affect moral and social behavior" (O'Donovan, 1984, p. 264).

The law referred to was passed in England in 1623 and was made into an Act to prevent destroying or murdering of bastard children, on the presumption that a woman who concealed the death of her illegitimate child was guilty of murder. The law was designed to regulate illicit sexual conduct.

---

* Life imitates art as two legal cases illustrate. In 1923 a mother was convicted of manslaughter for the murder of her daughter's newborn. The Appellate court reversed the conviction because of insufficient evidence (*People v. Kirby,* 1923). Another mother took her 16-year-old daughter's newborn and left the child in a nearby garage where the child died from neglect. The baby, she claimed, would have caused trouble for her daughter and herself. She also killed the newborns of her two other daughters, who had delivered out of wedlock (*People v. Westfall,* 1961).

Since mothers could easily dispose of or hide their murdered infants, a law was passed against concealed pregnancies which was also aimed at illegitimacy. The rate of convictions rose, but despite the penalties, neonaticide remained commonplace (Oberman, 1996). The only way to rebuff the supposition of neonaticide was the testimony from another person that the child had been born dead — "even if the woman could prove that the child had been born alive and then died of natural causes" (Lansdowne, 1990, p. 43). The law was never applied rigorously and by the 18th century, it had fallen into disuse. The legal effort, however, did play a role in later literature.

The Heart of Midlothian

Sir Walter Scott's *Heart of Midlothian* was an historical novel set in 17th century Scotland and was based upon a Scottish law of 1690 that was almost the same as the earlier English one. The principal themes were about justice, rebellion, and social order. The parts of the plot centered on the act of concealment of pregnancy were based on an anonymous account received by the author of Helen Walker, a country woman who, 80 years before, refused to lie in court to save her sister's life and then had walked to London to seek a reprieve for her (Scott, 1830/1994).

The principal themes of the novel included the conflicts between English and Scottish cultures and between the emerging commercial urban development and traditional rural values. Scott also observed the problems of authority, social order, rebellion, and justice. Trained as a lawyer, Sir Walter Scott attacked the legal system as being rigid and corrupt, but necessary for the maintenance of social stability (cf Murphy, 1994).

In the novel, the heroine was Jeanie Deans, whose sister, Effie, a young Puritan girl, was seduced by George Staunton, a leader of the Porteous Riot (an actual historical event). He was the black sheep of a prosperous family and was reckless, dissipated, and irresponsible. Forced into hiding because of his role in the Riot, he was unable to help Effie. Effie gave birth to a baby boy in the woods, helped by an evil midwife named Meg Murdockson, who disappeared and took the newborn with her. Effie lost consciousness and, upon wakening, discovered that her infant was gone. She was accused of neonaticide because she had concealed her pregnancy and the baby had disappeared.

Her sister, Jeanie, refused to lie under oath that she knew of the pregnancy and Effie was convicted of neonaticide and condemned to hang. Even though she was pressured to do so, Jeanie felt she could not lie as a matter of honor (Cohen, 1993). However, she was determined to save her sister and walked to London to try to obtain a pardon from the Queen. Effie was granted clemency and sentenced to 2 years in exile. She then married Staunton, who had resumed his role as a gentleman, and she became a lady. Scott, in true Victorian fashion, needed to make the couple pay for their transgression. After all, Effie had borne a child out of wedlock and, though she had not murdered her baby, she *had* broken society's rules. Her son, called "The Whistler," had been reared by ruffians and smugglers. When his father, Staunton, learned of his existence and attempted to find him, the boy killed him unknowingly during a fracas and robbery attempt. The lad subsequently escaped and went to America to live with the Indians. Effie later retired to a convent. Scott (1830/1994) reminded his readers of the great truth: "that guilt though it may attain temporal splendor, can never confer real happiness; that the evil consequences of our crimes long survive their commission" (pp. 531–532).

The novel, though overly long and weakened by too many plot lines, possessed one element pertinent to this study. Scott captured the problem still extant even in our more enlightened times, that is, that so many young women refuse to acknowledge their pregnancies and manage to keep them a secret. Many even give birth alone and unaided. Although Scott based his partly realistic plot on the Law of 1690 (which was replaced in his own time by more lenient legislation), the reader is confronted by the gender discrimination of the law and society which seemed to be applicable to women only, as if they conceived and bore illegitimate children with no males involved. Scott also used the theme of illegitimacy and infanticide, as Ledwon (1996) pointed out, to emphasize the power of the mother in society. "The mother holds the power of life or death over the newborn infant, particularly if she conceals her pregnancy from society. The threat of the murderous mother is the threat that maternity … no less than that of paternity, may be only a legal fiction" (p. 16).

Popular culture of the 17th and 18th centuries reflected the same interest in the fallen women that Scott later recaptured in his novel. Scottish ballads recalled tales of seduced girls and their babies. The best known and most realistic was a song entitled, *Mary Hamilton,* which was revised and sung for almost a century. Mary Hamilton, the woman in the song, announces bravely that she has killed her newborn and she mounts the scaffold almost in defiance of a society which denigrated women's sexual and emotional needs: "Sae, weep na mair for me, ladies,/ Weep no mair for me;/The mither that kills ain bairn/Deserves weel for to dee" (Symonds, 1997, p. 57).

Adam Bede

One of the most widespread themes in the didactic novels of the 19th century was that of innocent, humble country girls who, after coming to the city, were seduced by predatory upper-class men and then abandoned to their terrible fates (Gillis, 1983). The purpose of these novels was not only to exhort young women to avoid temptation for moral reasons, but also to vividly illustrate the very realistic consequences of shame and despair which befell women who did not protect their virtue. George Eliot (1859/1981) played upon this theme in *Adam Bede*. Her narrative was based on a true experience that her aunt had had with respect to a young woman who had been convicted of infanticide and was to be executed.

The novel portrayed the interplay of class, gender, and communal mores in the development of the tragedy of neonaticide. The story was centered in the village of Hayslope where Adam Bede, a young carpenter, fell in love with Hetty Sorel, the young ward of tenant farmers (the Poysers). However, Hetty became involved in a secret liaison with Arthur Donnithorne, the local squire's grandson and heir, which resulted in her pregnancy. Overwhelmed with apprehension, she left the village, delivered her baby in another town, and then abandoned the baby to die. She was arrested for neonaticide and condemned to hang, although her sentence was later commuted to transportation — a terrible exile where she died alone. Arthur, her lover, filled with remorse, served 10 years in the army and then came home to resume his role as the local landlord and squire. Meanwhile, Adam Bede, suffering from Hetty's betrayal and her tragic fate, developed greater tolerance and patience for human frailties. He subsequently married Dinah, the local evangelical Methodist minister.

Eliot's novel depicted real people: rural tenant farmers and artisans as they struggled to earn a living and establish communal relationships. It was a "shame" society in which there were rigorous mores and social codes which Arthur and Hetty broke. Eliot, ever the Victorian moralist, however, was both sympathetic and accurate in creating portraits illustrating the complexity of motives and behavior. She used the story of neonaticide to demonstrate that even decent people, driven by inner weaknesses, could commit the most horrible crimes. Neonaticide in this case was never condoned, but the idea of mitigating circumstances, or clemency, became more acceptable, even though Eliot punished her characters for their moral lapses (Alley, 1993).

Beloved

The novels and plays discussed previously treated the cases of women who had been seduced, lured, or driven by erotic desires. They were complicit in their victimization in that they had yielded to temptation and defied their communal mores. They paid a great price for their moral frailties, far greater than their male counterparts — a matter to which we will return later — but both the men and women shared the blame for their victimization. There were other women, however, who were not willing partners in their predicaments of unwanted pregnancies. They were truly victims of the social system either because they were slaves or lived in harsh patriarchal societies.

Under the institution of slavery, the master claimed the woman's maternal history and her identity as a mother. She was subjected to sexual exploitation and to his will with no choice in the matter (Tobin, 1993). The slavery system had a particularly deleterious effect on mother and child. The mother was separated from her children, and was usually so enervated by hard work that she could do very little for them anyway. There were cases of slave women who offered resistance to that institution by refusing to bear children, i.e., sexual abstinence. Others used primitive contraceptives and abortificient drugs, and in a few cases practiced infanticide. Still, other slave women attempted escape, but some abandoned their babies knowing that the master and other women would take care of them (Fox-Genovese, 1988).

Toni Morrison (1988) used filicide as a technique to force readers to confront the nightmares of slavery in her novel, *Beloved*. In her book, Morrison, like Eliot, based some of her plot on real episodes in history and intertwined them with African-American myths. The plot is set in the period immediately after the Civil War. It tells the story of Sethe, a slave woman, who kills her second oldest daughter, Beloved, to spare her the dehumanization of slavery. Morrison used infanticide and filicide to illustrate the brutalization and spiritual degradation brought to fruition in slavery and the subsequent caste system in the South.*

Sethe's own mother had been raped, after which she abandoned her babies and attempted to escape. She was branded and hung. Sethe, herself, had married and given birth to three daughters. After the death of her good master, Sethe and her children escaped to freedom, but she was caught while nursing her youngest. Fearing for her daughters at the hand of the new — and harsh — master, she committed the one filicide, but was stopped before she could commit the other two. Sethe was tried for filicide but was defended by a white abolitionist lawyer who turned her case into an attack on the institution of slavery. She served 3 months in prison, and then went home to her surviving children at the home of her mother-in-law in Ohio. Haunted by the ghost of her murdered child, Sethe was ostracized by the community which regarded her act as evil, whatever her motives had been.

Morrison's novel used the acts of infanticide and filicide to raise questions about the motives that haunt and drive people — and especially those arising from brutal and degrading environments such as slavery and poverty. These murders also forced the reader to re-think what good and evil are. Sethe's deed, reprehensible as it was, represented "individual defiance to the oppression of slavery and the beginnings of claiming and defining the self, of breaking the physical and psychological boundaries of oppression" (Jones, 1993, p. 625).

---

* Margaret Garner was a slave mother who committed filicide in 1856. She had attempted to escape with her family and when faced with recapture by her master, killed one child and wounded two others to spare them the travails of slavery (Weisenburger, 1998).

Woman Warrior

Just as Toni Morrison was involved with the psychological effect of slavery upon women's lives, Maxine Hong Kingston, a writer, was more concerned with gender relationships and women's adjustments to the larger community. Her book, *Woman Warrior* (1989), somewhat autobiographical, speaks of a woman caught between two cultures. She was an ethnic Chinese, writing in the English language, but part of a family who was literate in Chinese. Kingston mixes family stories and Chinese myths in a fascinating tapestry.

Her book opens with the tale of the author's aunt, No-Name. It is a cautionary story for young people who might presume to defy the mores and bounds of the community. No-Name is so named because she disgraces her family and is, therefore, denied her identity and personhood. No-Name becomes pregnant out of wedlock in a society which tolerates no deviance and in which illegitimacy is the ultimate shame. On the night she gives birth, the villagers, furious at her sin, punish her by raiding her family's home, destroying the furnishings and killing the livestock. Humiliated and guilt stricken, the young woman drowns herself and her baby in a well.

The lesson was clear. Women were carefully monitored and their conduct scrutinized. Any deviations from established codes would not be tolerated, and any disgrace would also involve her family. The woman's role was clearly defined — to be subordinate as wife and mother to the will of the man, but clearly not to be defiled outside of marriage.

Alan's Wife

At the end of the 19th century (1894 to 1914), feminists used drama to express their visions of motherhood. Women began to protest their subordinate roles in both family and community. In examining their roles, they perceived their functions as serving either their husbands or their children or both. *Her needs, desires, and aspirations had to be suppressed in order to best serve the interests and needs of her family. She, therefore, could not exist for herself* (Fitzsimmons and Gardner, 1991, p. xii). *Alan's Wife*, written by Florence Bell and Elizabeth Robins at the turn of the century (1901/1991), was a protest against their culture's assumptions.

The heroine, Jean Creyke, kills her handicapped child. She does this because her husband is dead and she fears that if and when she is unable to care for the child, he will be placed in harm's way. She characterizes her deed as one of love and in the last act unflinchingly accepts her death sentence. Even this gesture is part of the feminist dialogue, for Jean can escape the death penalty for infanticide if she claims she was insane when she acted. Jean refuses, hoping to be reunited with her husband in death (Wiley, 1990). The play is essentially an "indictment of an uncaring society" in which Jean takes complete control and responsibility (Bell and Robins, 1901/1991). It is not a very good play and fortunately has not been revived. Though it is ostensibly about women's place in society, the unresolved problem is that of euthanasia — a topic that has preoccupied political debate and will be discussed later.

Saved

In the 20th century, especially in the idealistic period of the 1960s and 1970s, many became critical of a society besieged by a new technocracy and unsettled by cultural change and its instability. Child homicide became the vehicle by which one playwright criticized this society. Edward Bond (1965), in his play *Saved*, was not interested in gender relationships. His drama, produced in England in 1965, reflected his anger at a society corrupted by materialism and greed which he considered to be the outgrowth of an evil capitalist system. He used the murder of a child as a metaphoric device to engage our attention as to how the bottom strata of the community behaves in a "consumer-based and technologically driven society" (Hay and Roberts, 1980, p. 39).

The play is centered on a casual but lusty affair between two disreputable characters who consummate their affair in a careless and loveless fashion. The child who is the consequence of their sexual attachment is later murdered for no apparent reason other than as part of a meaningless whim. The horrible scene of men stoning a baby on the stage evokes the audience's visceral dismay, partly because those in the audience believe that children are meant to be protected because they are totally vulnerable. Through Bond's use of overt filicide, he called attention to the "cultural and emotional deprivation of our children that makes them dead even before they are assaulted" (Hay and Roberts, 1980, p. 51). The use of child homicide made this play very controversial, and it has provoked enormous emotional and angry reactions.

To Summarize ...

It is apparent that neonaticide, infanticide, and filicide have provided themes and plots for literature from ancient times to the present. The literary imagination offers an incisive illumination of the various past and contemporary cultural attitudes regarding women and maternity. Novels, dramas, popular songs, and narratives involve us in the various socioeconomic, psychological, and emotional environments which led to child homicides. Through analogy and metaphor, the artist depicts the ambivalence of the one who commits neonaticide — the intensity of despair and abhorrence coupled with sympathy for the mothers and their victims.

Often, the message conveyed is that society not only affirms the female's proper role, but also decrees what happens when she deviates from it. In other words, it is the society that is condemned through the act of a parent murdering a child. That the act was not simply the product of the author's imagination is evident when one examines historical and cultural patterns regarding these crimes, as will be done in the following chapter.

Neonaticide in Theory and in History: Who are the Perpetrators of Neonaticide?

2

Because child homicide has always occurred, social scientists and other professionals mystified by such unnatural behavior have long searched for a variety of answers. They have perceived nature as a benign force and life among other species as utopian. The search has been in varied and sometimes overlapping fields including sociobiology, cultural anthropology, and history.

Sociobiological Perspectives

As biologists and anthropologists advanced their knowledge of genetics, they extended their observations to other species, using newer scientific models based on closer scrutiny. These examinations of social and instinctive behaviors were more subtle and sophisticated, exemplified by the insect studies of William Hamilton in the 1960s, and then followed by the works of George Williams, Robert Trivers, Richard Alexander, and Edward O. Wilson, who carried on the studies of altruism and mating selection among animals.

This newer form of analysis, known as evolutionary biology or sociobiology, is a systematic study of the biological basis of all forms of social behavior including sexual and parental conduct for all living things. Destruction is not uniquely human; it occurs in living organisms among plants and animals and other mammals including primates. Most sociobiologists were more interested in animals than plants and were primarily zoologists. Older notions of animals' lack of cruelty, hierarchy, and even murder had to be discarded as sociobiologists observed animal behavior more closely. Hrdy (1992) studied primates (langur apes) very closely and discovered numerous examples of infanticide. Males killed babies that were not theirs in order to pair with their mothers. They also perceived animal species as seeking to maximize their reproductive needs and cooperating only to enhance their genetic interests (Hrdy, 1992). Reports of infanticides and cannibalism among non-human primates were noted (but not necessarily as a regular practice). "What is distinctive in human species is selective removal on the basis of conscious intent" (Dickemann, 1975, p. 1008). Anthropologists discovered evidence that there have been instances in human groups such as the Ache hunters-gatherers in Paraguay that permit infanticide on the grounds of infidelity and fatherless children (Wright, 1994). Ache hunters are very cooperative and the society seems benign, but if a father dies, the chances of a child being killed increases by four fold. "It's not uncommon for orphaned children to be thrown into their father's grave"(Zimmer, 1996, p. 73).

In the mid-1970s, studies of the genetic basis for some human behavior presented new ideas about evolution. Wilson's book (1980) was widely discussed and his theories gained some acceptance. He examined the behaviors of insect and animal life and began to discuss the integration of neo-Darwinian explanations of both genetic and animal behavior as pertinent to human development and behavior. He spoke of attempting to create data on the widespread incest taboo, infanticide, mental retardation, and schizophrenia, merging the efforts of biology with those of psychology, anthropology, and sociology to create a broad-based social science effort. Sociobiology became the analysis of social behavior as it emerged from organic evolution. The research devolved on two levels: an abstract method which depended upon mathematical models of genetics, ecology, and demography, and the concrete which analyzed specific problems of the species and their physical and social evolution.

Research, observations, and statistical analysis concluded that species' behavioral patterns, including humans, generally adapted to the best outcome for reproduction or the genetic continuation of future generations. Therefore, cooperation within a family, tribe, pride, or den is achieved as a means to bring about the desired goal of reproduction and, according to Daly and Wilson (1988), this idea has been "abundantly confirmed by recent research on nonhuman animals, and there is a growing body of empirical studies indicating its applicability to human sociality, too" (p. 520). Sociobiology thus became concerned with the complexity of social organization based upon demography, ecology, genetics, and other components of behavior in societies.

Some of these explanations are based on studies of altruism, aggression, and cooperation accompanied by the use of Darwinian natural selection. Mutations that occur as a result of natural and environmental adaptation are included in these theories (Dawkins, 1976). Thus sociobiology has created a model that makes evolution a part of social behavior as well. The models established among animals are clear and decisive, but when they were extrapolated to human behavior they were not as precise and, moreover, they aroused emotional distress among many scholars and thinkers (Lumsden and

Wilson, 1983). These concepts were difficult to accept because of the belief that sociobiology implied genetic determinism to human growth. Thus the propagation of these studies could only result in the preservation of racism and sexism. The propensity toward aggression or dominance could lead to acceptance of destructive human traits. Political ideology colored the emotional content of the debates (Montagu, 1980). Some scholars felt sociobiology was based on questionable speculation that would support the dominance of patriarchal society and a laissez faire attitude toward social problems. There were others who criticized sociobiology on a sounder basis. They argued that while biological imperatives were sound in the evaluation of insect and animal behavior they cannot be relevant to what is essentially the essence of humanity: the products of human consciousness, art, music, and philosophy. While they conceded that some human tendencies can be elucidated by zoological theory such as kin relationships and the incest taboo, as well as some sexual practices, the critics stressed that human beings have created a variety of social institutions and communities because they have free will and creativity. It is this mental agility that leads to culture beyond the descriptions of biology (Gould, 1980). Quadagno (1979) asserted that "in terms of logic and method, sociobiology cannot be applied to the analysis of complex human social behavior" (p. 109).

Others questioned the accuracy and validity of the models and scientific data (Williams, 1981). In contrast, Peter Singer noted "that the account of ethics sociobiologists offer is incomplete and therefore misleading. Nevertheless, sociobiology provides the basis for a new understanding of ethics. It enables us to see ethics as a mode of human reasoning which develops in a group context, building on more limited, biologically based forms of altruism" (1981, p. 149).

In response to its many criticisms, and as a result of continued research which was empirically based and scientifically rigorous, sociobiologists advanced insightful descriptions of the reproductive behavior of humans as well as animals. They also became more circumspect about the dominance of genes and began to explore the cultural contributions to human development (Durham, 1990). Scientists began to carry research even further afield and to conceptualize evolutionary theories about the mind and human intelligence.

Man was a product of both his genes and culture (which included history, economics, and environment) — "unique and remarkable properties of the human mind resulting in a tight linkage between genetic evolution and cultural history," according to Lumsden and Wilson (1983, p. 20). Genes and culture are inextricably linked in a circular fashion: genes provide the means of development and learning to absorb the culture which is, itself, consequently altered to adapt to change. This causes some people to function more adroitly in the modified society, and they then reproduce their altered genes.

"In sum," according to Lumsden and Wilson, "culture is created and shaped by biological processes while the biological processes are simultaneously altered in response to cultural change" (1983, p. 118). They began to elucidate a more ambitious program that sought to unite the biological and social sciences even more closely. They conceived of a theory of gene-culture as co-evolution which was a further extension of sociobiology and what they considered a further push to integrate the social and physical sciences. They hoped to forge new links between biology, economics, and even history. They further established three criteria by which sociobiology could be judged: 1) it must create rigorous explanations that have been speculative tenets of the social sciences; 2) it must be testable and it should be predictive (which at the present is not true for any of the social sciences); and 3) it should give rise to new questions as well as "identify previously unknown parameters and laws to be woven into a network of verifiable explanations from genes through the mind to culture" (Lumsden and Wilson, 1981, p. 346). Wilson's newest work, *Consilience*, has continued that search for the unity of human knowledge (1998).

Richard Alexander attempted to relate morality to biology by showing that "evolved human nature and morality are compatible, and … the great value of evolutionary understanding lies in its guidance, in developing appropriate and useful ideas and hypotheses about human activities and tendencies" (1987, p. 10).

Evolutionary psychology developed from the works of sociobiology as psychologists began to explore the mind in the same way that biologists were examining genetic human behavior (Buss, 1999). According to these thinkers the brain must have evolved according to the same evolutionary process as other organs. Pinker (1997b) claimed that the mind resembles the computer-modules designed to perform certain tasks. Therefore, these modules are pushed by their genetic instincts to love, cherish, and take care of children and parents. The interest in the relationship between genetics and culture created a new attention to how the mind works (Pinker, 1997b) which has been described as "the investigation and characterization of the innate psychological mechanisms that generate and regulate behavior" (Durham, 1990, p. 193). There was hope that the new psychology would help connect the new sociobiology and human behavior even more closely. The result was the belief that man's need to adapt to an ever changing and hostile physical environment necessitated genetic tendencies that fostered free will in order to be able to meet the challenges (Pinker, 1997b).

As research increased and became more refined, many scholars began to attribute new significance and value to the studies even if they still were uncertain of some conclusions. Wright (1994) argued that many of our ethical judgments may have biological origins, and if we want to develop a mean-

ingful morality we need to continue to learn more about our basic psychological drives. Continuing in this vein, Wright discussed the reasons
homicides occur.

Primitive societies also decried neonaticide, but those who carried it out
as social policy did so only for the following reasons. Unhealthy or handicapped infants were killed, as were those children born under difficult or
threatening circumstances (i.e., the mother had younger children and/or no
husband or in the case of twins). The population controls among primitive
peoples are consciously limited by abortion, infanticide, or prolonged abstinence. It was duly noted that among nomadic peoples restriction of population was necessary to fulfill nursing obligations and mobility of the group.
There was evidence of wide-spread abandonment of "deformed infants," and
in many communities there was frequency of female infanticide. These practices were believed to have dated from the Upper Paleolithic times (Carr-
Saunders, 1922, p. 113). The conflict between environmental demands of a
nomadic society and fertility needs were illustrated by the Australian aborig-
ines. Women on the move had to carry their children and goods, and they
could carry only one child. To facilitate the groups' mobility, efforts were
made to control fertility by prolonging nursing periods for as long as 3 or 4
years. Primitive abortion was tried and if that failed, neonaticide was practiced. Deformed children were smothered, and if the mother died in childbirth or while nursing, the child was also killed (Hughes, 1987).

These circumstances do not exist in developed or modern societies.
Certainly there is ample food and medicine, and today even single parenthood is acceptable. However, the studies of Daly and Wilson (1988) show
that a large percentage of child homicides in Canada are the murders of
stepchildren. Further, Wright suggests that some crimes are "committed by
the natural fathers who have begun to doubt — consciously or unconsciously
— that they are" (1994, p. 390).

Despite approbation and acceptance by some scholars, others still feel
uneasy about the implications of these biological studies. There is the fear
that human nature is being reduced to biological or genetic tendencies which
limit the chances for the amelioration of injustice and the ability to recreate
our societies (Rothstein, 1998). The speculations of sociobiology caused some
to question whether our laws should be modified to include genetic factors.
Jones (1997) claimed that while evolutionary biology revealed its influence
upon some responses, men were still capable of rational behavior and free
will. However, he continued, "the law should orient itself to take into account
the evolutionary influences that can help generate new legal strategies for
regulating human behavior" (1997, p. 1125).

Part of the new synthesis in the evolving work of the evolutionary biologist was the incorporation of anthropology and what came to be known as

cultural evolution (Durham, 1990). As noted, anthropologists have long studied ancient and modern primitive societies. Carr-Saunders (1922) was the first to show evidence of infanticide on a world-wide basis — and consequent studies have not abrogated much of his evidence.

Some sociobiologists claim that "all organisms, including people, are products of the historical process of differential survival and reproduction … " (Daly and Wilson, 1984, p. 487). While that factor may be appropriate for primitive peoples in hostile physical environments where there is a lack of sustainable food and shelter, it is inapplicable in modern societies where other psychological and cultural behaviors prevail under conditions of relative plenty. Factors such as illegitimacy, youth of the mother, stepparent households, or mental illness of the parent are more predictive of both neonaticide and infanticide than mere survival needs today (Daly and Wilson, 1984).

Killing of offspring was also observed across diverse cultures. These homicides were linked to the enhancement of the status and welfare of the family and were best illustrated by the case of Rajputs and other castes of northern India. Dickemann's study (1979) tried to explain the killing of daughters. Based on sociobiological analysis, she claimed, "Lineage needed wealth and high social status in order not to perish in bad times. The great cost of dowries hampered the accumulation of wealth, therefore higher-caste families often killed their female infants … because of the nature of the marriage system" (p. 50).

If this practice is so widespread and neonaticide persists even in the most technologically advanced societies where the notion is abhorred, then is this crime a part of evolutionary process and sociobiological in its origins? Pinker claimed that neonaticide was a way of conserving the family by sacrificing the infants in a harsh and unforgiving environment, and women's brains led them to these sacrifices (Pinker, 1997a). Sociobiologists point out the significant argument that nature provides bonding between mother and infant — in the nursing process — and leaves a gap of a day or two before the mother can nurse, during which the maternal instinct is not aroused. It enables the mothers and society to provide a space in which the infant can be abandoned and/or exposed. Thus they claim that "both biology and cultural tradition seemed designed to permit mothers, for a brief period, to practice infanticide" (Hrdy, 1984, p. 50).

Granzberg (1973) claimed that twin homicide was more likely to occur in societies that lacked sufficient facilities to enable mothers to properly rear two children simultaneously while tending to necessary chores for survival. His findings have been challenged by others who contend that twin homicide occurs more often in aggressive societies or those in which women have inferior status (Lester, 1986). Ball and Hill (1996) supported Granzberg's thesis by more rigorous analysis and concluded "that infants who are twins may be subjected to infanticide not because they are twins per se but because by virtue of being twins they manifest attributes that would cause them to fall into one of several categories under which any infant, singleton or twin, would be killed" (p. 863). The prevalence of this behavior, however, gives some credence to Pinker's assertions.

Despite the belief that neonaticide is part of "human nature," anthropologists also declare that primitive societies often display contradictory attitudes toward infanticide "that is both universally practiced and universally condemned" (Carr-Saunders, 1922, p. 115). Both abortion and infanticide were practiced occasionally, but they were considered socially undesirable, and, therefore, subjected to strict social regulation. Infanticide and neonaticide may be allowed only if they occur before the child has been named and accepted as a bona fide member of its society (Carr-Saunders, 1922). The less eligible a child is for membership in the group, the less seriously the act of killing the child is viewed. The fact that societies create sanctions against unrestricted infanticide suggests that mothers, though loving and nurturing, do kill unwanted infants (especially if they have borne and reared a number of children) (Carr-Saunders, 1922). Scholars should also be cognizant of the high mortality rate caused by natural causes in primitive societies.

Evolutionary social scientists deduce, therefore, that teenagers, faced by the birth of a child and desperate at their condition, will resort to established genetic patterns of behavior (Pinker, 1997a). Similarly, the findings of Daly and Wilson, in their studies, have statistically illustrated that infants in Canada and Great Britain are 60 to 70 times more likely to die at the hands of a stepparent than a natural parent, confirming evolutionary biologic analysis that stepparent homicide is the pattern observed in other creatures such as insects, birds, primates, and other mammals (1988). Thus these scholars suggest that another facet of selective infanticide has been observed in both nature and among men.

Despite this evidence, the conclusions are still highly speculative. Neonaticide is not widespread, although we are more aware today as the 20th century ends of instances of child-killing. This crime has never been prevalent or acceptable. Neonaticide since the Middle Ages has not been a culturally-supported matter, but rather an individual one. As already noted, all child homicide was condemned by Judaism, Christianity, and Islam. Yet the historical tradition records a continual account of instances of child abandonment and neonaticide. Amighi (1990) hypothesized that, given the difficult lives of average persons in unsophisticated cultures, "the infanticidal mother is expressing resentment against the new infant who is adding to her burdens or that an emotional detachment is evoked to permit her to abandon or kill her infant" (p. 135).

Cross-Cultural Perspectives

A Brief Look at Asian Cultures

Neonaticide or abandonment of baby girls was part of a long Chinese tradition based, as it was in India, on custom and economic necessity (sons were the only support for aged parents) as girls needed dowries which reverted to the new families. This made daughters a burden unless their marriages could provide upward social mobility by creating alliances with more powerful families. Opposition to this custom co-existed with the practice (Waltner, 1995). By the end of the 19th century there were attempts to bring relief to Chinese children through the creation of hospices and the suppression of some neonaticide (Leung, 1995). The 20th century Chinese Revolution and its rush to modernization led to the adoption of a one-child-per-family policy for many years which is only now being eased. Nevertheless, it is believed that many girls may have been killed and their bodies hidden, or neglected so that they died from disease, especially in the poorer rural districts, with none of these deaths recorded as infanticides. As in India, new technology, when available, allows for gender-directed abortions, although they are discouraged by the government (Hull, 1990; Johansson and Nygren, 1991; Li, 1991).

The urban populace have mostly cooperated and accepted the stringent regulations for childbearing. Contraception and sterilization are the preferred methods of fertility control, and women are sometimes coerced into having abortions although physical force is no longer used. Penalties such as fines and loss of privileges are used to enforce birth control policies. A sex imbalance which favored male babies over female seemed to suggest continuing female sex selection and neonaticide as well as female adoptions. The opposition expected in the countryside led the government to acknowledge parental preference for boys by allowing the couple, after a 5-year wait, to try for a second child if the first was a girl. In some areas, as the government moderated its policy, it even allowed a try for a second child if the first birth had been a male. In some underpopulated areas, even third and fourth children are sometimes permitted. The government's relaxation of its regulations, plus strict statutes against infanticide and antenatal sex selection, seems to have reduced lopsided gender ratios (Hesketh and Zhu, 1997).

Even in those societies in parts of China and India where daughters were perceived as a drain on their families' assets and were frequently abandoned, present day changes have been dramatic. The Indian government has sought to restrict population growth and to deter the sex selection that became possible with the availability of ultrasound in some locations, with mothers opting for abortion early in pregnancy if the fetus was female. As in China, the efforts to limit family size have been more successful than the efforts to limit sex selection.

In Japan it was long believed that the peasant population suffering economic distress limited the size of their families accordingly. However, more recent studies have shown that the limit was adopted not because of economic distress, but rather to increase their standard of living. The way to limit families in earlier centuries was believed to have been by abortion and neonaticide. Even that view is questioned by newer demographic studies which indicate that child homicides did exist, especially in pre-modern times (Hanley, 1983), but in relatively small numbers. Japanese fertility was controlled by the custom of long nursing, mobility, primitive contraception, and a high infant mortality rate from disease (Cornell, 1996).

Cultural Causes in the West

Homicidal mothers come from varying social classes and differing locales: rural, suburban, and urban. Studies in both the past and the present indicate that while the neonaticidal and infanticidal actions are similar in the end result, psychological and environmental circumstances vary widely, as do the periods in which the crimes occurred.

In medieval times, infanticide and neonaticide were viewed with horror along with parricide, heresy, witchcraft, and murder as crimes challenging to the established order. Whenever there was clear evidence of neonaticide in the records throughout late medieval and early modern Europe, it seemed there was a preponderance of illegitimate children killed by single girls or widows. What made the crime even worse in the eyes of many was the fact that these newborns had not been baptized (Riet, 1986). For most women, such pregnancies were socially disastrous and the woman and her family were disgraced (Ruggiero, 1992; Wilson, 1988). They were even more fearful of the public humiliation imposed by church authorities, loss of livelihood, and the certainty of social isolation and poverty (Shorter, 1975; Wrightson, 1982).

The church was more concerned that neonaticide was evidence of extramarital affairs, adultery, or illegitimacy (which was rarer then) than in the crime of murder. The absence of effective birth control devices meant that options were few for couples both in and outside of marriage. One factor that remained stable throughout history was the "association between infanticide and illegitimacy" (Kellet, 1992, p. 2).

What was more common in medieval times than actual murder was what could be considered homicidal neglect, e.g., children drowning in wells or falling into ditches, scalding deaths in boiling pots of water, or wandering away outside. Parents toiled long and hard and such neglect "would have been a fairly efficient means of ridding oneself of unwanted and demanding burdens but also the death would be acceptably accidental, at least by secular law standards" (Damme, 1978, p. 7). Another common cause of death of the young infant was "overlaying." It was the custom in poor families for infants to sleep with parents, and in many cases death of the child was probably deliberate, or so it seemed, especially because so many more female babies died than males (Damme, 1978; Kellum, 1973; Sauer, 1978).

During the Middle Ages and early modern times, there was widespread credulity in which the belief in witchcraft was widespread. Sometimes the midwife or the wet nurse would be accused of witchcraft as women arrested for neonaticide or infanticide sought exoneration by claiming that they were possessed. One of the more heinous superstitions used when encountering a dead child was the belief that Jews had killed him for use of the blood in rituals, rather than seeking the perpetrators of either neonaticide or infanticide. These latter beliefs persisted into modern times, as attested to by the Fokhancy affair in Rumania in 1859 and the Beiliss Affair in Russia in 1913. "Christians lose their children and the enemies of the Jews charge the latter with having kidnapped or killed them in order to use their hearts and blood for sacrifice … . These things happen under the completely false pretence [sic] that children were abducted and murdered by Jews …" (Schultz, 1991, p. 282). In these ritual murder accusations "the motivations ascribed to the Jews' 'crimes' was either to mock the Easter celebration or to celebrate the Passover" (Kellum, 1973, p. 376). There were even a number of instances of poor Christian parents offering to sell their children to Jews to be killed, and as late as 1699, a poor woman offered to sell her baby for that purpose to Meier Goldschmidt, court jeweler to the King of Denmark (Trachtenberg, 1943). Parents were so harried that they were willing to sell their children for what they thought were nefarious purposes.

An Historical Perspective

Neonaticide between the 15th and 19th centuries was relatively rare. The penalties were often given great publicity. In the period of the 16th and 17th centuries, infanticide was considered ungodly and legislators were anxious to suppress it. Of all kinds of homicide, neonaticide was easiest to conceal in spite of the fact that there was little privacy in the villages and communities. Women of the village kept a wary eye open for suspicious behavior on the part of young women, especially those who were considered vulnerable to seduction such as single women (virgins or widows). Domestic servants most frequently became pregnant and had illegitimate children during the Ancien Régime because they were most vulnerable (Riet, 1986). As Shorter (1975) cogently observed, people in much of Europe and some of Colonial New England were densely grouped in villages and hamlets, rather than in the rural farms of the northern U.S. In those areas, surveillance and community controls were far stricter because privacy was difficult to maintain. There was relatively little social and physical mobility, and the local courting customs were enforced in order to prevent illegitimacy and other social ills (Shorter, 1975). Nevertheless, when pregnancy occurred, it was often hidden and denied if the woman was unable to get married. When babies' bodies were discovered, it was even more difficult to determine how they died. Hence laws were passed against the concealment of pregnancy in order to attenuate the problem of neonaticide and reduce the instances of illegitimacy (Wrightson, 1982).

English courts of the 17th and 18th centuries revealed the same motives and the same denials of pregnancy (Hufton, 1974). Most instances of both abandonment and child murder occurred in instances of bastardy, which by the 17th century was considered a matter of social disgrace (Illick, 1974; cf Francus, 1997). Hoffer and Hull (1981) speculated that for many women "neonaticide was a deliberate form of delayed abortion. It involved concealment, and probably was the most common among poor, unwed mothers" (p. 157). Abortion, before the last part of the 19th century, was perilous and sometimes ineffective, so delivering the baby and either killing it by neglect or force at birth (sometimes *in utero*) seemed more prudent. In these cases women sometimes had the assistance of friends, lovers, and especially midwives (Illick, 1974).

A study of neonaticide in Bavaria in the 19th century, based on a series of police dossiers, revealed data about the women that parallels modern problems for some pregnant women and reinforces the knowledge of the universality of this type of homicide. Servant girls faced no shame, no censure — their problems were to keep their jobs, and the majority did work up to the very moment of birth. Thus these girls made no preparation for the births or even the babies. Their motivation for killing did not derive from extreme conditions. Generally it was because the father denied paternity or would not give them support. There was usually no prospect of marriage, and for some, extreme poverty made another mouth to feed difficult. Typically, the accused showed few feelings of sorrow or guilt; they probably regarded it as a late abortion. Schulte (1984) speculated that the lack of remorse was tied to the prevalent attitudes in poor peasant Bavaria, where there was great fertility and even greater infant mortality. Survival of children in large families depended upon the will of their parents. They generally felt that killing the baby was no different from the barnyard animals they frequently killed for food.

A similar analysis of neonaticide and child abandonment in 19th century Corsica revealed cultural differences. In southern Mediterranean society, factors of honor and shame played a paramount role in the motivations of the behavior of Corsican women. "Sanctions deriving from notions of female honour were thus the usual cause of neonaticide, overriding economic necessity or any feeling towards children as such" (Wilson, 1988, p. 764–765). The law of 1810 was harsh toward the crime; the punishment was death while other homicides carried the penalty of life imprisonment. However, judges and prosecutors lessened the punishment by allowing for extenuating circumstances or convictions on lesser charges (Wilson, 1988). The mothers prosecuted for neonaticide had characteristics resembling those of women from other countries. The overwhelming number were unmarried, few were widows, and few were married women living apart from their husbands. The major difference was that in Corsica there were few servants and farm workers; most women lived at home with their parents. Poverty in these cases was not the major cause of homicide, and in many instances the babies were killed by accomplices — the lover or the woman's mother. The primary motive was the wish to avoid dishonor and shame (Wilson, 1988). In Belgium, too, "living honor was strong and the social pressure also more unbearable" (Leboutte, 1991, p. 182).

A factor that further promoted despair in Catholic countries was a strong patriarchal culture which allowed fathers to avoid legal responsibilities for the support of their illegitimate children. In addition, they were legally protected from any attempt to identify them as the parent (Kertzer, 1993). There was a high rate of neonaticide among servant girls who were vulnerable to both seduction on the one hand, and often the overt attempt to use the sexual encounter to capture the commitment of marriage on the other. Once pregnant, the woman faced shame and dismissal; to avoid such a fate, the young girl concealed her pregnancy and destroyed the baby. In both France and England, household servants formed the largest proportion of such women (McBride, 1976).

The increased number of unwed pregnancies in Victorian Europe was partly the result of the urbanization and modernization occurring in western Europe. The sudden influx of people into the cities, with their inherent anonymity and poor living conditions, made the seduction of young women easy. Squalid social and economic conditions in domestic and factory labor led to deplorable behavior. Children were left unsupervised and, in the earlier part of the century, child labor also led to premature sexual experimentation (Edwards, 1981). Young women were victimized and harassed in both the homes and the factories where they worked, with pregnancies resulting in the loss of their jobs as well as shame and blame. Sometimes the young women became involved, in hope of or because of the promise of marriage. The men could disappear, leaving the women to bear the consequences of their amorous dalliances (Tilly, Scott, and Cohen, 1976). (This has not changed too much over the decades.)

Since girls who were pregnant would be raising illegitimate children, they frequently felt their only choices were neonaticide or abandonment. On the other hand, the more protected upper class young women could always be sent abroad if they became pregnant, and they did not have to face the same consequences as their poorer sisters. (This, too, is still true in many situations.)

The passage of the Poor Law of 1834 in Victorian England and its cruel treatment of the indigent also contributed to the rising number of neonaticides. The single mother could no longer receive aid from her local parish. She had to keep her child in an institution called the "poor house," where the poor were sequestered and separated by sex. The law also relieved the father of responsibility, for the sole purpose of the law "was to make girls realize the harsh consequences of sexual delinquency so they would guard their chastity and bastardy would decline" (Sauer, 1978, p. 27). The Poor Law was especially cruel because most of the time it prohibited financial aid to women with illegitimate children. Even so-called deserving women with children (widows or deserted married women with children) received piddling welfare payments (Thane, 1979). The harsh bastardy provisions against the unmarried woman eventually turned public opinion against the law, because many began to realize that the woman was an innocent victim of seduction (Henriques, 1967; Thane, 1979). "The larger proportion of neonaticides was attributable to the women of limited resources who, through isolation and desperation, often concealed the birth of their child, killing the infant within the first twenty four hours through exposure or other means" (Barlow and Clayton, 1996, p. 215).

After the 1870s, the decline in the birth rate in industrialized societies became the norm as information about contraception and abortion was disseminated in the middle classes. Contemporaries viewed neonaticide as a crime of unmarried women (usually seduced and abandoned mothers) despite the fact that there was a decline of illegitimacy later in the century. The reality of continuing neonaticide rested on bad socioeconomic conditions — the punitive bastardy legislation embodied in the Poor Law with its refusal of "outdoor" relief, the difficulty of getting fathers to support their children, and the inability of women to find work. Many thought that the Poor Laws forced more neonaticide and abandonment (Behlmer, 1979). Chances of adoption for infants were slim. Foundling hospitals accepted few of the children. Neonaticide thus appeared to be an appropriate response to the economic pressures for many mothers. As family planning spread at the end of the century and abortion became more common, there appeared to be a decline in neonaticide (Behlmer, 1979). Imperial Germany's statistics on abandonment, neonaticide, and abortion reflected many of the same tendencies seen elsewhere. Neonaticide declined as convictions for abortions rose precipitously (Richter, 1998; Sauer, 1974).

Poverty rather than shame was the primary motivation for neonaticide in 19th century U.S. In Philadelphia, hundreds of dead infants were found in cesspools and streets; 483 were found in 1 4-year period and 41 cases of homicide went to trial between 1860 and 1900 (Friedman, 1991; Lane, 1986).

Friedman claimed that infanticide was also a crime of immobility, while abortion as an alternative to neonaticide was more commonly practiced in the U.S. (Friedman 1991; Mohr, 1978). The U.S., as a more mobile society, had many men who moved frequently, seeking opportunity on the frontier. However, the new cities developing in the West also gave many women a chance to change identities and conceal their single parenthood, but poor women locked in urban slums had little choice. It was here that more neonaticide occurred. Infanticide was rarer in the West than in either the East or the South. "There were no prosecutions for infanticide in Alameda County, California between 1870–1910 and no newspaper accounts of such crimes. In Oakland, California this was an exceptionally rare crime" (Friedman, 1991). Records of infanticides in 19th century Ohio corroborate findings that we noted in early Europe. In insular communities bounded by common values, language, and snoopy neighbors, social behaviors inhibiting infanticide were enforced (Wheeler, 1997).

Death rates for girls in Colonial America, and even later for girls under age nine, were sometimes twice those for boys. Sheila Johansson, a demographer, claimed that the growth of modernization in the 19th century meant that boys' labor contributed to the cash crop economy while daughters' work had no monetary value. Girls, therefore, were overworked and underfed in poor rural areas, leading to a higher death rate than for boys. In urban settings where girls could find employment in factories, they and their brothers died at more equal rates (Burke, 1984).

Abandonment

Amighi (1990) examined a cross-cultural group of myths, folk tales, and rituals, and found that stories of "maternal or parental abandonment of children are very common and found in many cultures. They may express ambivalence toward children" (p. 135). In addition, given the difficult life of the average person in many unsophisticated cultures, Amighi hypothesized "that the infanticidal mother is expressing resentment against the new infant who is adding to her burdens or that an emotional detachment is evoked to permit her to abandon or kill her infant" (1990, p. 138). Either feeling could lead to neonaticide or abandonment even in more sophisticated societies.

Abandonment was far more frequent in the past than murder. Some mothers were hesitant to kill their newborns outright, and they often nursed the hope that their babies would be cared for by compassionate strangers. Infant abandonment became prevalent throughout Europe during the late Middle Ages from southern Europe to Russia as an alternative to neonaticide and filicide. Parents abandoned babies when they were unable to support them because of poverty, shame, illegitimacy, or incestuous relationships, or when inheritance or other resources might be compromised. Most abandoned babies in the early Middle Ages were rescued and brought up as either adopted members of the household or as laborers. European society as a whole did not place serious sanctions against the practice, but rather tolerated or regulated it. The sale of children had been common in ancient and medieval Europe (Boswell, 1988). As illegitimacy rose in numbers in the 15th, 16th, and 17th centuries, so did the number of abandoned babies. The causes of this phenomenon varied, as did the causes of neonaticide. Poverty brought about by seasonal change, bad economic conditions, plus the inadequacy of fertility control, plagued the family's welfare. Sometimes parents abandoned their babies and hoped that they could reclaim them later (Kertzer, 1993). In periods of catastrophe or crisis, more male children were left, but generally there were more abandoned girls (Gavitt, 1994; Trexler, 1973).

The number of abandonments increased so dramatically that governments were forced to create foundling homes. By the time of the Reformation, foundling homes had become a part of the architectural landscape of urban northern Italy, and they had been established in France, Spain, and Portugal. These institutions, by establishing a locus, gathered all of the troubling aspects of child abandonment in one place, hiding the babies from the public eye. At first, they were additions to hospitals, and then they became "substantial institutions generally run by lay boards in close consultation with the Church" (Boswell, 1988, p. 418). The creation of these institutions made abandonment quite common in Catholic Europe, but it was not as widely practiced in northern Protestant areas where there were no foundling homes. When the Catholic church of the Counter-Reformation era imposed the strict definition of legitimate sexual relations as those only engaged in after a religious ceremony, infant abandonment became more frequent. The view of unwed mothers raising their own children was seen as encouraging sinful behavior, but many desperate mothers, and their families, wanted to protect their babies. The foundling hospitals continued to increase throughout the 18th and 19th centuries as the state began to supervise the welfare of poor mothers and children and regulate families, reproduction, and sexuality (Tilly, Scott, and Cohen, 1976).

One of the devices which made abandonment easier because it provided anonymity while lessening guilt was the rotating wheel, called a *ruota* in Italy, *la tour* in France, and a *roda* in Portugal. This was a

> revolving cylinder with an opening on one side of its revolving surface; its closed side faced the street. An outside bell was placed nearby. When a woman wanted to abandon a new born child she merely had to alert the person on duty by ringing the bell, and straight way the cylinder, revolving on its axis, would present its open side to the exterior; it would then receive the infant and continuing the motion, convey the child inside the hospital (Donzelot, 1979, p. 26).

Abandonment existed on a large scale in France, and the many foundling hospitals there facilitated this practice as opposed to just leaving the baby on a doorstep. Most babies were born in public institutions and many were brought into hospitals by midwives or were "delivered anonymously at hospital gates" (Wrightson, 1982, p. 13). The abandoned children were sent to the country to be nursed because bottle feeding was not really available until the late 19th century and wet nursing was the cheapest way of caring for babies. The practice was especially prevalent among poor women who had to work in factories, mines, or domestic service. The mortality rates were appallingly high (Fuchs, 1984, 1992; Sussman, 1975). "Institutional neglect by well-intentioned but overburdened and under-financed charitable institutions made what was probably the largest contribution to infanticide in modern Europe" (Rose, 1986, p. 14).

In Britain, the national mortality rate for infants was 15–16%, but babies left with baby farmers reached a 90% rate. Most deaths were probably unintentional, occurring because poor rural women lived under appallingly squalid conditions and were ignorant of any notion of cleanliness, but "parents often took out burial insurance on their children and, to increase benefits often insured children in several clubs, making a profit on their death (McKee, 1984; Sauer, 1978). Baby farms were also a prominent feature of the working class in many 19th century American cities. It was both a way for neighborhood women to pool their resources to care for their babies, enabling them to work, and also "in its worst abuses a latent system for the disposal of unwanted babies" (Broder, 1988, p. 130). Mothers who wished to abandon babies they could not afford would simply leave them at a baby farm and disappear. "In this way, baby farmers often served as unwitting and unwilling agents in the process of abandonment" (Broder, 1988, p. 139). The economic dislocations caused by the Civil War and Reconstruction, plus the South's postbellum industrialization, produced suffering and poverty, resulting in a marked increase in the number of infant abandonments and homicides (Green, 1999).

The Basque country was the one area of Europe that had unusually low rates of abandonment in the 18th and early 19th centuries. Despite a high illegitimacy rate — one-fourth to one-third of all newborns — there were few problems. In this society there was no shame attached to single mothers because a large number of babies were born in concubinage relationships (often involving priests). The extended family was the prevalent model and thus they were able to sustain and integrate the illegitimate children. Unlike Mediterranean Europe and even northern Europe, there were no institutions that could care for foundlings. Instead, the laws required the fathers to assume responsibility for their children, and often mothers relinquished their children to the fathers' families (Valverde, 1994).

As the country modernized its laws and customs to conform with the rest of Europe, the number of abandonments began to rise sharply. The church enforced its ban against sex as sinful, insisted that the priests become more celibate, and declared unmarried motherhood unacceptable. As in the rest of Europe, the extended family declined, fathers were no longer required to support their children, and the increase in poverty contributed to the factors that were inimical to the welfare of lower-class newborns (Valverde, 1994).

In France, admissions of abandoned babies rose from 40,000 a year in 1784 to 138,000 in 1822. By 1830 there were 270 revolving boxes in use throughout France, with 336,297 infants legally abandoned during the period from 1824 to 1833. Between 80 and 90% of the babies died within the first year of life (Harris, 1977). By 1874 in France, the French legislators regulated the wet nursing "industry" to ease the high infant mortality rate. They also hoped to discourage mothers from working outside the home, and considered regulations to protect children and women's labor (Cole, 1996). The *tours* were closed, and mothers could no longer anonymously leave their newborns. Instead, the mothers were taken to a government bureau where they were interviewed and their inability to care for the babies was reviewed before they were admitted to the hospitals. Mothers felt encouraged to keep their children, even when illegitimate, since the government provided assistance. The result was a drop in abandonment, as the women preferred help which enabled them to keep their children (Litchfield and Gordon, 1980).

Penalties of the Past

Whenever there was clear evidence of neonaticide in the records throughout the late medieval period and early modern Europe, it seemed there was a preponderance of illegitimate children killed by single girls or widows. One factor that has remained stable throughout history is the "association between infanticide and illegitimacy" (Kellet, 1992, p. 2). The church worried that an unbaptized infant's soul would be damned to eternal punishment, and retribution for that crime was heavy (15 years' public penance rather than 7 years), but punishments were often mitigated (to 7 years) if the guilty women were poor (Kellum, 1973). What was most clear in the penances prescribed by ecclesiastics was that they were addressed to females only, never to men or even to parents. Illegitimacy was not condoned. However, Damme (1978) points out, as do many others, that church punishments were moderate because "it was merely a recognition by the church of a method of population control by the poor that may have been necessary, in many cases, for survival" (p. 4).

As the Middle Ages waned into the Renaissance and the 16th and 17th centuries, jurisdiction over crimes passed to the secular courts as the emer-

gence of the modern state diminished the power of both Catholic and Protestant churches. Gradually the church authorities became more determined
to regulate the sexual and social behavior of their members, and the acceptance
of unwed motherhood became intolerable. The war against illicit sexual relations and their products — illegitimate babies — became most intensive in
the 16th century, a time of profound religious rivalries and a fear of witchcraft.
Neonaticides continued as social and economic pressures did not abate for
the poor. In addition, court records show that most of the reported neonaticides were illegitimate babies, indicating the significance of the stigma of
bastardy (Damme, 1978). The criminal statutes became brutally severe in these
cases, allegedly because of the difficulty in enforcing the laws and, therefore,
the greater need to instill fear as a deterrent for these crimes. Princes, hampered by lack of police and modern methods of detection, compensated by
providing a "fiercely retributive character to punishment" (Ransel, 1988, p.
13). Hanging was not enough; the punishment had to be *awful*.

The penalties prescribed for the crimes were appalling. In late medieval
France, guilty mothers were burned or buried alive after torture. The codes
of the Holy Roman Empire, as issued in 1332, followed medieval German
precedent and included live burial, drowning in a sack, or impaling. These
sentences were replaced in the 17th century by torture and decapitation.
The punishments varied from country to country ranging from simple
beheading to burning or burial alive. After the witchcraft hysteria of the
17th century subsided, the harsh persecution of women began to abate, and
there were fewer indictments and executions in England, France, and then
the rest of Europe.

However, inadequate forensic and scientific techniques, faulty diagnoses,
and cover-ups made child homicide difficult to assess. To satisfy the need to
promote order and to legislate "proper" sexual behavior, states began to pass
laws creating a presumption of murder in those cases where the unmarried
woman was alone at the time of birth and the baby was later found dead.
This was written into French law in 1156, 1586, and again in 1708. Unless
the woman could prove that the child was stillborn or died naturally, she
could be convicted of infanticide. Similar laws appeared in England in 1624,
Sweden in 1627, Wurttemburg in 1658, Scotland in 1690, and Bavaria as late
as 1751, in which failure to declare a pregnancy could result in the charge of
infanticide if the baby was not found alive. The single mother became a social
pariah, reduced to prostitution or other socially denounced means to stay
alive. These pressures often led her to hide her pregnancy and to kill the
newborn (Symonds, 1997).

Similar laws were also passed during the Colonial period in the U.S.,
notably in New England and Pennsylvania, and as late as 1855 in New Jersey
(Rowe, 1991; Wheeler, 1997; Zimmer, 1996). The laws in the U.S. varied

widely, but reflected their roots in the English common law. "The aim was to punish 'lewd and dissolute women' who produced 'bastard children' but lacked enough 'natural affection' to keep them alive" (Friedman, 1991, p. 654). Similar laws were passed in Canada beginning in 1758, and their legal records indicated that the vast majority of women charged with this crime were unmarried (Saunders, 1989).

The rate of conviction rose for a short time, but, despite the penalties, neonaticide remained commonplace (Oberman, 1996). When babies' bodies were discovered, it was difficult to determine how they had died. Forensic medicine did not exist and it was impossible to differentiate a stillbirth from a murder (Wrightson, 1982). The only way to rebuff a supposition of neonaticide was testimony from another person that a child had been born dead — "even if the woman could prove that the child had been born alive and then died of natural causes" (Lansdowne, 1990, p. 43). The law was never applied rigorously and, by the 18th century, fell into disuse.

Gradually, because the crime was perceived as so "unnatural," it came to be regarded as a result of mental disturbance. As early as the 15th century in France, mercy might be granted on this ground, although only after a long imprisonment, and in many German states by the 18th century, sympathy for the mother was reflected by acquittal or reduced sentences (Kord, 1993). In England, the same defense was used and there were many cases where it was successful, even if some women, who were clearly deranged, were executed. Attitudes in both England and Scotland gradually became more humane, and clemency was given more often. In England, the Law of 1624 was repealed, but the Law of 1803, although less severe than the earlier law, still provided capital punishment for women who killed their newborns. The final clause declared that single women acquitted of murder, but who had concealed their pregnancies, could be imprisoned for 2 years (even if the child had been stillborn) (Jackson, 1996). The same easing of the law's severity occurred in Scotland. It became more and more difficult to convict women of infanticide. From 1799 until 1809, 26 women were accused of infanticide but there were no convictions. In 1809 a new law reducing the penalties to 2-year imprisonment made convictions rise again (Symonds, 1997).

Sympathy for women increased during the 19th century, based partly on a more compassionate view of young women's suffering as a result of being victims of seduction and sexual exploitation. That, plus the belief that puerperal insanity was a legitimate defense in cases of neonaticide, led judges and prosecutors to reduce the punishment by allowing for extenuating circumstances or by convicting them on lesser charges (Showalter, 1980; Wilson, 1988). Juries, too, acquitted large numbers of women indicted for similar reasons. By the 20th century, in some jurisdictions, the treatment for women involved in child homicides differed from other murder cases by using the rubric of extenuating circumstances to reduce the severity of punishments (Fuchs, 1992).

From its inception as a sex-specific crime in 1623, infanticide has been concerned with theories about women. The initial object of the laws of secret pregnancy of 1623 (and later) in England, Europe, and the U.S. was to punish single women for becoming pregnant and for refusing to live with their sin. Thus "the crime was created to affect moral and social behavior" (O'Donovan, 1984, p. 264). In the 19th century, attitudes changed toward women; people became more ambivalent and sympathetic. As ideology altered the feminine role to perceive women as more dependent and weak, but also as the mistress of morality and culture in the home, any deviation from the ongoing standards of motherhood meant that the female was obviously mentally ill. Her problems were caused by her gender and biological destiny, and thus she was more vulnerable, requiring protection and avoidance of the world outside the domestic sphere.

To Summarize ...

Combining the contemporary studies of sociobiologists with a survey of the perception of child homicide over many centuries in western Europe and, to a lesser extent, the U.S., provides a vital context for regarding the same crime today. We continue to have religious influences, social disapproval of illegitimacy *and* unwed motherhood, and conflicts on how to deal with those who kill infants. However, we come to study the crime with the recognition that it is not something "new" in this world and that many of the pressures that caused young women to kill their newborns in the past still exist, as do the difficulties of knowing how to handle them.

Motives for Murder

3

As we have shown, cultural mores, economic development, and technical-medical progress have created communities that can provide more favorable and nurturing environments for families. Yet the problem of child homicide remains, though on a smaller scale than in the past. Women's status and rights have been firmly established on more equal terms in Western societies. They have gained the vote, and, in general, have access to more control of their reproductive functions. Young people enjoy more freedom from adult supervision, have greater economic opportunities, and have a far longer adolescence than formerly. The rising divorce rate and the earlier physical maturation of youngsters have abetted earlier sexual activity. The pressure to engage in sexual intercourse is substantial. This has led to a dramatic increase in teenage pregnancy which has just begun to slide in the past few years. When a boy urges a girl to have intercourse — "everyone does it!" — what alternatives does she have? (She could say "no," but may be weighing this against the consequences in terms of future dates, peer popularity, or other factors.) If she "does it" and becomes pregnant, again what alternatives does she have? Homicide is one tragic option, whether as neonaticide by a panic-stricken mother at the time of birth, infanticide by an ill-prepared parent in the child's first year of life, or filicide even later.

What are the salient characteristics of homicidal mothers? They differ in socio-economic background, community, and education. But though different in these instances, they do possess other similarities. The women are usually young and single. The majority of them live with parents, guardians, or relatives. They are often, but not always, poor. Most are not married or do not have committed relationships. They keep themselves isolated and are unwilling to admit even to themselves that they are pregnant. Yet the studies both in the past and present indicate that while the actions (neonaticide or infanticide) are similar in behavior, psychological and environmental circumstances vary widely.

Why Murder?

Why are children the victims of their parent's inability to cope with life? Are children expendable? What can stir a parent to kill a child, especially a newborn? People are horrified when parents kill their children, and the media focus varying amounts of attention on such crimes. Professionals and the lay public alike need to understand why these incidents occur and what family, public agency, educational, and legislative actions can and should be undertaken to reduce them. (We believe that it is unrealistic to expect that such cases can be totally eliminated.)

In 1984, Christoffel wrote that homicide warranted review as "the only leading cause of death of children under age 15 to have increased in incidence in the last 30 years ... " (p. 68). Several other studies published in the 1980s and 1990s sought the risk factors involved in neonaticide, infanticide, and child homicide (Cummings et al., 1994; Emerick, Foster, and Campbell, 1986; Siegel et al., 1996; Wilkey et al., 1982; and Winpisinger et al., 1991). They tended to agree that these factors included young, usually teenaged, unmarried women from poor, often non-white backgrounds, with less than a high school education, and who had had little or no prenatal care. Of course, not all of those who commit neonaticide or infanticide are teenagers; some are chronologically mature women who may have other motives for their actions. Further, many of the recent cases we have found involve young women from middle-class, white backgrounds, often college students. The one factor our sample appears to have in common with those cited is the lack of prenatal care.

As we indicated earlier, child homicide can be divided by the age of the victim into neonaticide, infanticide, and filicide. Child-killing can also be divided by murderer(s). In neonaticide, the perpetrator is most often the new mother who has usually given birth unattended (Kunz and Bahr, 1996; Smithey, 1998). Occasionally, she has the child's father with her, as in the Grossberg-Peterson and Sims' cases. The murderer in infanticide and filicide is usually one of the victim's parents, more rarely both parents. Occasionally in these cases, the murderer may be a non-parent who is acting *in loco parentis*. Kunz and Bahr (1996) found that U.S. government and other data "suggest that children are at greater risk when they and their parents are young" (p. 349), but age is not the only criterion for either victims or perpetrators. Overpeck and her colleagues (Overpeck et al., 1998), studying linked birth and death certificates for children born from 1983 to 1991, found 2776 cases of infant homicide for which they were able to identify a number of risk factors. [They were not, however, able to find birth certificates for 2.0 to 2.8% of the deaths in that period and found that this was more common "for infants who were less than 28 days old when they died than for those who were older" (p. 1212).] They concluded that the strongest risk factors for infant homicide "were a maternal age of less than 17 years, a second or subsequent birth for a mother 19 years old or younger, and no prenatal care" (1998, p. 1213). Having completed fewer than 12 years of education, especially for those mothers over age 19, was also a high risk factor. As we read reports of both neonaticides and infanticides, there was graphic support for these conclusions.

The most recent available data from the National Center for Health Statistics of the Centers for Disease Control and Prevention indicated that "infant mortality rates were higher for mothers who began prenatal care after the first trimester or not at all" (MacDoman and Atkinson, 1999, p. 5), with an infant mortality rate of 35.6 per 1000 live births in 1997 for those who had no prenatal care at all (MacDoman and Atkinson, 1999, p. 10). The highest frequency of infant mortality by the age of the mother was for the group aged under 20 years, and by the highest frequency of infant mortality the years of education for the mother was in the 9 to 11 years of education group, another risk factor noted previously. Early neonatal deaths (less than 7 days) were at a rate of 3.8 per 1000 live births, but there is no correlational data to tie any of these factors to each other conclusively.

McKee and Shea (1998) compared their sample of 20 adult women charged with infanticide or filicide with those studied by Resnick (1970), d'Orban (1979), and Bourget and Bradford (1990). Eighty percent of their subjects had a diagnosable mental disorder, and 35% were mentally retarded or diagnosed with Borderline Intellectual Functioning. McKee and Shea's subjects were also much more likely to be categorized as "low income" than was true in the other studies reviewed here, with most of these women being unemployed. Just over 20% were in adult abusive relationships. Given a detailed background, McKee and Shea found that "These women lacked adequate resources with which to cope with the stressors preceding the children's deaths" (1998, p. 685). Furthermore, the "great majority of these killings were apparently not due to impaired judgment from intoxication but, rather, were the result of distorted reality contact or were impulsive, unplanned acts evolving from extreme levels of situational stress, frustration, anger, depression, or a combination of these" (p. 685). They rarely used weapons.

The motives for these crimes may vary considerably from one case to another, and especially with the age of the victim. In some cases, denial is operative; in others, uglier motives surface, like revenge against a third party. As to method, suffocation or drowning of neonates, horrible as they are, do not carry the sadistic quality seen in many of the child abuse cases ending in infanticides and filicides.

Neonaticide

What sets the stage for a parent — usually the mother as already noted — to kill her newborn or to abandon the child to almost certain death? There are many questions evolving from this one. For example, does she acknowledge or deny, even to herself, the fact that she is pregnant? What are her resources? What are the (typically young) woman's relationships with her own parents? What is the role of a young woman's religious training? *Is* neonaticide a belated alternative to abortion, or is abortion, as some claim, early neonaticide? Do attitudes and laws regarding abortion have any relation to neonaticide? What is the role of the social climate of a particular era with respect to out-of-wedlock motherhood? What alternatives to neonaticide exist in a given society at a particular point in time? In short, what are the social, political, and sexist ramifications of neonaticide in addition to the criminal nature of the act itself?

Resnick's classic study of neonaticide (1970) suggested several motives for neonaticide. In considering them, however, we must remember that abortion was not legally an option in the U.S. at the time he wrote and also that the perception of illegitimacy changed markedly between the late 1960s and the late 1990s. Furthermore, his reasoning was based on the 37 neonaticides he found in a review of world literature in the period 1751 to 1968, hardly a sizable sample for that expanse of time. These reminders do not negate his work; they simply sharpen our interpretation of his findings. Although Resnick found that 83% of the neonaticide reports he located were motivated by the baby being an "unwanted child," he asserted that "illegitimacy, with its social stigma, is the most common motive" (1970, p. 1419). One would have to question that today, as being an unwed mother is not seen in quite as negative terms at all levels of society as was true 30 years ago. For some young mothers, shame and guilt may still be primary motives for doing away with the unwanted baby in some way; for many others, shame and guilt are not part of the picture, although they may still have other motives for neonaticide.

On the other hand, Resnick also included as a motive denial of the pregnancy by the "mother" to herself, with the apparent expectation that the child would be stillborn or somehow magically disappear. When neither of these occurred, the young mother would do away with the neonate herself. In many other cases, he found that the girl felt she could not reveal her pregnancy to *her* mother, fearing anger, punishment, or rejection. These situations are still prominent as motives for neonaticide. They raise the question of the nature of the relationship between the girl and her parent(s). On the one hand, there may be little communication between them; on the other hand, mother and daughter may be close, but the daughter may be aware that her parents view her behavior as a reflection of themselves. This would increase the daughter's denial or inability to cope because of the shame it might bring.

Resnick also mentioned rape or extramarital pregnancy as motives for neonaticide. However, if the rape is reported to the authorities, abortion of the fetus would be permitted in many jurisdictions (although not in Brazil, as we have noted elsewhere). That depends, also, on the point in the pregnancy at which the rape is reported. A case in Michigan was reported (Philadelphia: Channel 6, July 17, 1998, 5:30 p.m. news) in which the court would not allow an abortion of a 12-year-old's pregnancy because she was in her 27th week and Michigan law prohibits abortion after the 24th week except to save the mother's life. In this case, apparently the girl's parents were not aware of her condition until she was in her 25th week. At her age, irregular menses are quite common and would not have raised the possibility of pregnancy if other symptoms were absent. (Note: the abortion was finally allowed, in her 29th week.) She had been impregnated by her 17-year-old brother, who was subsequently indicted for rape, pleaded guilty to fourth-degree criminal sexual conduct, and hoped to avoid deportation for his felony (Associated Press, 1998).

Extramarital pregnancy is another matter, as a married woman has more options available to her and presumably would be more active in resolving her situation than a passive teenager. She could conceivably pass off the pregnancy as one originating in her own marriage, although this may be risky if the resulting child looks too much like the biological father or if her husband had been absent for 10 or more months. She might be able to obtain an abortion on the grounds of risk to her mental health. She could also, of course, commit neonaticide.

Scrimshaw (1978) alleged that "mortality may sometimes be a response to high fertility instead of a stimulus to it" (p. 383). This may involve "underinvestment" in unwanted children in terms of their care, feeding, and response to their illnesses. It happens in terms of gender, a child born in fewer than 3 years after birth of the next older child, twins. And " ... it is possible that sex preferences and the sex composition of the 'ideal' family can significantly affect mortality within the family" (p. 389).

To most people, the murder of one's newborn or infant is beyond contemplation or comprehension. Indeed, it is most often **un**premeditated even by those who commit neonaticide or infanticide. That being the case, we have to look beyond simple intent in our attempt to understand why these crimes occur. Oberman (1996) put the case well:

> Neonaticide is not so much about a lack of economic resources as it is about a lack of communication and community. As is the case with infanticide, neonaticide is not merely an individual problem; it is a reflection of an atomized society that places little value on the mental and physical well-being of its most vulnerable constituents. Those who would prevent neonaticide must begin by identifying and remedying girls' vulnerability long before they become pregnant (Oberman, 1996, p. 73).*

* Reprinted with permission of the publisher, Georgetown University and American Criminal Law Review. © 1996.

Part of that vulnerability is simple naiveté; they know little or nothing about contraception (although that may be due to religious teachings) and even less about the need for prenatal care if they do engage in intercourse and become pregnant. For those who deliver their babies and choose to raise them, they know frightfully little about child care or child development. (In our concluding chapter, we will review what is being taught in the schools and a number of programs which appear to have greater effectiveness than the traditional health education courses.)

Psychological Explanations

One can look at the psychological aspects of neonaticide from the viewpoint of the individual alone or recognize that the individual is also a member of a family and community. "At the individual level, the girls involved in neonaticide cases possess so little self-esteem that they are incapable of acting to protect themselves. Their insecurity almost certainly contributes to their becoming pregnant in the first place, and it leads to their paralysis once pregnant" (Oberman, 1996, p. 71). In addition, many of the girls fear that they will be excluded from their families when they are found to have had sex and to be pregnant. In Oberman's (1996) opinion, their fear may be justified. She found that many neonaticide cases

> show evidence of families that are remarkably disinterested in their children's lives. Those who commit neonaticide lack relationships with open, caring, reliable adults — adults who will recognize the signs of pregnancy, confront the girls about their situations, and initiate the difficult conversations about the alternative resolutions to pregnancy, including motherhood. This isolation from loved ones, even within the home, clearly constitutes a structural factor that contributes to neonaticide" (Oberman, 1996, p. 71).*

Such isolation is not always the case. The fear of being rejected may be real, but is based on recognition by the daughter that her parents think she is perfect and her knowledge that her pregnancy is "letting them down."

With young women, unintended pregnancies do not necessarily lead to marriages. The prospect of single parenthood with all of its physical and emotional responsibilities, perhaps leading to dropping out of school and the abandonment of hopes and plans for the future, can also consciously or subconsciously propel an adolescent to neonaticide. Mapanga (1997) has addressed several of these problems with respect to adolescents, but they also hold true for unmarried young adult women.

* Reprinted with permission of the publisher, Georgetown University and American Criminal Law Review. © 1996.

The Role of Shame

As Massaro (1997) has suggested, "*shame* has become in the 1990s what *self-esteem* was in the 1980s … The shameworthy ones are usually Others — typically, general categories of others unlikely to pen a response: unwed mothers, deadbeat dads, urban youths … " (p. 646). It is interesting which group leads the list. She adds that shame is potentially destructive rather than reintegrative, that "it is a call for *humiliation* of offenders, first by the state and then — less predictably but likely nonetheless — by the offenders' community" (p. 647). Shame is not a new way of dealing with pregnancy among the unwed, for it has been used by parents, the clergy, and others for centuries to keep (or try to keep) unmarried girls from having sexual relations, or, failing that, from having babies.

With respect to neonaticide particularly, what is the role of shame? Does the girl deny her pregnancy, even to herself, out of shame at her sexual behavior, for pregnancy was an admission of having had sex and indeed would provoke feelings of shame (Ehrenreich, 1998)?

Shaming will clearly promote one end: it communicates the shamer's disgust for the offender and the offense. And it plainly "is cheaper than imprisonment and may in some ways be less cruel to offenders. I argue, however, that when judges and other officials express their disgust in this fashion, they risk recommitting the very act that justifies punishment of criminal offenders, that is, the treatment of others as mere objects" (Massaro, 1997, p. 649). Public shaming might have two results with respect to the individual. It could act as a "potentially devastating incursion into one's idealized sense of self: It is a narcissistic defeat" (Massaro, 1997, p. 660). For some, however, it may evoke greater rebellion, more outrageous and maladaptive behavior. In the latter type of situation, it may be that the young woman remains in a state of denial of the crime she has committed, or, at the other extreme, she assumes the attitude that "if I've got the name, I'll play the game."

An example of the influence of religious background is found in a case presented by Green and Manohar (1990). The patient was an only daughter among six children of a family that practiced a strict Protestant faith, lived in a socially isolated community, and avoided contemporary ways of living, which were regarded as sinful. After a severe beating by her father, one of many over the years, she left home at age 18 and subsequently entered into a common-law relationship. At age 23, unmarried, she delivered her baby alone and it drowned in the lavatory bowl. She was initially charged with second-degree murder which was subsequently changed to infanticide, and she was admitted to a psychiatric hospital.

The dynamics of the case appeared clear. From the perspective of her religious cultural background, to be pregnant out of wedlock was considered "a very wicked sin. To have obtained an abortion would have been considered even worse. Although the patient had left home in an attempt to set up an independent lifestyle, it was clear that her parents' attitudes continued to have a marked hold over her. Before the birth of the baby she had never been able to inform her parents that she was living in a common-law relationship" (Green and Manohar, 1990, p. 123). When hospitalized, she claimed to have no memory of having pregnancy tests, or of having been pregnant, and said that she did not realize she was in labor until the baby appeared. As Green and Manohar (1990) pointed out, the fact that she had seen a physician and was told she was pregnant is quite unusual in cases of neonaticide. "The case illustrates the importance of physicians diagnosing pregnancy in unmarried mothers ensuring that there is proper exploration of the impact of pregnancy on the mother's psychosocial status" (p. 123).

A team of psychiatrists (Silva et al., 1998) has made a strong case for considering the impact of the individual's cultural background in evaluating those who commit neonaticide. In the case on which their article was focused, the young woman's family was opposed to out-of-wedlock sexual activity, birth control methods as alternatives to abstinence, and abortion. She was not in denial of the pregnancy as many other 18-year-olds have been, but thought about seeking abortifacent herbs in Mexico or leaving her baby at a church. Unfortunately, the pregnancy had continued long past the time when the herbs might have been effective and the baby arrived before she could abandon it safely.

Denial of Pregnancy

In both the past and the present the most mysterious and yet the most common trait exhibited in neonaticide is the denial of pregnancy itself. An interesting phenomenon is that, in most cases, the women's families and friends also deny it. The girl or woman gains little weight as compared to most pregnant women and is able to disguise that with boxy blouses or sweaters. If she misses her menstrual period, she attributes that to some other cause. When she actually delivers the baby, often in a restroom, she says that she felt the need to defecate and was totally shocked when a baby appeared. It is not only a matter of *saying* this; she actually believes it. "That discomfort I feel down below must be a pre-menstrual cramp or a little constipation," she thinks to herself. Alone, possibly frightened but often in total denial, the girl or woman delivers a newborn baby whose very evolution she has denied for as long as 8 or 9 months. The delivery is either relatively easy and brief, or the young woman exerts monumental self-control in not making a sound during contractions or even during the delivery itself. The existence of this child is so threatening to her and to her way of life that she suffocates or drowns or shakes the life out of the newborn. "Denial and rationalization of symptoms and denial of pregnancy may result in inadequate responses at the time of childbirth, and that may result in the death of the newborn" (Finnegan, McKinstry, and Robinson, 1982, p. 674). Even those who delivered in a hospital, however, had come seeking aid for stomach pains, flu, or other sources of pain, not for deliveries of babies whose existence *in utero* they and those close to them had denied.

This denial behavior is not a contemporary phenomenon. Records of English courts of the 17th and 18th centuries revealed similar denials of pregnancy, and that had been observed also in France and in the American colonies (Hufton, 1974). Court records in Victorian England indicated the isolation, denial, and concealment of pregnancy (Higginbotham, 1989). Most of the servant girls in 19th–century Bavaria had their babies in privies, and treated the births as evacuations — which did not affect the rhythm of their work. They denied the pregnancy and "subsequently told the judge that they had not known that they were pregnant. They had certainly lost 'something'; they did not know it was a child" (Schulte, 1984, p. 85).

Our contemporary society has seen similar behavior. Although motives may differ, social and economic circumstances may be disparate, and even the ambience is different, young women seem to react to their dilemma in the same way. Women in the past and present who commit neonaticide generally have made no plans for the births or care of their children. Massive denial of the gravid state is a prominent feature of this clinical situation, with the denial so powerful that it affects not only the young woman's own perception, but also those of her family, friends, teachers, employers, and even physician.

Five cases in Iowa reported in 1987 exemplify this pattern of behavior (Saunders, 1989). In February 1987, a 19-year-old college freshman drowned her 9-lb baby boy in a college dormitory toilet after denying and concealing her pregnancy. She pleaded guilty to a charge of child endangerment and was sentenced to 10 years in prison. A 14-year-old girl gave birth to a living baby girl who she hid in a closet, where the infant died of exposure. She was tried in juvenile court for endangering the life of a child; her sentence was withheld from the press. A 4¹/₂-lb baby girl was found abandoned in a ditch, dead from exposure. Her mother, a 17 year old, was subsequently found and charged with murder. Her sentence was also withheld. A 28 year old claimed that she did not realize she was pregnant until her newborn was found dead in a toilet. She was sentenced to 20 years for endangerment and neglect of a baby. Another 28 year old was discovered dead from blood loss after delivering a 5-lb baby who was found dead from exposure. No one knew she was pregnant. These cases echo the scenario played out in the past: the mothers denied or concealed their pregnancy.

Other studies provide additional evidence. In Oberman's (1996) study, of her 47 cases of neonaticide, 19 denied the pregnancy to themselves, 10 concealed it from others, and 43 delivered without assistance, which is consistent with other studies. Similarly, in the study by Overpeck et al. (1998), "95 percent of infants killed during the first day of life were not born in a hospital, as compared with 8 percent of all infants killed during the first year of life … " (p. 1214).

Denial of pregnancy can also contribute to prenatal conditions that render the newborn either underweight, ill at birth, or possibly mentally retarded. This is because the young woman has not had any prenatal care and generally is not following a diet or physical regime that would be helpful to the pregnancy and developing baby. A 17-year-old high school senior in Eastern Pennsylvania was raped twice, saw the school nurse periodically for what were noted as menstrual cramps and spotting, bled profusely midway through her pregnancy and thought it was a miscarriage due to the second rape, and gained only 10 lbs during her whole pregnancy. "While these circumstances seem hard to believe, it is important to bear in mind that Lisa was a naive, 17-year-old girl who felt ashamed and afraid and who confided in no one" (Atkins et al., 1999, p. 7). She delivered a full-term baby girl who was not breathing, hid her in an overnight bag at her hosts' home in New Jersey and then in the garage at her own home. Taken to the hospital shortly thereafter, the doctors found signs of the delivery and "Lisa" admitted to what had happened.

Wheelwright (1998) related the case of a 21 year old in Manchester, England, who endured 17 hours of labor alone which ended in a breech delivery. In another case, a young 20-year-old student at a local community college had a premature infant alone at home, refusing to summon the aid of her sleeping family. She had a long difficult labor and was discovered hemorrhaging in the bathroom the next morning. She was taken to the emergency room where medical intervention saved her life. The doctor's testimony indicated that the problem of her self-delivery could induce shock. Her premature baby later died (*State v. Maurico,* 1987).

Crittenden and Craig (1990) noted, in a study done in Dade County, Florida, that there were a high number of spontaneous births and subsequent drownings of newborns in toilets, echoing results found by Mitchell and Davis (1984) who had conducted an earlier study in the same county. The new mother commits neonaticide and will deny that, too, as ever having happened. Whether in cases of drowning or other birth settings, often the girl or woman throws the little body, wrapped in a bag, into a trash can. "Out of sight, out of mind!" Clearly, the baby never existed.

One of the more sensationalized cases was that of Melissa Drexler, the so-called "Prom Mom," who arrived at the site of her high school prom, excused herself to go to the ladies' room, and shortly thereafter came out and allegedly danced at her prom (Hanley, 1997). She was arrested when a maintenance worker found the body — while the prom was still on and Drexler, herself, was dancing and enjoying herself. One friend was quoted as saying that, to her knowledge, Drexler did not know she was pregnant, while the mother of another friend commented that she certainly did not look $8^1/2$ months pregnant when shopping for a prom dress a few weeks before the event (Goodnough and Weber, 1997). In a less publicized incident, a 20-year-old college student gave birth alone during the night (3 a.m.), wrapped the baby in a blanket, and took the baby to the basement, placing the baby in a wood-burning stove. She then took a bath, retrieved the baby's remains, placed the bundle in her car's trunk for later disposal, and then attended her college classes the next morning as if nothing happened (*State v. McGuire*, 1997). This echoes the view of Brozovsky and Falit (1971) who suggested that the denial can be so potent, it affects not only the pregnant young woman, but also her family, friends, teachers, employers, and even her physician.

Denial was not even mentioned by Nadeau (1997) in her discussion of a revised typology of filicide; nor was neonaticide mentioned in the work of Resnick (1992) on the alternatives available to a pregnant girl (abortion, mothering, adoption). Yet, there are a number of psychologists, psychiatrists, and obstetricians who have written about both the hysterical denial of the young girl and the more psychotically-based denial of a young woman who suffers from a chronic mental illness. The difference is clarified by Spielvogel and Hohenor (1995):

> It is common for primaparous women who are unfamiliar with symptoms of pregnancy and for those who are ambivalent about being pregnant not to recognize their pregnancy until the second trimester. When pregnancy is denied throughout most or all of gestation, significant risk to the infant and mother may result, such as ... neonaticide. Persistent denial can occur in women with otherwise intact reality testing (nonpsychotic denial) and in those with a thinking disorder and general deficits in cognitive functioning or reality testing (psychotic denial) (Spielvogel and Hohenor, 1995, pp. 220–221).*

Additional reasons for nonpsychotic denial may include young age, anger toward the baby's father, rejection of the fetus, childhood psychological and sexual traumas, and "conflicted or inhibited sexuality in response to strict religious or parental prohibitions of premarital sex" (Spielvogel and Hohenor, 1995, p. 221). Separation from the partner or stress arising from other interpersonal problems may also precipitate a denial of pregnancy

---

* Spielvogel, A.M. and Hohenor, H.C. (1995) Denial of pregnancy: a review and case reports, *Birth*, 22(4), 220–221. Courtesy of Blackwell Science. With permission.

(Brezinka et al., 1994), as may social isolation (Finnegan, McKinstry, and Robinson, 1982). In the case of adolescents, particularly, they may not reveal or discuss amenorrhea or other symptoms even if they visit their health caregivers, and thus they receive no prenatal care. They do not plan to do away with the baby after birth; they simply refuse to think of the baby in any way at all, and "it" is what they perceive rather than a baby. Whether the neonate is killed as part of the denial or as a result of panic following the birth is often difficult to determine.

As previous cases illustrated, the denial of pregnancy and absence of prenatal care add to the risks of childbirth. Not only does the young woman risk her life, but she risks possible severe damage to the baby in terms of brain damage, malnutrition, and a variety of defects. This may well have been the case with Amy Grossberg, who apparently had some bleeding during pregnancy and then had seizures and eclampsia following her unattended delivery (McCullough, 1998; Most, 1999). According to testimony at the sentencing hearing reported on CNN's "Burden of Proof" (July 9, 1998), Brian Peterson, father of the baby-to-be, claimed to have asked Amy twice to have an abortion, which she refused to do for fear that her mother would find out, and also to have neonatal care, which she also refused to do. She also wrote Brian letters in which she hoped that "it" would disappear (Most, 1999).

Margaret Spinelli, a psychiatrist at Columbia University who had worked with nine neonaticidal women, said that their denial could be linked to a dissociative disorder in which the pregnancy is denied so firmly that it is compartmentalized and separated from the conscious self (ABC News, 1997). She believed that there should be two psychiatric evaluations by specialists in perinatal psychiatry of these young women prior to their being handled by the legal system.

Psychological/Psychiatric Diagnoses

Psychotic denial of pregnancy may occur in women who are chronically mentally ill, possibly schizophrenic, and who may have lost custody of other children earlier. Another possibility is cognitive and ego impairment, allegedly occurring in connection with a close but ambivalent relation with the young woman's mother (Milden et al., 1985). Here, both mother and daughter tend to be in denial of the pregnancy. Some young women believe that they are suffering from a blood clot or water retention which is contributing to an enlarged abdominal area, or may misinterpret the symptoms of labor (Spielvogel and Hohenor, 1995). All of these young women need to be cared for during pregnancy and helped during delivery to avert postpartum emotional disturbances and fetal abuse or neonaticide (Miller, 1990; Spielvogel and Hohenor, 1995). One psychotic woman in her fourth pregnancy had a history of three consecutive unassisted home deliveries and subsequent neonatal deaths. Not knowing what to do, she placed two of her newborns in a garbage can and left the other unattended in her apartment. The woman was hospitalized in the psychiatric unit for her fourth delivery, and gave birth to a healthy infant whom she gave up for adoption (Spielvogel and Hohenor, 1995, p. 224).*

Defense attorneys for those who have committed neonaticide or infanticide frequently claim that the young woman was suffering from a reactive psychosis or post-partum depression which made her commit the crime (that she was mentally ill). Postpartum psychosis, sometimes mistakenly tied to neonaticide, may have applicability to infanticide, i.e., murder of the infant after the first 24 hours but before age 1 year, but is not really a factor in neonaticide. This is because the onset of this condition is usually a few days to a few weeks after childbirth (Schroeder, 1993). It was mentioned in the *Diagnostic and Statistical Manual of Mental Disorders, Third Edition* (American Psychiatric Association, 1980), but was considered an "atypical psychosis" rather than a discrete entity (Munoz, 1985).

Whether there is a diagnosis incorporating denial as well as a psychotic episode at the time of delivery resulting in the neonate's death, and called "neonaticide syndrome," is debatable. Wolman's classic *Handbook of Clinical Psychology* (1965) refers to the psychoanalytic perception of denial as a defense against the perception of a painful reality (p. 322). Kaplan and Sadock (1996), dealing with the content of the American Psychiatric Association's *Diagnostic and Statistical Manual of Mental Disorders, Third Edition* (1980), have a similar definition of "denial" as a defense mechanism and briefly mention infanticide as one risk of untreated postpartum psychosis. There is no separate citation of "denial," "infanticide," or "neonaticide" in the American Psychiatric Association's *Diagnostic and Statistical Manual of Mental Disorders, Fourth Edition* (1994). For an attorney to attempt to use "neonaticide syndrome" as a defense for one of the young women charged with neonaticide is difficult, for it does not meet the *Frye v. United States* (1923) or *Daubert v. Merrell Dow Pharmaceuticals, Inc.* (1993) tests of acceptability within the professional community.

An example of the confusion can be seen in two neonaticide cases involving the same psychologist. In the first case, a 21-year-old woman was said by her therapist to be suffering from "neonaticide dissociative disorder" and, after pleading guilty to involuntary manslaughter and concealment of a homicide, she was eventually sentenced to 30 months of probation, continued psychotherapy, community service, and other obligations (Taylor, 1998). A

---

* Spielvogel, A.M. and Hohenor, H.C. (1995) Denial of pregnancy: a review and case reports, *Birth,* 22(4), 224. Courtesy of Blackwell Science. With permission.

few months later, another 21 year old pleaded insanity as a defense, having been diagnosed by the same psychologist as having "acute stress disorder," a condition that made her "unable to appreciate the wrongfulness of her actions" (Illinois Report, 1998). The attorney in the second case no longer planned to present evidence that her client suffered from neonatal dissociative disorder because, she was quoted, "that term is not generally recognized in the psychiatric community" (Illinois Report, 1998).

The existence of a neonaticide "syndrome" became a source of argument and appeal in the case of Stephanie Wernick, a college student who asphyxiated her newborn son, denied she had ever been pregnant, and was convicted of criminally negligent homicide (*People v. Wernick*, 1996). She had claimed insanity as a defense. Wernick's expert witnesses were allowed to testify that she had denied she was pregnant, that such denial occurs in almost all cases of neonaticide, that she may indeed not have known that she was pregnant, and that she suffered a brief reactive psychosis upon giving birth. They were not allowed to say that she suffered from the so-called "neonaticide syndrome" or to cite relevant clinical experience, and this decision of the lower court was upheld twice on appeal. In two other cases of neonaticide in the Chicago area, one attorney was ready to present an insanity defense while the other was not. The one who chose not to raise this defense said that if the defense was used, the defendant had to admit having committed the crime, and other defenses, such as having an alibi or alleging that someone else murdered the newborn, could not be used (Chen, 1998).

In a study of 60 women who had killed one or more of their children (N = 76) between 1970 and 1996, Lewis et al. (1998) found that 52% "were found incompetent to stand trial and an even higher percentage found not guilty by reason of insanity (65%)" (p. 614). The victims ranged in age from birth to 26 years, with a median age of 2.50 years. Further, it was found that "Although 25% of the total sample used a gun or a knife, 36% of the psychotic mothers used these weapons compared to only 5% of the non-psychotic mothers" (p. 615), and the children killed with these weapons were significantly older than those killed by other means (smothering, poisoning, drowning, beating, starvation, etc.). Although neonaticides were included in this sample, the use of a weapon to commit the crime was unlikely.

Reaction and Revenge

Depending upon the era in which a case occurred, and the state, some homicides of pregnant women may be viewed as neonaticides, i.e., the fetus, especially if viable, killed before birth is regarded as a newborn for the purposes of prosecutorial charges. These murders usually occur when the male does not want the child (if he is the father) or wants to punish his wife/girlfriend for becoming pregnant by another man or even by him. Such an incident occurred in California when Larry Apodaca raped and assaulted his pregnant ex-wife, claiming that he would not permit her to bear anyone else's baby. After sustaining the beating, she delivered a dead fetus (about 22 to 24 weeks). The defendant was convicted of second degree murder of a fetus, rape, and assault (*People v. Apodaca*, 1978). A similar incident involved another angry ex-husband who, discovering his ex-wife was pregnant, physically attacked her, causing a miscarriage (*People v. Keeler*, 1970).

Infanticide and Filicide

Infanticide, the killing of a child older than 24 to 48 hours but up to 1 year of age, is the result of a different set of motives. Silverman and Kennedy (1988) asserted that immaturity and psychological stress were pre-eminent motives in infanticide. These can be understood to some degree when the age of many of the perpetrators is considered as well as the absence of proper preparation for parenting or the aid of support systems. Reaction to stress or family arguments, or a desire for revenge against the child's other parent, can lead to infanticide (rarely to neonaticide). The stress may be rooted in poverty, ill-health, having too many children, or lack of a support system. It is taken out on the vulnerable baby, who may be crying, have wet a diaper, or just be "there" and "in the way" as it were.

As we noted earlier, when births are shown in almost complete detail in soap operas or "family" television shows and on the Internet, there seems to be little excuse for anyone to be uninformed about infantile behaviors and bodily functions. What psychological factors operate to repress such knowledge in the minds of homicidal caretakers? Child neglect, as in inadequate feeding, and child abuse, as in violent shaking of a baby, are often the basis of charges against the homicidal parent(s); infanticide does not have to result from drowning or stabbing as can be seen in cases throughout the country. Why do these parents (or those serving in that role) batter and kill children who cannot control their behavior because they are too young to do so? When social welfare agencies exist in virtually every community in the U.S., why are some parents so overwhelmed by child care that they murder children rather than seek outside help?

In cases where the parents separate, one parent may kill their child(ren) rather than permit the other to have visitation or shared custody, or, conversely, to avoid paying child support. Such a "revenge" motive, one of several postulated by Resnick (1970) is an example of warped thought processes, and may lead to a defense at trial of mental illness. It is difficult to ascertain whether these cases of infanticide and filicide are committed more frequently by fathers or by mothers, although the motive may be quite clear in some individual cases. One might hypothesize that a parent against whom the other parent has secured a "protection" order, typically the father, is more likely to commit this crime as part of his crusade of revenge against the children's mother. However, it is difficult to secure accurate statistics to test such a hypothesis.

Brody (1998) cited research by Daly and Wilson, evolutionary psychologists cited earlier, who found "the rate of infanticide was 60 times as high … in stepfamilies as in biologically related families" (p. F1). They and others who take the evolutionary perspective believe that the "underlying trigger" for abuse and conflict in stepfamilies "lies within inherently selfish genes, which are biologically driven to perpetuate themselves" (p. F1). This is seen in lower animal family groups, they assert, where a male that takes over an existing family typically kills offspring from the female's earlier matings.

Personal Gain

In at least some cases, beyond the ken of most people, babies are killed for the parent's financial gain. That is, the parents have taken out life insurance on the children and collect when the children die from "Sudden Infant Death Syndrome" (SIDS), drowning, arson, neglect, or some other cause. Several cases have been reported, usually after prolonged investigation, and tend to evoke antipathy in the minds of the public. One such case involved a woman in Chicago who was charged with suffocating her 7-week-old daughter in order to collect $200,000 for the child's supposed SIDS death. The money would have been used to support her gambling habit (Chase, 1999). In another, the Mitchells of Kentucky were accused of starving their 2-year-old son to death; they had $60,000 paid-up insurance on each of their three children (Bridis, 1997). In yet another case, parents in West Virginia were charged with the arson death of their five children, arranged so that they could collect on their homeowner's insurance policy (Sharp, 1997). Ellen Baker Boehm, mother of two sons and a daughter, killed her boys by smothering them and then attempted to electrocute her daughter — all with the goal of collecting on the insurance she had taken out on their lives (Costen, 1995).

It should be noted that murdering a child to collect on the child's insurance is not a modern phenomenon. In 18th- and 19th-century England, infants and young children died from burns, suffocation, drowning, excess medication, starvation, and indifference, just like today. "Under burial society rules a member, ordinarily a parent, received as beneficiary on the death of his or her insured child a payment from the society that considerably exceeded the combined cost of the insurance premium and the burial" (Forbes, 1986, p. 189). It was very difficult to prosecute the parents in these burial society cases. Laws were passed in the 1889 to 1908 period, however, that made it a felony to benefit from the death of a child (Forbes, 1986) .

There are also murders of babies that are initially labeled "crib deaths," or SIDS deaths that, in cases where multiple instances occur in the same family, are subsequently recognized as infanticide. The authorities may begin to suspect that they are dealing with a parent who enjoys the role of victim ("Poor woman!") even if there is no life insurance to collect. Waneta Hoyt in upstate New York lost five children in this way in the 1960s, and has only recently been accused and convicted of murdering her children (Firstman and Talan, 1997; Pinholster, 1995; Toufexis, 1994). Arthur and Marie Noe in Philadelphia lost 8 of their 10 children to SIDS, with a 9th stillborn and the 10th who died 6 hours after birth — all between 1949 and 1968 (Fried, 1998; Gibbons, 1998). Thirty years after the last alleged SIDS death, Marie Noe was arrested and charged with eight counts of murder (Loyd, 1998). She pleaded guilty to second-degree murder in March 1998, and 15 months later was sentenced to 20 years' probation, with the first 5 years as house arrest (McCoy, 1999). She gave few reasons for the murders and was to meet with psychiatrists monthly in an effort to understand what drove her to the infanticides. Another case very similar in context was that of Cheri Welch, who claimed that her 7-month-old baby had died of apnea reflex (similar to SIDS). Her 2-week-old boy was brought to the hospital bleeding and breathless. He was saved, but hospital personnel became suspicious of child abuse. Subsequent investigations revealed the death of another girl baby. At the same time, Welch claimed she was the victim of a rape. The authorities arrested her for the murder of two babies and attempted murder of the third. Psychological testing indicated that she suffered from borderline personality disorder or Munchausen Syndrome by Proxy (MBP). She was convicted of first degree murder and sentenced to life imprisonment (*U.S. v. Welch,* 1994).

Whether the mother cannot cope with the stresses of parenting, seeks to collect insurance benefits, or is mentally ill, differs in each situation. As many experts have said, one SIDS death can be a tragedy; even two can be due to a tragic genetic flaw; but three or more certainly warrant investigation. According to psychiatrists, these parents suffer from a form of Munchausen's Syndrome, an unusual condition in which someone feigns or induces illness, usually in an attempt to get attention and care from physicians and possibly others. In the variation known as MBP, the parents injure their children or cause them to be ill. According to one report, "Parents have even been caught by surveillance cameras attempting to smother their offspring in their hospital beds" (Toufexis, 1994, p. 64). The mothers tend to display frequent or bizarre symptoms of illness in the absence of real illness, labeled "Factitious Disorder by Proxy" in *Diagnostic and Statistical Manual of Mental Disorders, Fourth Edition* (American Psychiatric Association, 1994). This latter behavior tends to be indicative of child abuse as well as parental illness.

In these cases, the mother (unconsciously) seeks to gain sympathetic attention through her MBP activities. Here, the infant or child is repeatedly brought to the hospital suffering from shortness of breath, diarrhea, or some other symptom, either falsified or induced in the child. A falsified history can create a damaging self-image in the child as being chronically ill, and the unnecessary medical tests to determine the cause of illness can themselves do damage (Kahan and Yorker, 1991). While in the hospital, the child is fine and healthy; a few weeks at home, and the child is back at the hospital with new symptoms. After several such incidents the child may die, with the death attributed to a respiratory or other illness — unless someone checks the child's hospital records, as is normally done where child abuse is suspected. Artingstall (1998) provides a number of helpful clues to use in differentiating child abuse cases from those where the MBP syndrome is the dominant factor.

It should be noted that fathers are rarely involved directly in MBP cases, although it is suggested that they may be helpful in describing a child's symptoms (Kahan and Yorker, 1991). More likely they will support the wife's sad tales.

In Summary

These theories and motives relevant to killing one's child obviously cover a wide range of contexts and perspectives, as well as a range of children's ages. Apart from the socioculturally sanctioned motives, it is possible to find several of these motives operating within any society at a given point in time, and, indeed, within the individual who commits the crime. In the coming chapters, we will focus first on the unnatural deaths of newborns and then on infants and young children.

Neonaticide and Its Alternatives

4

Teenaged girls today range from the truly naive to the pseudo-sophisticated, from those who maintain their virginity to those vulnerable to peer pressure involving sexual relations to the promiscuous. They are exposed to sexually explicit films and song lyrics which almost assume that sexual relations among the young are the norm, while their parents debate with school boards as to whether there should be sex education in the schools and if there should, how much information and what kinds should be included. Surrounded by titillating stimuli, but with insufficient factual information to help them cope with it, pre-adolescents and adolescents alike are often ill-prepared to prevent pregnancy or to deal with it.

As Pipher (1994) has pointed out,

> … girls are scared of many things. They are worried that they will be judged harshly for their bodies and lack of experience. They are worried about getting caught by their parents or going to hell. They fear pregnancy and STDs. They worry about getting a bad reputation, rejection and pleasing their partners. They have seen sex associated with female degradation and humiliation, and they have heard ugly words describing sex, words that have more to do with aggression than love. So they are fearful of being emotionally and physically hurt. For the most part, girls keep their anxiety to themselves. It's not sophisticated to be fearful (p. 207).

Add to this confused picture the fact that many girls also live in stressful family environments where their psychological and perhaps other needs are not being met, and one has a situation where these girls become highly vulnerable to sexual activity. They are often afraid that if they refuse to have intercourse with boys, they will be rejected, and they want desperately to be loved by someone. Indeed, some girls in this situation seek to become pregnant because they believe that at least the babies will love them unconditionally. Unfortunately, they seem to be unaware of the time and care needed by, and the demands of, infants. This can lead later to infanticide by unprepared caretakers of either gender.

No sexual intercourse
Sexual intercourse with contraceptives
vs.
Sexual intercourse without contraceptives
\> \> \> Pregnancy occurs
Abortion
vs.
Carry to term \> \> \>
Mother the child
vs.
Place for adoption
vs.
Abandon
vs.
Commit neonaticide

Figure 1 What are the options?

If the girl or woman elects not to have intercourse, obviously there will be no pregnancy. If she chooses to have intercourse, but only with the use of contraceptives, there will be no pregnancy as long as the contraceptive is effective. If no contraception is used, there is the risk of pregnancy, and then there are other choices to be made, as seen in Figure 1.

The adolescent girls who become pregnant are considered to have immature cognitive development in that they take risks without weighing the potential outcomes of their behavior. According to Stoiber, Anderson, and Schowalter (1998), several studies have shown that the bent toward risk behavior plus situational factors such as educational disadvantage, school failure or school dropout status, and strong peer pressure to have sex contribute strongly toward adolescent pregnancy. In addition, they reported that parents did not discuss sexually transmitted diseases, pregnancy, conception, or contraception with their children. Strong peer pressure, in the form of higher scores on the "powerful other" locus of control sub-scale in terms of health decision-making, was also a significant finding in Morgan's study (1995) of sexually active suburban middle-class adolescent girls and pregnancy. She hypothesized that they might be more susceptible to peer pressure than others, which might place them at higher risk for unintended pregnancy than more self-reliant peers. On the other hand, the ability to control impulses and delay gratification requires a sense that there are choices to be made and consequences of choices. A third perspective, that of Stevens-Simon and McAnarney (1994), suggests that childhood physical or sexual abuse is a common antecedent of adolescent pregnancy and is tied as well to the birth of smaller and less mature infants.

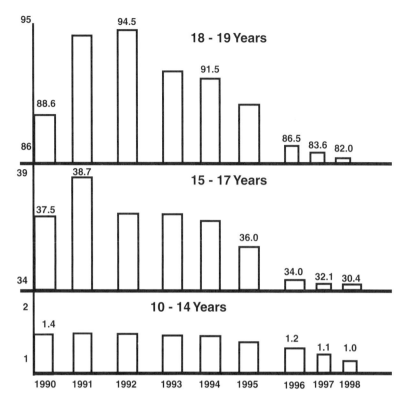

Figure 2 Birth rates for women under 20 years of age, 1990–1998 (per 1000 in specified group) — all races and divided by age group.

Although the birth rate for teenagers has been declining in recent years, according to the National Center for Health Statistics (Ventura, Mathews, and Curtin, 1999b), a different estimate suggests that about 11% of girls aged 15 to 19 years get pregnant each year, or approximately 1 million pregnancies (Benoit, 1997). The Alan Guttmacher Institute reported, in 1998, that the rate of adolescent pregnancy was declining, with 101 pregnancies per 1000 girls aged 15 to 19 years in 1995 as compared with 117 per 1000 in 1990 (Lewin, 1998). These figures may be incomplete and a slight underestimate according to Henshaw (1997), who analyzed 1992 data for the Institute. None of the sets of data account for all of the pregnancies, either because they have excluded pregnancies among even younger girls or because of unregistered births (and deaths, such as neonaticides). The National Center for Health Statistics does, however, show that the number of births per 1000 for girls aged 10 to 14 years has declined from a high of 1.4 in 1991 to 1994 to a low of 1.0 in 1998 (Ventura, Mathews, and Curtin, 1999b) (Figure 2). This translated in 1998 to 9,481 births.

Not all of those who commit neonaticide, however, are teenagers (or younger). This is apparent if we examine data from available studies or ones we have collected ourselves. In the cases we found with mother's age reported between mid-1994 and mid-1999, 52 were teenagers or post-adolescent (ages 13 to 20 years) and 33 were 21 years of age or older, with a median age of 19 years. In addition, of 6 recent cases where the newborn was found alive and the mother was later identified, 4 were aged 12 to 17 years, one was aged 38 years, and the other was a 43-year-old mother of 8 other children. In Oberman's (1996) study, the median age of those who committed neonaticide was 17 years, but this means, obviously, that half of her sample of 47 were older than 17 years.

Adler (1984) pointed out that several studies of adolescents indicated that both males and females lacked appropriate information about contraceptives, and that where the youths *were* cognizant of the need for contraception, it was the girl who was expected to handle this, not the boy. However, if the girl did use a contraceptive method or sought information about preventing pregnancy, this was admitting to herself (and perhaps others) that she planned to have intercourse. The use of contraceptives was also often seen as violating religious instruction. Either of these reasons provoked feelings of guilt in the girl. Vance (1985) similarly commented on the ignorance and naiveté of many teenaged girls: their "lack of motivation to take responsibility to prevent pregnancy; ... fear of asking for help in preventing pregnancy; and inner feelings of denial based on false assumptions that 'it can never happen to me'" (p. 274).

If pregnancy does occur, and this is a more frequent outcome than the youths anticipate, denial tends to persist throughout most of the pregnancy, if not through the delivery itself. Both prenatal care and abortion are typically avoided as either of these would be an admission to the self, and others, that the girl was pregnant (Bluestein and Rutledge, 1992).

The denial may be the result of paranoid schizophrenia, borderline or inadequate personality disorder, or a kind of hysterical amnesia designed to avoid admitting to the moralistic self even that she had participated in sexual intercourse (Milden et al., 1985; see also Brozovsky and Falit, 1971). "What happens to the babies, secretly growing inside the mothers who are unaware, and, by extension, unable to make any antepartum decisions — to terminate or continue the pregnancy, to seek prenatal care, to plan to relinquish the babies for adoption or to raise them in their own families?" (Milden et al., 1985, p. 256).

Options in Pregnancy

As shown in Figure 1, if the girl admits to herself, even briefly, that she is pregnant, she has two principal options: abortion or to continue the pregnancy. If she chooses the former, she enters an arena full of conflicts; if she chooses the latter, she then has other decisions to make.

Abortion

Even to contemplate an abortion means that the female has admitted to herself that she is pregnant. That is not a universal truth among women of childbearing age. Should the woman do so, termination of an unwanted pregnancy is an option for many girls and women, although not in good conscience for those who are Roman Catholic or followers of several other faiths. In the United States, abortion *is* legal in the first trimester, subsequent to the *Roe v. Wade* decision in 1972, and in some jurisdictions even during the second trimester. Whether the pregnant woman is a teenager or an adult, access to abortion must be available if she is to choose this option. Such access may depend on her age, the state in which she lives, her socio-economic class, and the dangers which may exist in her community relative to abortion. (The many factors affecting availability are discussed more fully in Chapter 8.)

Adler (1992) identified five types of pregnancy and found that each provoked a different type of response following an abortion. "A woman's responses following abortion are likely to be a function both of her desire for pregnancy and of her feelings about abortion" (p. 20), with those least desirous of pregnancy and least antagonistic toward abortion obviously having the most benign responses. There are differences between unplanned and unintended pregnancies, between those that are pre-marital and those that are extra-marital, between those of adolescents and those of adult women, and between knowledge or ignorance of the pregnancy of the female's family, all of which lead to varying perceptions of and responses to abortion. There is also the initial admission to herself that she is pregnant, rather than being in denial which would lead to the pregnancy being carried to term. Studies suggest that those adolescents who choose to have an early abortion do so because they recognize their immaturity as potential parents, and that they face far fewer physical risks from the abortion than from pregnancy, as well as few adverse psychological effects (Adler, Smith, and Tschann, 1998).

According to data supplied by the Population Division of the Department of Economic and Social Affairs of the United Nations Secretariat only five members of the U.N. "currently prohibit abortion even to save the life of the mother" (Ellsworth, 1998). These are Andorra, The Vatican (Holy See), Malta, El Salvador, and Chile. The other 185 nations permit abortion in varying degrees for specific reasons:

To preserve the woman's physical health	63%
To preserve the woman's mental health	51%
In cases of rape or incest	43%

In cases of possible fetal impairment	42%
For economic or social reasons	31%
Upon request	25%

The fact that abortions may not be legal for all reasons in all locations does not mean that they do not occur. To the contrary, the U.N. found that about 20 million unsafe or illegal abortions were performed in the early 1990s, with approximately 90% of those in developing nations, and more than 69,000 deaths annually from such procedures (Ellsworth, 1998).

Sanger, a professor at Columbia University Law School, has asserted that anti-abortionists have created an atmosphere that contributes to neonaticide through condemnation, stigmatization, and fear. "By denying the complexity of abortion decisions — by insisting that abortion is evil and that there is nothing more to say on the subject — antiabortion absolutists contribute to the fraught, panic-stricken atmosphere in which deadly denial becomes possible" (Sanger, 1997, p. A49). In other words, if we pretend the situation doesn't exist, it will disappear.

The Committee on Psychiatry and Law of the Group for the Advancement of Psychiatry (GAP) considered the right to abortion in the pre-*Roe v. Wade* era — 1969 — and averred that the effects of being unwanted (for the child) and having an unwanted child (for the mother) were highly negative for both. Further, they suggested that "those who believe abortion is murder need not avail themselves of it. On the other hand, we do not believe that such conviction should limit the freedom of those not bound by identical religious conviction" (1969, p. 219). They cited Erikson's consideration that mutilation of a child's spirit, by being an unwanted child, is the most deadly of all possible sins, and forced motherhood as being equally bad for a woman. Erikson's view is still valid some decades later, although this should not be seen as advocating abortion, but rather as recognizing the roots of negative self-esteem, child abuse, and other undesirable outcomes. David's longitudinal study (1992) of unwanted children born to mothers who had been denied an abortion similarly found negative effects on their psychosocial development that were apparent in adulthood.

An extreme case involving abortion and religion is one in which a 10 year-old girl in Brazil was raped. When she was 3 months pregnant she applied for an abortion, which is permitted in Brazil in rape cases, and was supported at the time by her father. The judge withheld his ruling for several weeks, awaiting information on possible harm to the girl if the abortion were performed. The Health Minister supported the girl's application, but some Catholic clergy opposed it, with one priest asking "What crime has that child [the fetus] committed?" (Reuters, 1997). [The dispute as to which life is the more "valuable" is also seen in Islamic writings. Abortion is forbidden, although it *may* be justified in cases of rape where the woman has reported the rape and has sought immediate medical attention. Ebrahim (1991), for example, is inclined to support abortion in rape cases, but then asks "… would that be just? After all, the fetus has committed no crime. How then could its life be terminated?" (p. 85)] Apparently a retired obstetrician and a priest persuaded the Brazilian father to reverse his stand and he withdrew his approval of the procedure (Mathis, 1997). An angry editorial writer saw this turn of events as a clear-cut case of child abuse from a mental health as well as physical health perspective. "The life of the innocent unborn is, though contentious, a reasonable matter for debate in most cases. In this one, however, there is another innocent child and, when it comes down to the value of life, hers has supremacy. How dare the father, the doctor and priest seek their own satisfactions and soothe their own consciences at her expense" (Mathis, 1997).

Judaism, in general, opposes "abortion on demand," or in cases of unwanted pregnancy, but supports it if the mother's life is in serious physical danger, or, more rarely, if it would endanger the mother's psychological health (this would be considered a valid reason for an abortion) (Werblowsky and Wigoder, 1965). The emphasis on the mother, the "most proximate life," as more than one rabbi has put it, obviously differs from that of anti-abortion groups who place the fetus' "life" above that of the prospective mother. Full human rights, in Jewish law, are extended only to a *born and viable* being.

Carrying the Pregnancy to Term

If abortion is ruled out and the pregnancy continues to delivery, the young woman who has not denied her pregnancy is confronted with choices again: mother the child, place "it" up for adoption, abandon "it" alive at a location where someone will find "it," or kill "it." The term "it" is used advisedly, for most of these young women do not regard the entity they are carrying as babies even when they are born. The problem is described clearly by Resnick (1970): "[W]omen who seek abortions are activists who recognize reality early and promptly attack the danger. In contrast, women who commit neonaticide often deny that they are pregnant or assume that the child will be stillborn. No advance preparations are made either for the care or the killing of the infant" (p. 1416). The denial usually means that the girl has no prenatal care, even when problems arise, for she denies to her doctor any relationship between symptoms such as nausea or weight gain and pregnancy. A very busy doctor may take her at her word. The lack of prenatal care resulting in damage to or the death of the fetus may be cause in itself, in some jurisdictions, for the state to charge the woman with manslaughter or "depraved indifference" to the welfare of another.

Mothering

For some young women, perhaps themselves "love children" raised by unwed mothers, the choice is to keep the children. Perhaps they simply consider this a normal life pattern, and it may be so in their communities, or perhaps they think of what might have been their lot in life had their own mothers not raised them. Or, as one 14-year-old mother put it, she decided to keep her baby "for selfish reasons. I wanted someone who I knew would love me" ("So You're Going to be a Mother," 1999, p. 24). What some may not realize is the tremendous change in daily routine, let alone lifestyle, which occurs as soon as the baby is born. For many new mothers, the sudden loss of control of one's own use of time is not only a shock, but also an emotional and, possibly, physical strain. There is also a loss of privacy, and, possibly, physical, emotional, and financial support. According to Ogle, Maier-Katkin, and Bernard (1995), achieving the status of being regarded as a "good mother" requires nurturing ability, willingness to make great sacrifices, and some kind of "inherent knowledge" which not only causes great stress for the mother, but may be especially remote experientially for the younger mother.

Psychiatrists, psychologists, and social workers in the 1950s viewed unwed mothers as mentally ill. "They remarked frequently that unmarried mothers got pregnant easily, had few miscarriages, little nausea, no food fads, no moods, and no delivery complications; and exhibited an unusual degree of contentment" (Solinger, 1990, p. 46). These were generally, however, young women already admitted to maternity homes and well past their first trimesters when seen.

The fact that the girl hadn't prevented or terminated her pregnancy was seen as conclusive proof of psychological disturbance by psychiatrists in the pre-*Roe v. Wade* era (1945 to 1965). No one referred to the legal obstacles in the way of both contraception and abortion at that time. "Displaying surprising willingness to expect criminality in girls and women, they were willing, as well, to deepen their blame of the victim by using her law-abiding behavior to justify the diagnosis of mental illness" (Solinger, 1990, p. 47). Why did they become pregnant if single? "Girls and women were driven into sex and pregnancy, professionals determined, as a result of both gender dysfunctions and family dysfunctions … The most typical patterns appeared to be a weak father and a hypochondriacal and controlling mother, or a strong but neglectful father and a frustrated mother" (p. 47). Mothers got the most blame for the daughter's pregnancy, i.e., the daughter allegedly felt unloved by her mother. As recently as 1988, a Pennsylvania couple was charged with endangering the welfare of their child because they allowed a young man to visit her in their home although they were aware that he and their daughter (age 13 years) were having intercourse, as a result of which the girl became pregnant. Although the jury voted to convict, they were found not guilty of neglect by the trial court (*Commonwealth v. Campbell*, 1990).

The perspectives of that pre-*Roe* era are interesting to consider a few decades later:

- White girls and women who were illegitimately pregnant before *Roe* could only anticipate rehabilitation and ultimately a "normal" life if they relinquished the baby for adoption.
- If a white girl or woman had a sex life or a baby before marriage at that time, she was considered by those in the psychiatric mainstream to be "sick." Any evaluation of her sex life could only be done *after* marriage.
- White unwed mothers suffered in that earlier period because they had no legal basis to control their own lives. "The application of psychiatric theory to single pregnancy further legitimated the use of science to punish women for their unsanctioned sexual experience and to limit their control over their own bodies and their own children" (Solinger, 1990, p. 52).

Although many adolescent girls in both earlier periods and today choose to mother their children, it is too often a case of poorly prepared and poorly informed "children raising children." This usually serves neither of them well, as the young mother has no time to develop her individuation, educational potential, or even physical health, and her lack of parenting skills, as well as the earlier lack of prenatal care, can affect her child's physical and cognitive development negatively (Coley and Chase-Lansdale, 1998). Although the health risks to these children are cause for concern, so are the increased risks of abuse and involvement with law enforcement (Corcoran, 1998).

Milden et al. (1995) compared nine cases of denied pregnancy in the literature with eight cases of denial that they had seen in their university hospital. Five of the nine women gave birth at home, with three of them committing neonaticide; in the hospital sample, seven of the eight young women kept their babies. The latter group were principally from low socio-economic status, black, single-parent families, but the patients were very involved with their mothers. Their decisions to mother their babies were not typical of what is found in the professional literature.

Sometimes the adolescent mother continues to live with her family and has help from *her* parents, but it takes substantial internal resources and external support for her to mature successfully and to rear her child responsibly. The headline on one newspaper article says it all: "The secret of motherhood: Birth may come naturally, sometimes unexpectedly, but nurturing must be learned" (Straight, 1998). Arnoldi (1999), who became a mother at age 17, raised her daughter, worked, sent the daughter through college although she herself had not graduated from high school, and now shares her story with adolescents, especially those in high school equivalency programs. (A number of school districts, usually in large communities, have special programs for students who are parents which provide not only nursery care while the mother attends classes, but also parenting education. These will be discussed later.) The father, also usually adolescent, may feel a sense of having proved his manhood, but that does not necessarily extend to taking personal or financial responsibility for his child.

Relatively few studies have been focused primarily on a continuing involvement of the father with the adolescent mother and their baby. In a study of 105 adolescents aged 14 to 18 years, most of them from rural or small urban areas of lower socio-economic status, and pregnant with their first children, it was found that those who had continuous involvement with the babies' fathers were less frequently the subject of abuse or custody revocation investigations than the young women who were less involved (Cutrona et al., 1998). His support throughout the pregnancy and immediate postpartum period, especially when she was confronted with negative life events, appeared to enable the young mother to provide better parenting and a better childrearing environment (as measured 6 months after delivery) than was true for her peers who did not have these significant relationships in operation. Many young parents unconsciously accept, even expect, a dependency on the government to provide for their basic needs and those of their children. As Benoit (1997) put it, "In other words, government can psychologically become the surrogate parent" (p. 409).

With changes in the welfare laws in the late 1990s, many dependent single mothers found themselves no longer eligible for welfare checks. One of the difficulties, however, was that many of these women had inadequate preparation for any kind of job, let alone one that would pay for child care if their children were of preschool age or needed after-school care.

On the other hand, even if the fathers remain involved, there are risks if the father is, himself, an adolescent. There are not only conflicts arising between the roles of adolescent male and fatherhood, but there may well be unrealistic expectations of infant development and behavior (Robinson, 1988). This can lead to infanticide or filicide as will be discussed later. Or, in an effort to provide financial support to his baby and its mother, the youth may drop out of school, leaving him in a negative competitive position in the labor market.

Clearly, not all of those who choose to mother the baby are adolescents or even unwed. It is still difficult in many locations for unmarried women to be accepted as mothers, although there are many more of them today than in mid-century. One has to hope that they are mature enough emotionally to be nurturing mothers; regrettably, this is not always true and some of their children develop psychological problems or become victims of child abuse or homicide.

A Comment on "Illegitimacy"

The child born out of wedlock has never had an easy time in life. To begin with, said child has been labeled illegitimate (one of the kinder terms), unfathered (impossible!), misbegotten, baseborn, or bastard. (Comment: Why the child has to bear the brunt of one of these hostile descriptions when the child had nothing to do with his own creation is unclear.) When the child is considered "unfathered," it simply reflects the fact that either the mother does not know who he is or fails to identify him for reasons of her own, perhaps including fear of his anger. The Georgia General Assembly, in 1988, substituted the phrase "born out of wedlock" for the nastier terms to get rid of the stigma attached to the latter (Thompson, 1998). The child is not acknowledged or entitled, generally, to a parent's estate, especially not in the hierarchy-conscious British tradition, unless specific mention is made in a will. For all these reasons, the unwed young mother perceives this "thing" as less worthy or legitimate than a baby born to a married couple. If that is the case, as Ehrenreich (1998) so aptly put it, the "thing" is trash and can be discarded as one throws out trash. As we know, this happens too frequently.

Having an out-of-wedlock baby and unmarried motherhood are not necessarily synonymous, nor are they as frowned upon today as used to be true. Many women who opted for careers before marriage and who chose not to marry because they feared the possibility of divorce, do want to be mothers. As they approach or pass age 40, they realize that their chances of achieving that goal are declining. Those who can afford it may seek single motherhood through AID (artificial insemination by donor) rather than having to deal with an identified father who might make claims on the resulting child. There will, of course, be those who condemn the woman for her choice, or later label the child negatively; others will cheer her on. (Some of these women choose instead to adopt a child, often a baby from overseas.) Not too many years ago, these very wanted children would have been harshly labeled bastards like any others born to unwed mothers. Today, one has to recognize that there are different faces of unwed motherhood which earlier generations chose not to recognize or accept.

Place for Adoption

In the U.S. from the beginning of the 20th century through the 1930s and 1940s, illegitimate babies were regarded as tainted, resulting from sins committed by the mothers. Girls were expected either to raise them by themselves or give them up for adoption. Legislators and caregivers, concerned over the new mothers' shame and desperation, often required mothers in maternity homes to breastfeed their babies for 3 months or more in order to create bonds that would prevent abandonment of the babies by their mothers (Solinger, 1992).

Society regarded unmarried pregnancy as shameful. Bridal virginity and conception after marriage were vital elements of American culture. Hence, part of both official and private policies was to encourage and facilitate adoption of illegitimate babies. Single motherhood was not an acceptable choice (at least not for most white women). Therefore, aided by a sizable number of white couples who wanted a child, adoption was encouraged and widespread. Often babies were taken from the mothers at birth and placed via adoption agencies or private brokers — lawyers, doctors, and nonprofessionals — who sometimes regarded the babies as commodities (Solinger, 1992).

Most black women did not have the same support as their white peers, and there was less pressure put upon them to give up their babies. White women were perceived as sinners, but in the racial ambiance of the pre-war years (and even later) prejudice labeled Afro-American girls as irresponsible and amoral, but loving toward their babies. Social workers tended to ignore the plight of black single mothers because they believed that these women would provide for their babies. Those who perceived black mothers in the same way as white mothers wanted them to place their babies up for adoption, but there were few black families able or willing to adopt. Moreover, grandmothers occupied a nurturing role in Afro-American culture and often helped to raise the babies. That suggested that single motherhood was more acceptable in that community. Some politicians viewed these women in a more punitive fashion, demanding that they be sterilized or removed from welfare rolls. As more young white women had babies and copied the Afro-American pattern, the stigma was reduced (Solinger, 1992).

By the end of World War II, socio-economic changes affected attitudes about sexual behavior. Breastfeeding regulations and other institutional policies became more and more difficult to sustain. The demographics of singles' pregnancies and new courtship mores had been altered by new methods of birth control and the nascent development of the women's movement, all of which led to growing sexual freedom. Increasingly, birth control methods and abortion were considered better alternatives to motherhood than adoption, especially after the development of birth control pills and the court decision in *Roe v. Wade* (1973).

For many young women, even today, mothering their babies is not seen as a viable choice, for they recognize that they have neither the means nor the abilities to be mothers, or their families perceive having children out-of-wedlock as a disgrace. Placing the child for adoption means that not only does the young woman have to admit to herself that she is pregnant, but she also has to admit this to other parties as adoption takes advance planning as well as appropriate medical care. If she spends part of her pregnancy in a maternity residence, she is likely to receive counseling on her options, including adoption. At least one study (Mahler, 1997) indicates that although the adolescent mother may regret having placed her baby up for adoption, she is not highly depressed. Rather, she more likely turned to education or employment than those who kept their babies. This finding was based on a study in the period from 1987 to 1992, when the rate of adoption was already dropping, as more recent statistics show.

Adoption was typically the response to unwanted pregnancy through the 1960s. The National Center for Health Statistics reported in 1999 that "Between 1989 and 1995, about 1 percent of babies born to never-married women were relinquished for adoption, down from 9 percent among such babies born before 1979" (Chandra et al., 1999, p. 1). The decline in numbers is even more marked if only the babies of never-married white women are considered: "In the early 1970's, almost 20 percent of babies born to never-married white women were relinquished for adoption, compared with only 1.7 percent of such babies born in the first half of the 1990's" (Chandra et al., 1999, p. 9). In the earlier period, as already noted, fewer children of never-married black women were placed for adoption than babies of never-married white women, and that continues today. It is less often the option of choice today because of changes in the perception of adoption generally, or, according to Demb (1991), in the black community specifically because the babies available for adoption by non-family members are often the victims of their mothers' drug or alcohol addictions. (Note: Babies who are victims of fetal addictions are not, in fact, limited to the black community.) Other problems may also be present in the infant which make the child less "adoptable" because medical science today can save so many fetuses and newborns who would have died a generation and more ago from assorted ailments. Further, some minority clients fear that the difficulty of finding an adoptive home for their child may doom the child to a life in foster or institutional care (Folkenberg, 1985). It should be noted, however, that interracial adoptions that *could* provide a home, e.g., Caucasian parents adopting a Native American or African American child, are often frowned upon, even fought, by members of the minority group (Schwartz, 2000). On the other hand, an organization called "Pact — an Adoption Alliance" seeks to place African-American, Latino, Asian, and multi-racial children in adoptive families (Pact, 1996).

Sobol and Daly (1992) cited data from a variety of studies showing that the estimated percentage of unmarried mothers who placed their babies up for adoption dropped from 40% in 1963 to 14% in 1971, 7% in 1982, and 3% in 1989. Some of this decline may reflect changing social attitudes in this period, some is due to the legalization of abortion, and some to the increasing acceptance of unwed motherhood (Kalmuss, Namerow, and Cushman,

1991). The decline may also be due to the option of adoption never being brought to the attention of the young woman by family, physicians, or counselors. In yet other cases, placing the child up for adoption may be perceived as abandoning the child, although the opposite view would be "finding a family" for the child. Some research suggests that having a voice in choosing the adoptive parents is very helpful to the young birthmothers, regardless of the nature or amount of post-adoption contact (Cushman, Kalmuss, and Namerow, 1993).

Adoptions in the U.S. are arranged through social welfare agencies and private parties, usually attorneys or physicians. It is perhaps easier for middle-class pregnant girls and women to work with the private intermediaries than social workers, while the opposite may be true for the less affluent who may have had experience with welfare or other public agencies for other reasons. In either situation, the mother-to-be has to first admit to herself that she is pregnant and then be willing to admit this to someone else, who will now have a voice in how she fares during the pregnancy.

The practice may differ in other countries. For example, French law allows women total anonymity and cost-free delivery if they place their babies up for adoption. Psychoanalytic interviews with 22 women, 18 of whom took advantage of this law, revealed symptoms of earlier sexual and psychological traumas which contributed to their situation (Bonnet, 1993). In the other four cases, the women's denial was so total that they ended up committing neonaticide.

Contemporary adoption practice also has a controversy about the degree of contact, if any, that should exist after adoption between the biological mother and the child. This can provoke a variety of emotions in the mother such as anxiety, guilt, or even resentment, as well as in the adoptive parents who may be uncomfortable with an "open" adoption on the one hand or feel conflicted about a "closed" arrangement on the other. Appropriate counseling for the biological mother should include an explanation of all options with their respective advantages and disadvantages for all of the parties concerned (biological mother, child, adoptive parents). Even where there has been an open adoption, the girl may not have told her parents about the pregnancy or the placement, and may suffer guilt feelings about denying them their grandparental role (Carrera, 1997).

Abandonment

As we noted earlier, Amighi (1990) found many references to abandonment as well as "justifications" for neonaticide in both folk literature and social history. Feelings of resentment or emotional detachment could lead to neonaticide or abandonment even in more sophisticated societies. The ways in which the abandonment or neonaticide were carried out, discussed earlier, have certain similarities even with today's methods on the whole. One unusual practice in such cases, however, has been the abandonment of neonates in coin-operated lockers in Japan (Kouno and Johnson, 1995). The baby might have been placed in the locker alive or dead, and was not usually found until several weeks later, thus precluding finding the parent(s). An academic research committee in Japan studying infanticide found that mothers who kill their illegitimate newborns usually suffer from serious problems in coping with life's problems and requirements. They may change jobs frequently, for example. Their primary motives are poverty and fear of shame associated with having an illegitimate child. Mothers who kill their legitimate newborns, on the other hand, tend to be motivated primarily by already existing poverty which would be exacerbated by having more children (Bryant, 1990, p. 9). These findings do not differ significantly from those found in Western countries.

Abandonment of the neonate on church steps or near a hospital's emergency ward was another choice in the past and is still an option today. In earlier times, as we have already shown, foundling hospitals and orphanages were also available for abandoned babies. The Salvation Army had group homes where the pregnant girl could stay until she delivered, and the New York Foundling Hospital, an arm of the Roman Catholic archdiocese in New York City, cared for newborns abandoned in that area. Neither of these options was as widely available in the late 1990s as was true a few decades earlier.

Among the alternatives to neonaticide in different locations for dealing with an infant who is unwanted for various reasons are:

1. Exploitation of the infant as a resource, usually selling the infant.
2. Abandonment of the infant (with the expectation that it will be found), possibly placement for adoption.
3. Fostering out the infant — to a relative or other person.
4. Wet-nursing — releases mother for other roles.
5. Oblation — child placed with religious institution.
6. Reducing overall reproductive effort — delegating care to others.
7. Reducing parental investment in particular children (Hrdy, 1992, pp. 413–414).

"From the perspective of reproductive strategies, abandonment of an infant should be the default divestment strategy for parents terminating investment; infanticide would only be a last resort when this option is curtailed" (Hrdy, 1992, p. 415).

Although the new mother cannot see herself rearing the child, she cannot bring herself to kill the newborn. She also cannot bring herself to admit to someone else that she has been pregnant and has delivered a baby, but she also recognizes that this *is* a baby and not an "it." Sometimes the mother leaves the infant somewhere, wrapped in towels or a blanket and maybe with a note attached; in other cases, the baby is left on top of a trash bin or in a restroom. The use of trash cans or larger dumpsters for this purpose has led, in Italy, to the placement of signs on the bins that say, "Not for babies" (Levene, 1998). If the baby is found in time, there is a good chance for survival and, ultimately, adoption. The mothers are usually not located. Indeed, three of the cases that came to our attention between July and October 1997 were abandonments, with only one of the mothers identified (Vanessa Gomez). A girl in Pittsburgh left her 6-day-old infant, wrapped in a blanket outside a hospital emergency room with a note that said she was "only 12 years old, and I can't take care of him" (Associated Press, 1997b). In another case, a woman walking her dog in suburban Los Angeles found a 6-hour-old baby boy in a shallow grave (Associated Press, 1997a). The newborn was subsequently placed in foster care. Earlier, a 19-year-old girl, herself the daughter of an unmarried mother, delivered herself and wrapped her unwanted baby in a paper bag she placed on a trash can (Ratner, 1985). This was her second pregnancy, but neither her own family nor her boyfriend's (with whom she was living) recognized she was pregnant. Fortunately, the sorry story of this late adolescent's family history and self-deprecating image resulted in a plea bargain with a suspended sentence and a probationary period in which she was to have psychological counseling.

Not all cases of abandonment have the happy ending of the neonate surviving and gaining a home. Consider the situation in Oklahoma: "Fifteen abandoned newborns were found dead in Oklahoma between 1987 and 1997, according to a report by the University of Oklahoma Health Sciences Center. Just this month [February], three abandoned newborns were discovered. Two were dead" (Ruble, 1999). Whether the increase is factual, or simply a matter of better record-keeping, can be a matter of debate.

Neonaticide

The final option, and one rarely mentioned in the literature, is neonaticide. According to several sources, approximately 250 neonaticide cases are reported to the Department of Justice annually, but the Department has said that it does not keep separate records for such cases and the National Center for Health Statistics maintains data on infant deaths divided by "early neonatal" (less than 7 days) and "late neonatal" (7 to 27 days), and as "28 days of age or less" and "1 year and under," depending on the table examined, but not for neonaticide per se (i.e., age 24 hours or less and as a result of deliberate or inadvertent acts by the mother at or immediately following delivery). Not only are separate records not kept, but there is some question as to whether all cases are reported since some of the babies' bodies are never found.

As already noted, the girl or woman may have denied the pregnancy even to herself. She is convinced, at the time of delivery, that she is having stomach cramps or needs to defecate. Delivery is unassisted. Frequently the baby is born as she sits on the toilet, then falls into the bowl and drowns. Or, if she is squatting on the floor, she may simply smother the newborn with her hand or a towel to prevent anyone hearing the baby's cry. Those who attempt to cut the umbilical cord use any handy tool — scissors, razor blade, nail file. The infant is then wrapped in something (a towel, plastic bags) and discarded; the blood is mopped up from the floor with rags or towels; and the young woman goes on her way — to bed, work, school, or out with friends.

Brozovsky and Falit (1971) and others have characterized those who commit neonaticide as young women who deny and conceal their pregnancies so convincingly that those around them also deny it, a point made earlier. Further, they determined that in 1967, 45.6% of the infants killed in the first year of life were victims of neonaticide. In Canada, the term "infanticide" was used to refer to what we call neonaticide, and in 45 cases reported in 1974 to 1983, 69% of the offenders were under age 21, 69.3% were single, and the most common occupation reported was "student" (Silverman and Kennedy, 1988). As many researchers have pointed out, "Most neonaticides are the results of unwanted pregnancies and births. Mothers tend to be younger and unwed, and the inability of the girl to reveal her pregnancy to her mother, the stigma of having an illegitimate child, and the shame or fear of rejection are factors in many cases" (Bourget and Labelle, 1992, p. 668). Comparable data are not available in the U.S. Green (1990) asserted that neonaticide is almost certainly underreported in official figures. Further, he differentiated two groups of neonaticidal "mothers": 1) the emotionally immature who panic at the time of birth, and 2) the strong-minded who premeditate the baby's death at birth.

A number of cases have involved college women, and have thereby raised concerns at higher education institutions. The incidents "at colleges have raised questions not only about how well-acquainted students are with the medical services available to them, but also about the isolation that would allow a student to complete a full-term pregnancy in secret without being questioned by anyone on campus" (Geraghty, 1997, p. A49). Most colleges have facilities for confidential prenatal care; a few would require the pregnant student to move out of the dormitory. The need is recognized, however, to have both faculty members and dormitory advisers better informed about where to refer a troubled, possibly pregnant, student for help.

Among married women, extramarital paternity is sufficient reason (in their minds) for neonaticide, although there may be other reasons. In one case in Milwaukee, a 30-year-old mother of two had been impregnated by a married man. He ignored her attempts to discuss the situation, so she ultimately decided to abandon (and asphyxiate) the newborn (Doege, 1998). An ignorant young mother may not intellectually calculate the pros and cons of infanticide. But she may consciously arrive at decisions that place the value of the infant lower than the perceived value of something else, such as more freedom (Reece, 1991, pp. 704–705). Sometimes the new baby is seen as "one child too many," and the overwhelmed mother commits neonaticide (Zurzola, 1998). In a few cases that we found, the woman was on cocaine or another drug when she delivered herself and killed the newborn. Deliberate neonaticide may also occur when the newborn is obviously handicapped. In this case, it is perceived by some as delayed abortion (Rue, 1985). In any case, each of these mothers had a conscious reason, however warped, for killing her child.

Whether criminal charges of neonaticide or infanticide are to be filed against the mother often depends on the findings of an experienced pathologist. If such a charge is to be made, "then the pathologist must be certain that not only had the infant achieved separate existence but also that the cause of death was by a deliberate act or omission on the part of the mother" (Kellet, 1992, p. 13). Such acts might include failure to clear the baby's air passages (omission), failure to cut and tie the umbilical cord (omission), dropping the baby on a hard floor causing a skull fracture (deliberate), strangling the baby manually or by ligature (deliberate), smothering (deliberate), and drowning (deliberate). Concealment of the birth and abandonment after the birth have also been considered to be criminal acts, and have been punished in various ways depending upon the laws in a given period and country (or state).

In 75 of the 86 cases that came to our attention as having occurred from 1990 to 1999, the mothers were identified, charged, and, in many cases, tried or they pleaded guilty. Some of the babies were born alive and then killed, but at least ten more were found alive and rushed to the neonatal care unit at a hospital. Although the laws dealing with neonaticide and infanticide make reference to postpartum depression as a mitigating circumstance in these cases, the condition is not present in neonaticide as the clinically defined onset is a matter of weeks after birth, not hours or minutes. More often, the mother acts out of fear, shame, guilt, rejection, denial, and/or ignorance. This is not too surprising when one considers the youth of many of these "mothers." [For example, in the cases mentioned, **33** were 21 years of age or older, and the balance (**53**) were all in the age range of 12 to 20 years.] That almost one third were aged 21 years or older, several of them having been pregnant previously and could still be in denial or claim ignorance of their condition, does suggest, however, that committing neonaticide is not simply an adolescent reaction to an unpleasant or difficult situation.

Why Neonaticide?

As we have seen, there are a number of options available to pregnant women. In most cases, the babies are wanted and the mothers have prenatal care, normal deliveries, and go on to raise their children. In those cases where the pregnancy is unwanted, the women have choices and decisions to make. Sometimes they cannot deal emotionally with the pregnancies and deny them right through the moments when they deliver the babies. This is most often the situation with neonaticide or, less frequently, abandonment. At the other extreme, some take measures to abort the fetuses when they first discover their conditions. Those who exercise neither extreme at the outset or the conclusion of pregnancy can still choose to raise the children or to place them for adoption.

Why some women choose the neonaticide option rather than selecting another option leads to a number of hypotheses. Some have been examined in this chapter, and others will be discussed in the next chapter when the neonaticidal woman has to present a defense in court.

Neonaticide and the Law 5

As we are aware from European and Latin American studies of neonaticide and infanticide, the popular perception is that only poor, uneducated, young, lower-class females commit these crimes. The American stereotype often adds non-Caucasian to the description, and today has added middle-class and educated as well. Neonatal mortality is not always due to neonaticide, but Geronimus (1987) concurs with this later description, asserting that adolescent motherhood in the U.S. "occurs almost exclusively among socioeconomically disadvantaged populations," and that a large percentage of these are from the black population (p. 245). A study of cases in Rio de Janeiro (1990 to 1995) also supports this perception of disadvantage plus minority ethnic origin as a basis for committing neonaticide (Mendlowicz et al., 1998). The mother simply does not have the means to raise a child, whether it is her first or her third. What has become apparent in the 1990s, however, is that all four "traditional" descriptors may be too limiting and that the differences between the stereotype and reality may become critical issues in the prosecution of the young woman.

There is no question that, in most societies, women who kill their babies are regarded as having committed the ultimate sin. As Reece (1991) points out, however, our criminal justice system also postulates that a person is only punishable for a crime for which he or she can be held morally responsible. The question then arises whether a woman who commits infanticide while suffering from a post-partum disorder can be held morally culpable. "If so, then she deserves punishment. But if she is not morally culpable, because she fell victim to something she could not control, punishment would be inappropriate" (Reece, 1991, pp. 747–748).

Legal Ramifications

Throughout the literature, whether historical or contemporary, American or not, it is obvious that the crime of killing a newborn baby has resulted in a wide variety of charges.

The discrepancies and inconsistencies in sentencing rest on the nature of state law and the rule of precedent. Judges are constrained by the exigencies

Table 1   **Charges against Neonaticidal Mothers by Age Group and Type of Charge (N = 86)**

	Under 18	18 to 20 Years	21+	N =
Misdemeanor			1	1
Injury to child/child abuse	3		2	5
Manslaughter	6	5	8	19
Homicide[a]	13	16	18	47
Other	2		1	3
Unknown	5	3	3	11
	29	24	33	86

[a] Homicide includes charges of "Murder One," "Murder Two," and a non-specific charge of "Homicide."

of evidence and case law. In addition, the legal establishment makes no particular acknowledgement of the special circumstances of neonaticide. Prosecutors have, therefore, charged young women with a variety of crimes: murder in the first, second, or third degree; manslaughter; gross abuse of the corpse; and concealment of death (Bookwalter, 1998). Of the 86 cases mentioned in the previous chapter, we were able to determine the charges in 75 cases, as can be seen in Table 1. The two most significant factors in determining the fates of the mothers are whether the babies were born alive and their intentions toward their newborn.

In both instances, the prosecutors must prove their case either to the jury or to the presiding judge. The state must show *beyond a reasonable doubt* that the baby was alive and that it had an independent circulation (*Shedd v. State*, 1934). The problem of determining whether the baby was alive is often difficult because in most of the neonaticides the only witness is the defendant, and the pathologist's evidence is often not conclusive or contains conflicts. Convictions in these cases vary widely and are affected by the lack of precision in determining how the baby died. For instance, in one case, Stacy Myers delivered a baby in her friend's dorm room. After cutting the baby's cord with scissors she wrapped the baby in a garbage bag and left it on a windowsill outside her room. She had not informed her friends of her pregnancy. She was convicted of second-degree murder and sentenced to 15 years. The appellate court reversed this decision claiming that the prosecutors had not proved without a doubt how the baby died or even if the baby was born alive (*Myers v. Commonwealth*, 1994). Similar cases such as that of Elizabeth Ehlert had the same outcome. Ehlert killed her newborn by wrapping the baby in a garbage bag and dropping it in a nearby lake. Despite strong circumstantial evidence, and her past history of two abortions, the pathologists' reports were unable to ascertain a "live birth." Though she was convicted of first-degree murder and sentenced to 58 years, the verdict was overturned by the appellate court (*People v. Ehlert*, 1990; cf *Lane v. Commonwealth*, 1978;

Singleton v. State, 1948; *State v. Doyle,* 1978). In all these cases, the young women escaped punishment.

If the prosecutor cannot sustain the charge of first-degree murder because it is impossible to prove whether or not the neonate was born alive and the death premeditated, the charge can always be reduced to "gross abuse of a corpse" or "concealment of death." Manslaughter itself, which involves "unlawful killing without malice" (Ford, 1996, p. 531), may be subdivided as voluntary, involuntary, or aggravated, depending upon the jurisdiction in which the tragedy occurs. Since murder, even second-degree, presupposes premeditation or planning of some kind, and manslaughter does not, the denial or psychological dissociation which accompanies many neonaticide cases would clearly make manslaughter the more appropriate charge (Book-walter, 1998).

The divergence in charges and sentencing depends on the legislation of the various states which often vary. Further complicating the legal decisions are the problems of evidence. Frequently the pathological analysis and physical evidence which give credence to the prosecutor's case determine the charges. Examiners and forensic pathologists are important figures in these cases because they are the professionals who can (usually) determine whether or not the baby was born alive (i.e., breathed on its own after birth). Sometimes the experts disagree and, even when a confession is freely given, there is very little evidence to support the defendant's statement. Too often in the case of neonaticide, there is little physical evidence and the pathologists cannot prove whether the baby was alive at or after birth. This was even more true in the 19th and early 20th centuries as we found in cases from that period, although it was interesting to see that at least one of the techniques — trying to float the infant's lungs in water — was used more than a century ago and is still used (e.g., *Mary Harris v. State,* 1891; *John Josef v. State,* 1895; *Cordes v. State,* 1908; Editorial, *Dayton Daily News,* 1998).

Another factor influencing the disparity in the outcomes of neonaticide cases is that sympathy for the defendants often allows convictions for lesser crimes and consequently reduced sentences. The legal system has also been inconsistent in recognizing the psychological ramifications implicit in the crime and often ignores expert testimony in some cases (*People v. Wernick,* 1996). Barton (1998) concluded, "the same murder by the same mother could receive different treatment depending on the jurisdiction's laws, particular jury, or even the beliefs of a particular judge" (p. 619).

Variations in Charges and Sentencing

The outcomes of trials for neonaticide vary widely. As one example, Rebecca Hopfer of Dayton, Ohio, was convicted of neonaticide and sentenced to serve 15 years to life in prison for her crime. Appeals for commutation of her sentence were made to the governor (*Ohio v. Hopfer,* 1996). Her family and supporters alleged that she was "victimized" for being a white suburban teenager, i.e., no one could say she had been treated differently from a poor black teenager who had committed the same crime. The county coroner opposed any clemency action by the governor, saying that no such appeals had been made to the governor on behalf of a poor black woman, who had committed the same crime (Editorial, *Dayton Daily News,* 1998; France, 1997).

In contrast to this case, a high school senior (Anna) in suburban Chicago gave birth alone, left the baby in the toilet while she cleaned up blood in the bathroom, then wrapped the dead newborn in a towel and hugged it against her body as she went to sleep. Later that day she told her best friend what had happened, and the friend told her father, who then contacted the police. Anna was arrested, charged with first-degree murder, but was found guilty of involuntary manslaughter by a jury. She was placed on probation and ordered to perform 1000 hours of community service (Brienza, 1997).

Butterworth, a clinical psychologist in Los Angeles, is quoted as saying that the profile for these mothers is "a Caucasian under the age of 20 who comes from a middle- to upper-class home" (Puit, 1998). Examples that support his view in the mid-to-late 1990s include Melissa Drexler, also known as the "Prom Mom," and Amy Grossberg and Brian Peterson, all of New Jersey, as well as several college students across the country, each of whom committed neonaticide. In each case, the accused differ from the supposed traditional stereotype, and there was some feeling expressed in the press and elsewhere that "they should have known better" because they were better-educated, middle- or upper-middle class, had intact families, and had had more advantages than many other youths. If "they should have known better," there may be an implication that they should be more harshly treated under the law than if they had not had such advantages, as Hopfer claimed in her appeal. This is perhaps asserted even more so when the woman is in her 20s or older or has had other children, because the perception is that she is "old enough" to know better, and indeed about one third of the cases we found involved women who were in the age range of 20 to 43 years, some with other children.

Bacilia Lucero, a 22-year-old illegal immigrant from Mexico, who was living and working in northern New Jersey, gave birth to a girl in January 1997. With the help of a male cousin, she threw the newborn out of a third-floor window. The baby's body was found the next day and Lucero was subsequently arrested. The way in which her case was handled offers a sharp contrast to the treatment of Amy Grossberg and Brian Peterson, also residents of northern New Jersey, whose parents spent more than $1 million on their defense and whose in-prison time was no greater than $2^1/_2$ years. No one interviewed Lucero about her motives or her problems.

Neither young woman had wanted a baby, and neither was a danger to society, a threat to kill again, though Lucero was an illegal immigrant and possible flight risk. Yet after Lucero's arrest, her bail was set at $500,000, and when her family could not afford to pay it and her public defender lawyer could not get it reduced or raise any questions about the health of the baby, she was placed in a New Jersey mental institution. Her freedom was gone, and she would eventually plead guilty to aggravated manslaughter and be sentenced to twelve years in prison (Most, 1999, p. 207).

As Most, an area reporter, pointed out, Lucero's case did not receive the media attention or public concern that the Grossberg-Peterson case did. In addition, this pair of cases shows sentencing markedly different from the sentences given Rebecca Hopfer and Anna mentioned previously.

"In order to accommodate neonaticide under modern murder codes, one must equate an unattended birth — the most commonplace and natural event in human history — with the pathological behavior of the depraved-heart murderer. So doing has the curious effect of criminalizing the birth process when it takes place without medical supervision" (Oberman, 1996, p. 80). Of course, unsupervised births occur daily in many parts of the world, even today.

Another law professor wrote that some theorists look at mothers who kill as having violated their cultural image as life-giving and other-oriented, who are thereby entitled to honor and deference. This means that "Because she was a mother, we have to punish her more harshly than any man because she broke that hedonic bond; she killed her baby" (Schmall, 1996, pp. 286–287).

The charge of first degree murder generally requires premeditation, planning ahead of time. As we are aware from both cases and studies in the psychological and legal literature and from contemporary cases in the headlines, the younger women rarely plan to kill their babies. Rather, the newborn's death seems to occur as a result of the young woman's *lack* of planning and *lack* of support, isolation, and hysterical denial of the pregnancy altogether. Sadoff (1995), a well-known forensic psychiatrist, argues that neonaticide (and infanticide) occurs more often from fear, depression, panic, or mental disorder than from cold premeditation. His opinion with reference to neonaticide is echoed in statements by other psychiatrists. A psychiatrist in Arizona, for example, said that the minds of some of the younger women in these cases "are so clouded with denial and fear, some don't understand they are having a baby" (Fimbres, 1998). "Although one might argue that the defendant was negligent in her failure to anticipate the impending birth of a child, and in her failure to take precautions to insure the baby's survival, this hardly can be seen as premeditated murder" (Oberman, 1996, p. 80). Nevertheless, 8 of 47 defendants in Oberman's sample were so charged.

At common law, manslaughter was broadly defined to govern unlawful killings that did not involve malice aforethought … [I]nvoluntary manslaughter generally exists as a less severe offense than voluntary manslaughter or murder, and is applicable in circumstances where the defendant's conduct lacked a murderous intent, but involved a high degree of risk of death or serious bodily injury to the victim.

This definition applies to neonaticide in that the pregnant woman who fails to acknowledge her condition and to plan for her impending delivery poses a distinct risk to her offspring's well-being. Even if her behavior prior to the birth is both legal and unintentional, it can be argued that, once the baby is born, the woman's failure to seek assistance is either criminally negligent or reckless because a parent has a legal duty to furnish medical care for her child (Oberman, 1996, pp. 81–82).

The claim of "self-defense" has generally been rejected in involuntary manslaughter cases arising from neonaticide incidents, although in many cases, according to Oberman, the women could be seen as victims and their actions understood as almost inevitable responses to hostile environments. Manslaughter was the charge against 8 defendants in Oberman's neonaticide sample. Of the 88 cases that we have been able to track, 21 defendants were charged with or pleaded guilty to manslaughter. This was sometimes the result of plea bargaining down from a murder charge.

Should Neonaticide Be Punished? And If So, How?

There is no question that neonaticide, in its most basic definition, is a crime. As a crime, it should normally be punished. A whole flock of questions arises from these simple statements.

- Was the act premeditated? (If the mother denied the pregnancy throughout, can it be proven that she really knew that she was pregnant and planned to kill the newborn?)
- Should the death of the newborn be equated with the murder of an older child or an adult? That is, are all homicides equal?
- Is the accused a threat to herself (suicide) or to society (possible additional homicides)?
- Although imprisonment will punish the individual guilty of homicide, what else will it accomplish? (Revenge? Mental health treatment? Mental health damage?)
- If imprisonment is the decision, what term should the sentence be? (We have recorded widely varying sentences ranging from community service + psychiatric care + probation in one New York case to 25 years to life in another case.)

Since many mental health *and* legal professionals recognize that neonaticide is often the result of disordered perceptions and thinking, it seems very strange that in only 6 of the more than 85 cases we have tracked was reference specifically made to psychiatric treatment or counseling as part of the sentence. Current practice seems to continue that which was reported by Resnick (1970), especially with respect to neonaticide: "Mothers who commit neonaticide are more likely to be sentenced to prison or probation, whereas mothers who commit filicide are more likely to be hospitalized" (p. 1418). Why is this so? Is part of the penalty in neonaticide cases punishment for the woman's (or girl's) sexual activity outside of marriage?

Consider yet another case, this one involving a girl of 14 who cut her newborn's umbilical cord with scissors, wrapped the baby in a plastic bag that she then placed in a kitchen trash can, and claimed that she had not even known she was pregnant (*People v. Doss*, 1991). She was convicted of first-degree murder and sentenced to 20 years in prison, with both the conviction and the sentence upheld on appeal. Although she had to have known that her behavior would kill the infant and that she was not in danger from the neonate — so that technically she met the criteria for first-degree murder — in what ways will imprisonment for 20 years (or even less) rehabilitate her, help her to be a more effective adult, or even protect society?

Lisa, the mid-adolescent referred to in Chapter 3 (Atkins et al., 1999), eventually pleaded guilty to manslaughter, was sentenced to 4 years in prison, but was paroled after 10 months. Prior to the trial, she suffered from post-traumatic stress disorder which involved nightmares, depression, over-dependence on her parents, and suicidal thoughts. She and her parents were referred for therapeutic evaluation and counseling. Although this was all brought to the attention of the court at the time of sentencing, the state (New Jersey) argued that a prison sentence was necessary not only to punish Lisa and to deter others, but to "send a message" at a time when there were several similar cases before the courts (Atkins et al., 1999). There is little or no evidence to support imprisonment as an effective deterrent.

What defense can be entered in these cases? Frequently, the press reports pleas of innocence or "not guilty" by women accused of neonaticide. Typically, they denied their pregnancies and perceived that "things" (not babies) emerged from their bodies. In other cases, they might appropriately enter pleas of "diminished capacity," although this appears to be underused in the cases we have followed.

Anglo-American Laws and Sentencing

There is a significant difference in perspective between British and American law when considering neonaticide, mostly stemming from statutory revisions in the 20th century in the U.K. which moved away from the harshness of earlier legal views. Neonaticide is a crime that the law agrees is the killing of a newborn baby. American law does not recognize this as a separate category of crime, however, as the British and others do. "Neonaticide syndrome" is, itself, a legal construct rather than a psychiatric or psychological one, but it includes such elements as denial of pregnancy, concealment of pregnancy, and giving birth, usually alone, in an isolated setting. The denial aspect not only enables the prospective mother to avoid feelings of shame or guilt, but also means she does not premeditate the murder of the neonate.

British Law

British law has, since the Infanticide Act 1922 (U.K.) and Infanticide Act 1938 (U.K.), regarded post-partum psychosis as a means of reducing the charges for neonaticide and infanticide from murder to manslaughter, although in truth this condition is not applicable to neonaticide. In New South Wales (Australia), laws based on the Infanticide Act 1938 (U.K.) were adopted, enabling a judge to sentence a woman who had committed neonaticide or infanticide as if for manslaughter, which meant that a discretionary sentence could be given. This was considered to "offer a humane means of dealing with women who became 'temporarily deranged' as a result of the after-effects of childbirth" (New South Wales Law Reform Commission, 1997, p. 102). The New South Wales Law Reform Commission recognized that there may actually be different causes for neonaticide and infanticide, ranging from the hidden pregnancy of the single woman to the overwhelming socio-economic stress of another child to raise rather than only the postpartum psychosis. Accordingly, the Commission has recommended that the crime labeled "infanticide" be abolished in New South Wales. They anticipated that such child killings would then be handled with a defense of diminished responsibility. In England, the Criminal Law Revision Committee recommended altering the Infanticide Act 1938 to allow for environmental or other stresses, and it was entered into the Criminal Code Bill of 1989 as clause 64(1) (Mackay, 1993). Changes in attitude, even before passage of these laws, resulted, according to d'Orbán (1979), in shorter or suspended sentences, sometimes with mental health commitments, and with a small percentage serving short terms.

Overall, British law, and its derivatives in former colonies such as Canada and Australia, tend to view neonaticide specifically and infanticide to a lesser degree as events due to psychological disorder which require treatment rather than punishment. As dreadful as the crime is, in truth the homicidal mother is more a threat to herself than to society, one of the principal reasons for incarcerating someone in prison. The more recent laws also avoid the earlier legal connections to lactation and hormonal upsets as the basis for such tragic acts, which had had an anti-female aura. In almost all cases of neonaticide, after all, the mother had not begun to breastfeed the newborn, so that lactation was not a factor. Indeed, she had no emotional, let alone maternal, tie to the neonate, as we have indicated earlier. The baby is an "it," as Amy Grossberg and many others in her position have indicated. That leads to some interesting philosophical as well as legal questions.

Scottish law does not differentiate between neonaticide, infanticide, and other forms of homicide as English and Welsh laws do, but it does differentiate in practice between the sexes (Marks and Kumar, 1996). In 15 cases of infanticide committed by males, 12 of those convicted were remanded to custodial care; of the 8 women's cases, 2 were hospitalized (none of the men were), 2 were imprisoned, and the other 4 were placed on probation. In Marks and Kumar's earlier study in England and Wales (1993), they had found that 80% of the neonate cases were due to a relatively non-violent means (e.g., suffocation) or neglect, but in Scotland, they found more violence.

American Law

Iffy and Jakobovits (1992) pointed out that, as of that year, there was no American law that required consideration of the mother's mental state when she committed neonaticide or infanticide, other than the usual concerns in homicide cases about the defendant's ability to "know" and "appreciate" the wrongfulness of her acts when she committed them.

Unlike the British pattern and others, not only does each American state have its own laws for all imaginable infractions, but in some areas, as is true here, there may not even be a Federal law that acts as guideline. "With such great diversity among jurisdictions, it does not seem likely that a uniform policy of humanitarian response to infanticides resulting from postpartum psychosis will soon emerge" (Katkin, 1992, p. 281). One could add that a uniform policy toward neonaticidal mothers is equally unlikely, although moves toward a "policy of humanitarian response" may be encouraged by the work of Wexler and Winick (1991) and others in the approach they have called therapeutic jurisprudence. In addition, laws sometimes remain on the books long after they are appropriate or relevant. A third *caveat* is that there are situations where Federal law supersedes state law, as when certain crimes occur at a Federal facility (Assimilative Crimes Act, 18 U.S.C. 13) or among Native Americans (Major Crimes Act, 18 U.S.C. 1111). Thus there are few patterns to be found either in the charges against the neonaticidal parents or the sentences imposed, as seen in Table 2.

Sentencing Alternatives

Imprisonment appears to be the first goal of prosecutors when confronted with cases of neonaticide. As we have seen, a sentence of 10 years or more is

Table 2   **Sentences Imposed in Neonaticide Cases by Age of Defendant and Fewest Years Mandated to Serve (N = 46)[a]**

Length of Term[b]	Under 18	18–20	Age 21+	N =
Up to 4 years	5	5	6	16
5 to 14 years	3	5	3	11
15 years +	3	2	10	15
Life	2	1	1	4
N =	13	13	20	46

[a]   Includes 2 males.
[b]   Includes probation and prison terms.

not uncommon for the young woman convicted of some degree of manslaughter or murder. There is no provision for helping her understand or cope with her behavior, or even for educating her so that she can prevent a repetition of the behavior which landed her behind bars. As the murderer of her own newborn, she is held in the lowest possible "esteem" by other women prisoners, and may even be injured by them. Kaplan (1988) has reported on support group efforts to help these prisoners survive their incarceration without becoming more emotionally and psychologically damaged.

A second alternative, the one sometimes employed by British courts as noted earlier, is to hospitalize the girl or woman in a psychiatric facility where she can be treated for the condition which led to her crime or for the one which resulted from having committed it. Once confronted with the outcome of her behavior in court, there is a strong likelihood that the young woman could become suicidal or severely depressed. Treatment in the psychiatric facility would, in essence, protect her from herself.

Related to this is a sentence of x number of years probation combined with mandatory psychotherapy or counseling. Realistic sex education might also be part of this treatment. Tied to the probation may be a condition of several hundred or thousand hours of community service, often involved with educating younger students or perhaps working with babies and very young children who reside in orphanages or similar facilities.

Use of mental health treatment, whether in-patient or not, indeed even in prison, is a viable alternative to allowing the neonaticidal woman to become a victim of her own and others' most hostile emotions. It ties in very well with the therapeutic jurisprudence approach initially espoused by Wexler and Winick (1991) which we will discuss in the final chapter.

What About the Fathers?

"The adoption of the psychological explanation and a psychiatrically oriented cure for white single pregnancy [in the pre-*Roe* era] had a number of social functions. First, it spared the putative father from social opprobrium and responsibility — in fact, from professional attention of any kind" (Solinger, 1990, p. 51). Rarely was the male identified, let alone punished, for impregnating a woman half a century ago, nor is he today with the exception of rape cases (*if* the rapist is caught and convicted).

With rare exceptions, neonaticide is committed by the new mother who, as we have found, usually delivers the baby by herself. The fathers are nowhere to be found at the time, or even afterward, in most cases. There *are* exceptions: two cases cited by Resnick (1970), two more cited by Kaye, Borenstein, and Donnelly (1990), the Murphy-Stockwell case in 1995, the Grossberg-Peterson case in Delaware (where the murder took place) in 1996, and possibly one in Wisconsin ("Eau Claire," *Star Tribune*, 1998).

In one of the cases that Kaye, Borenstein, and Donnelly (1990) found, the man was from a wealthy family, had average intelligence, and was an alcoholic and psychopath, who had impregnated a fellow inmate at a psychiatric center. He wrote a document in favor of infanticide and felt, after killing his newborn son in the mother's hospital room, that he had saved his own social reputation and spared the woman a responsibility she could not handle. Found guilty of second-degree murder, he was sentenced to 25 years to life, but felt "'cheated' in that he was not allowed to enter a defense of justifiable homicide and therefore present to the court his view of infanticide" (Kaye, Borenstein, and Donnelly, 1990, p. 137).

In their second case, the father was present at the delivery of his deformed and cyanotic son, who was also diagnosed as having genetic abnormalities associated with trisomy 13 syndrome which is invariably fatal. After the baby was revived and the doctor was occupied with the mother, the man picked up his son, bent down, and smashed the baby's head on the floor, killing him instantly. He pleaded temporary insanity and was not convicted in either of two trials. Kaye, Borenstein, and Donnelly (1990) concluded that paternal neonaticide may be motivated by premeditation (for any one of several reasons), as was true in three of the cases they reported (two by Resnick and the first of their two), or by impulsivity, as happened in the last case summarized. Under these circumstances, the courts tend to be more punitive with men, who premeditate the neonaticide, and they give more severe sentences than they do to the mothers who are found guilty of the same crime (Kaye, Borenstein, and Donnelly, 1990, p. 138).

An Ohio newspaper editorial writer asked what his most radical position might be, recalled the view of a radio talk-show host who would not allow male callers to comment on abortion. The writer agreed that it seemed unfair for males to walk away "unscrutinized, unscathed, and largely unknown," while their female partners were criticized for their sexual activity (Brewer, 1994, p. 6A).

The Murphy-Stockwell case involved the burial of a newborn, alive, by Lisa Murphy Stockwell, 17, and her husband Billy Stockwell, 22, in May 1995 in Tennessee. The charge with the "legal equivalent" of first-degree murder against Lisa was reduced because she was found to be under the domination of her husband, and she was ultimately sentenced to 10 years in prison. Billy Stockwell was convicted of murder and sentenced to life (Donsky, 1997; Loggins, 1998).

There were earlier cases in which the partners were involved in either assisting the birth or in the destruction of the newborn. They are important, for all cases are based on precedent and they were often cited. For example, a case in 1895 revolved around the conviction of John Campbell for neonaticide. Both he and the mother, Nancy Cook, were indicted, but he, alone, was tried and sentenced to 14 years. His conviction was based on the sole testimony of Cook, who insisted that she had not seen the baby but had delivered a live premature child. Campbell took the child and disposed of it. No body or remains were discovered. The sentence was reversed by the appellate court on grounds that the testimony of Cook required corroborative evidence. However, the judges said that neonaticide presented the greatest difficulties in identifying the *corpus delicti,* body of a murder victim, and each case must depend upon its own peculiar circumstances. The decision also stated that the baby's death could be established without direct proof, if the circumstantial evidence was cogent enough. This precedent also contributed to the variations in sentencing and indictments (*People v. Campbell,* 1895).

Another similar episode involved a husband named Weaver, who was convicted of second-degree murder. He claimed the baby was born 40 minutes before he arrived home and he thought that the baby was stillborn. His wife (who already had three children from a previous marriage) went into labor unexpectedly and had a rapid premature birth. Weak and exhausted, she was unable to attend to the infant and lay alone for 40 minutes. When her husband returned she told him that she had a miscarriage and gave him the baby wrapped in a blanket, which he placed in the toilet and then called a doctor. The body was recovered but pathologists could not agree on whether the baby died from neglect or had died shortly after birth. As in the Campbell case, the decision was reversed for lack of evidence (*Weaver v. State,* 1931). It should be noted that in both cases the mothers were not tried at all.

In contrast, the judge who sentenced Amy Grossberg and Brian Peterson made the opposite decision; he gave Peterson a slightly shorter prison term and three years less probation (Dribben, 1998). Why? Because Peterson had plea bargained and pleaded guilty to manslaughter before she did. If he had really been more "chivalrous," a term used by the prosecutor, he would have driven her to an emergency care facility rather than meeting her at a motel for the delivery and disposition of their baby. As one columnist put it, "All is not fair in love and pregnancy. Since when does a boy worry about his reputation if he stumbles while drunk on the powerful cocktail of hormones and romance? How often do you read about a family disowning its son because he forgot to use a condom?" (Dribben, 1998).

A case in Eau Claire, Wisconsin, involved a 13-year-old girl, who was originally charged in adult court with the first-degree murder of her newborn ("Eau Claire," *Star Tribune,* 1998). A few months later, the judge allowed her case to be transferred to juvenile court where she was found guilty of delinquency on a charge of first-degree reckless homicide. Her sentence, according to the newspaper report, could be as much as 5 years in a correctional facility. The 13-year-old boy, who admitted sexually assaulting her, and who may have been the father of the dead neonate, was only ordered to spend 1 year in a group home. So much for equal responsibility.

Dateline NBC presented the neonaticide case of Audrey Iacona of Medina, Ohio on March 16, 1999. The search of her parents' home for the dead neonate was shown in detail; the court presentations by attorneys and witnesses were shown; her parents were interviewed; and the judge's sentence, in abeyance while it was appealed, was pronounced. There was one very brief mention of a boyfriend who was the father and knew it. He vanished into the landscape, while she was sentenced to 8 years in prison.

Each of these case illustrations contradicts the view of Resnick (1970) that "fathers appear to receive more severe sentences than mothers for neonaticide and filicide" (p. 1418), at least with respect to neonaticide. In the cases reported by Kaye, Borenstein, and Donnelly (1990), and in the Murphy-Stockwell case in 1995, Resnick's statement holds true, but, more often, the father is nowhere to be found, or *he* gets a slap on the wrist and *she* is sent to prison. Parness (1993) argued for legislation that would provide for criminal prosecution of and penalties for biological fathers for pre-birth damages, such as providing drugs to the expectant mother, physically abusing her, or lack of financial support during the pregnancy which might contribute to malnutrition or lack of care. He also proposed that pregnant females be given information on the responsibilities of expectant fathers when they are given information about their own prenatal care.

At the other extreme, there is a man suing his former girlfriend for getting pregnant and thus causing him to be liable for child support (Ryan, 1998). He blames her for not taking her birth control pills. As the columnist wrote, "Why didn't he take responsibility for birth control himself, either with condoms, a vasectomy or, as crazy as it sounds, abstinence, until he was ready for fatherhood?" As is widely known, however, this is too rarely the practice with males.

Concluding Comments

It is apparent that much more is at stake in the matter of neonaticide than the "simple" murder, premeditated or not, of a newborn by his or her mother. The question of when the fetus becomes a "child" legally varies from state to state. Even the feminist positions differ from each other to some extent because of religious concerns. The role of the male in contributing to what is considered neonaticidal behavior (e.g., drug addiction, sexual intercourse when the doctor has advised against it) has rarely been considered.

There are so many political/religious/philosophical positions taken on these matters, with no one group willing to listen to the others, let alone compromise with others to reach some rational stance, that it is unlikely that reason will prevail in these cases. As to how to sentence or treat those who commit neonaticide, there are wide variations among the different jurisdictions in this country — much more so than is true abroad, and there are alternatives that appear to be underused here which will be discussed in a later chapter.

Infanticide and Filicide by Parents and Their Surrogates

6

What may have been acceptable in one location or at one period in history, modern or otherwise, in terms of disciplining children or caring for them, may not be either socially acceptable or legally permissible in another place or at another time. Whipping children or socking them with fists, considered by some to be almost a parental "prerogative," is now perceived as child abuse. Not taking a child for medical care or starving a child is neglect and is regarded as a criminal offense. This was not always the case. A child who was beaten and woefully neglected in New York in the 1870s was removed from the abusive family only because, according to legend, the founder of the Society for the Prevention of Cruelty to Animals intervened on her behalf "and persuaded the courts to accept the case because she was a member of the animal kingdom" (Gelles, 1996, p. 10). The legend is just that, but it served to demonstrate the need for child protective services, and ultimately led to the founding of the Society for the Prevention of Cruelty to Children in December 1874 (Gelles, 1996). This is an interesting commentary on people's priorities, and one that has not changed for some people in more than a century.

What begins as child abuse — whether by malnutrition, shaking, beating, or other means — too often becomes infanticide or filicide, whether committed by the child's parent or by a parent surrogate such as a live-in partner, nanny, or someone else allegedly caring for the child. When the killer of an infant is the mother, the cause of her action is often attributed to post-partum depression by her attorney, and may well be. There are other motives as well, whether the killer is the mother or someone else. In this chapter, we will examine motives for child abuse which end as infanticide or filicide or homicide — outright — and we will look at the role of post-partum depression or other mental illness.

Motives

What is the situation, for example, when a young mother (age 20), kills her 9-week-old baby? Her husband, serving with the U. S. Navy, left one day after their daughter's birth to take a 14-week course in Texas, leaving mother and baby in Hawaii (Matsuoka, 1997). Did the young woman smother the baby deliberately in anger at the Navy for ordering her husband away and at her husband for obeying those orders (displaced aggression)? Was she under undue stress at trying to deal with the care of the infant alone and therefore guilty of killing without malice? Was she suffering from post-partum depression? If found guilty of murder, she was liable for life imprisonment without parole ("Accused Baby-Killer," *Honolulu Star Bulletin,* 1998). [She did, in fact, plead guilty to murder to escape incarceration "without possibilities," a reference to minimum sentences (Hall, 1999).]

Gartner (1991), using data from the World Health Organization, found that "Infants living in nations with a high proportion of teen births face significantly higher risks of homicide, as predicted ... Nations with higher rates of illegitimate births, teen births, and divorce have higher child homicide rates. For both age groups [younger than 1; 1 to 4 years], the family characteristic most strongly associated with homicide is teen births" (p. 236).

Before looking at the defenses raised in this and other cases, we should examine the motives of those who murder children, usually their own. Wilczynski (1997a) listed ten categories of motives, some of which we have already touched upon:

1. Retaliating killings (those in which one parent murders the children to get back at the other parent, usually an ex-spouse at the time).
2. Jealousy of or rejection by the victim (usually the father commits the homicide).
3. The unwanted child (the most common basis of neonaticide).
4. Discipline (overzealous corporal punishment of the child for crying or disobedience).
5. Altruistic.
    a. Primary (usually "mercy-killing" of very ill/retarded child).
    b. Secondary (possible post-partum depression; lack of support in parenting).
6. Psychotic parent (delusions about child).
7. Munchausen Syndrome by Proxy (direct physical actions of parent that lead to invasive medical investigations of child).
8. Secondary to sexual or ritual abuse.
9. No intent to kill or injure (neglect in the absence of criminal intent).
10. Not known.

The one motive most critical to our study of neonaticide, of course, is the "unwanted child" category. Secondary altruistic infanticides are at the root of many of the defenses to be discussed in the next section. Retaliation filicides are most often seen in cases of very hostile divorces where the more bitter parents will kill the children rather than let the other parents have custody of them, or to avoid having to pay child support. Wilczynski (1997a) does not include the child homicides involving cultural pressures, which we discussed elsewhere in this work such as killing one twin from a set or killing a female child in China or India. She does, however, hypothesize different meanings of child homicide by gender of the assailant:

> For men, filicide is more likely to be an expression of instrumental concerns and their desire to exert power and control within their family. For women, on the other hand, filicide reflects their simultaneous position of power and powerlessness, and expressive concerns are more likely to predominate. Therefore whilst filicide is a dramatic, severe, and relatively rare act, it reflects in extreme form the playing out of traditional gender roles. When taken to an extreme, both traditional male and female values can be literally murderous (p. 65).

In 1995, the U. S. Advisory Board on Child Abuse and Neglect presented its report to Congress: *A Nation's Shame: Fatal Child Abuse and Neglect in the United States*. Like Wilczynski (1997a), it distinguished between the parents by gender: "Enraged or extremely stressed fathers and other male caretakers are the perpetrators in most abuse fatalities, although most parenting and child abuse prevention programs target women. (Women are most often held responsible for child deaths from bathtub drowning, fires started by unsupervised children, dehydration and starvation.)" (Cavaliere, 1995, p. 34).

Shaking the baby, especially an infant aged less than 1 year, leads to brain damage and frequently to death, and is far too common. Spanking a baby of 10 weeks' age for sucking her thumb or for crying "too long" seems absurd to most people but these are examples of the "discipline" motive which underlies infanticide and filicide and which is frequently cited in newspaper reports of these tragedies. In another case, a man in Oklahoma beat, choked, and threw across the room the 3-year-old daughter of his live-in girlfriend because the child had wet her diaper (Weaver, 1998).

A different kind of child abuse has nothing to do with the child's behavior. Rather, it is the means the parent, often the father, takes to accomplish other ends. Two cases that horrified the nation when they came to public notice were those of Brian Stewart, who injected his infant son (11 months old) with HIV-tainted blood so that he would die and the father would not have to pay child support (Salter, 1998), and Ronald Shanabarger, who claimed he married his girlfriend, impregnated her, gave her time to bond with their infant son, and then killed the 7-month-old boy in revenge for a premarital "hurt" (Callahan, 1999). At the time of Stewart's arrest for his retaliatory crime, the boy was 7 years old and had a full-blown case of AIDS. The father was charged with first-degree assault (Thomas, 1998), subsequently found guilty, and was sentenced to life imprisonment (Associated Press, 1999). If (or when) the boy dies of AIDS, the charge could be changed to murder. Shanabarger readily confessed to having committed his infanticide on the eve of Father's Day and allegedly asked police to shoot him (Callahan, 1999).

What Kind of Parent ... ?

In the McKee and Shea (1998) study mentioned in Chapter 3, the authors attempted to define characteristics common to women who murder their children. They found several characteristics that appeared to span not only national borders among the English-speaking subjects, but many decades as well. The pattern suggested includes these factors: "nonaddicted, married, late 20's, low-income, mentally ill, new or recent mother of low-average intellect who, acting alone and without weapons, kills only one of her children, likely of preschool age" (p. 686). McKee and Shea pointed out that the rate of mental illness in their subjects and those of d'Orban (1979) and Bourget and Bradford (1990) far exceeds that in cases where the insanity defense has been used.

An example illustrative of the above description is that of Barbara Avery who was sentenced to 20 to 30 years for the murder of her 38-day-old infant who she had dropped down the garbage chute. Unable to find a babysitter, she disposed of the infant and then reported that the baby had been kidnapped. Upon police interrogation she finally confessed. The only defense witness at her trial was the psychiatrist who testified that she was of marginal intelligence with a mild mental deficiency. He also noted that she had personality disorder, though it was not a major psychosis (*People v. Avery*, 1980).

In a study of 42 women imprisoned for murdering children, Crimmins et al. (1997) found that many of them had themselves experienced inadequate mothering, lack of protection as children, years of frustration, and the use of violence as a means of "settling" disputes. They had such poor self-esteem and lack of a sense of self that they were unable to form emotional attachments to *their* children. Ostracized within the prison system, they expressed a need for some program to help them deal with the loss of their children, as well as programs related to domestic violence and parenting. [It is interesting to note that a support group for women convicted of infanticide had been set up at the Bedford Hills Women's Prison in New York state in the mid-1980s and has continued (France, 1997).] McQuaide and Ehrenreich (1998) also asserted the need for more psychological support systems in women's prisons, with awareness of ethnic differences built in, in part to assist women in developing more positive relationships with their children.

Seven of nine women imprisoned for fatally abusing their children similarly had suffered abuse, physical and/or emotional, in *their* childhoods (Korbin, 1986). Like the men (to be described next), the women in this sample suffered from additional problems including neglect as children, poverty, spousal abuse, lack of effective support networks, and other risk factors.

What is wrong with the men who commit infanticide or filicide? In one small study (N = 12), it was found that, "Most of the filicidal men grew up with multiple developmental stressors: Exposure to violence, parental abuse, separation from parents, parental death. Most of the subjects had psychological or neurological problems that increased vulnerability to abuse, neglect, and further developmental deviation. As adults, most lived in poverty and isolation from social supports" (Campion, Cravens, and Covan, 1988, p. 1143). In addition, substance abuse contributed to impulsive behavior in at least half of the sample.

Marleau et al. (1999) similarly found that the majority of their subjects (8 out of 10) had personality disorders which, when combined with situational factors such as financial or domestic stress, contributed to committing the filicide for which the subjects were hospitalized in Montreal from 1982 to 1994. Four of the subjects were psychotic at the time of the filicide; four others were under the influence of psychoactive substances at the time; and six of them tried to commit suicide following the filicide. None of the subjects had been in therapy prior to murder. Several of the cases involved an extended suicide plan ["in which a person develops a suicide plan but cannot leave 1 or more significant persons behind," (Marleau et al., 1999, p. 59)] or were seen as altruistic homicide in which the person was killed for the victim's own good (in the eyes of the perpetrator). Only one case was seen as motivated by revenge against a separated spouse, although a second case resulted in accidental filicide where the real target was the murderer's spouse.

An example of stress acting upon personality disorder was the problem affecting Jim Galloway's behavior. While babysitting, he had shaken the infant so violently that the baby died. Galloway was sentenced to 30 years without parole for murder and a concurrent 5 years for endangering the welfare of a child. The appellate court affirmed the sentence, but the Supreme Court of New Jersey reversed the conviction and had the case remanded. That decision was based on the New Jersey law code, in which the judges "upheld that all mental deficiencies, including conditions that cause a loss of emotional control, may satisfy diminished defense"(Heimmel, 1993, p.19).

What becomes apparent from these and other studies is that the homicidal father tends to be poorly educated (i.e., not a high school graduate), either unemployed and receiving welfare assistance or in a low-paying job, relatively isolated from social supports, and psychologically disturbed. It has been suggested that, if a parent is being evaluated and there is any possibility of suicidal or homicidal ideation, the evaluator ask questions about the parent's children — parent-child relationship, children's caretaker, parental responsibility — in an effort to pick up any possible threats to the children's well-being (Marleau et al., 1999).

Other Motives

Infanticide may also reflect maternal inadequacy rather than a post-partum disorder. That is, the mother (usually) is simply overwhelmed by the mechanics and responsibility of infant or child care and sees doing away with the infant as her only solution. That may have been the case of the young Navy wife in Hawaii as well as a number of other cases we have seen reported.

The mother may be depressed for some other reason, or be otherwise mentally ill. That is, her act has no criminal intent, but reflects her psychological state. Too often, her condition is minimized or shrugged off, with tragic results. This may have been the situation with the drowning by Susan Smith of her two young sons. As Gottlieb (1996), a psychologist, observed, if a woman with children is diagnosed as having a major affective ailment such as depression, then an investigation into the well-being and safety of her children is justified. If she is suicidal, there is a real risk that she might commit filicide so that her children will not be left alone and uncared for when she commits suicide.

A study of neonaticidal women adjudged not guilty by reason of insanity (NGRI) by Holden, Burland, and Lemmen (1996) supports this conclusion. Furthermore, Holden and colleagues found that the crimes of these women did not appear "to have been committed because the child was unwanted, by accident in the course of a beating, or as a means of revenge toward a spouse" (1996, p. 33). Lack of appropriate diagnosis is a critical factor here.

There is often an attempt to claim that the woman who commits neonaticide or other child homicide was emotionally disturbed to some degree at the time. In the Wernick case in 1996, mentioned earlier, for example, the defense asserted that she had suffered from a brief reactive psychosis. The prosecution's forensic psychologist, on the other hand, did extensive psychological evaluation and found Wernick to be a very self-centered and manipulative young woman, who was highly resilient, with impressive ego strength and an unusual capacity to face ordeals (Kirwin, 1997). As Kirwin testified at the original trial, Wernick did not meet the criteria for a brief reactive psychosis as defined in the *Diagnostic and Statistical Manual of Mental Disorders, Third Edition* (American Psychiatric Association, 1987) which included rapid emotional shifts, inarticulate speech, and overwhelming confusion. (Note: A battle of the experts, as occurred here, is not uncommon when there is a psychiatric defense.)

Other motives for killing a baby or a child include the parent's belief at one extreme that the child will suffer more by continuing to live than by dying, and, at another extreme, a mercenary aim. That is, in the first case, the child may have a severe, possibly terminal, illness and the parent sees himself or herself doing a "mercy killing" to spare the child continued pain (DePalma, 1997; Rue, 1985). This may be accomplished by giving an overdose of prescribed medicine, suffocation, carbon monoxide poisoning, or some other method. So-called mercy killings are also done by parents under severe wartime conditions when infants and young children might otherwise be tortured by the enemy. Two instances of this motive would be at Masada in the 1st century and in Bosnia in the late 20th century (Nadeau, 1997).

The mercenary aim would involve collecting insurance taken out on the child's life. This was apparently the motive of Susan and Billy G. Mitchell, mentioned in Chapter 3 (Bridis, 1997) and Ellen Baker Boehm, also mentioned earlier (Costen, 1995). Yet a third case involved a woman who allegedly insured her children's lives, killed them, and attempted to use the insurance funds to pay off her gambling debts (Simpson, 1999). She was convicted on federal insurance fraud charges after state prosecutors determined that murder would be difficult to prove.

There are also cases where the deaths of the children are attributed to the mother's drug abuse, as in the Charlene Wise case in Philadelphia in 1997. Wise had punished her 5-year-old daughter by putting her in the basement for several weeks, providing minimal food and water, until the malnourished child died. (She had punished her 8-year-old son in the same way, but to a lesser extent, and he survived.) Wise blamed her actions on her use of cocaine and other substances. As an interesting (and sad) side note, the city's Department of Human Services had closed its file on the family two months before the little girl's death (Loyd, 1999).

Faith Healing

A particularly difficult type of case to prosecute involves neglect of a child's medical needs by parents who are members of a religious sect (or a cult) that prohibits medical intervention. The difficulty arises because of the Constitution's separation of church and state and the alleged infringement on the parents' religious freedom of choice if the court forces them to obtain medical care for their child. One interpretation of *Prince v. Commonwealth of Massachusetts* (1944) is that parents may not force their religious beliefs on their children to the detriment of the children's welfare. On the other hand, the courts "balance the parents' fundamental freedom of religion and rights of privacy protected by the Constitution against the state's compelling interest in the preservation of the lives of its citizens" (Damme, 1978, p. 21). Some states, however, apparently exempt faith-healing parents from manslaughter or murder charges (Van Biema, 1998).

In a study of the Faith Assembly, founded in 1963, Hughes (1990) reported an investigation by and findings of the Indiana State Board of Health with regard to an unusually high rate of perinatal and maternal mortality within the group. Hobart E. Freeman, the founder and leader of the group, believed and preached that demons lived in medical drugs, three-fourths of physical illnesses have psychosomatic origins, medicines fail to heal, and hospitals fail to cure illness. On the other hand, if a child died even though the parents had not consulted doctors, Freeman said that the reason was that their faith was not strong enough for the child to be healed. The state began to prosecute members of the group for causing their children's deaths in 1984.

Members of the First Church of Christ Scientist ("Christian Scientists") prefer or mandate spiritual healing to medical attention, as do members of the Followers of Christ church and similar sects. Children, who cannot determine their own therapeutic needs, are often allowed to die rather than have life-saving medication or surgery. Neighbors or extended family members may report cases of such apparent parental neglect to local welfare or police authorities in hopes of preventing a death, but whether the child is then treated depends on state law. In a Minnesota case, for example, an 11-year-old boy, son of Christian Scientists, was treated by spiritual healing methods, but died of a complication of diabetes mellitus that was treatable by conventional medicine. The state indicted the mother and stepfather on charges of child neglect and second-degree manslaughter, but the indictments were ruled to be in violation of Constitutional guarantees and had to be dismissed (*State v. McKown, 1991*).

Child Abuse

Infanticide and filicide can also result from child abuse, or Wilcyznski's (1997a) case of "discipline," whether such abuse involves starvation, beatings, violent shaking, or neglect. Some of the 20 cases we documented (see Appendix B), as well as many others we did not track, resulted from a parent's frustration with the child's crying or other normal child behavior. A number of such deaths have occurred even when a child is nominally under the supervision of social welfare agencies either with a parent or with foster parents.

There are a number of common factors related to child abuse, according to Gelles (1997). Among these are family factors, including the stresses faced by a single parent rearing children alone; demographic factors, such as age at which the mother first gave birth; economic factors that include poverty, occupation, or unemployment; stress, including too many children born too closely together, or the added burdens of handicapped or senile family members; social isolation; and the perpetrator's own family history which may have featured spousal and child abuse. With respect to occupation, Gelles raises an interesting point: "Because blue-collar work requires following orders and deferring to authority, blue-collar workers tend to believe that their children should also follow orders and defer to authority" (1997, p. 61). Examined at another level, those who are employ*ers* may also expect others, including their children, to follow orders without question. If they were brought up this way (family history), the expectation is reinforced.

Educators, psychologists, physicians, and others have been required by state law, since the mid-1960s, to report suspected cases of child abuse to the police, and the social welfare agencies are then supposed to investigate the allegations and recommend whether or not the children should remain in the homes. More than 1 million cases were substantiated in 1993 and additional cases were never reported (Gelles, 1996). Sometimes the initial report is not made, for whatever reason the professional may give later. Too often the welfare workers are given too many cases to assess or are too believing of what a parent tells them and simply check off another visit to the home when the reality is that the child *is* being abused or neglected and they have not observed it. Many social workers and judges believe that preservation of the family is more important than the alleged child abuse. The end result is too often the death of the child, with or without multiple fractures, brain damage, or malnutrition.

A particularly relevant study here is one by Brewster and colleagues from the U.S. Air Force and Northern Illinois University (Brewster et al., 1998) in which the records of 32 infants, whose mean age at death was 4.92 months, were examined. The team reviewed five information sources [Air Force FAP Child/Spouse Abuse Incident Report, birth record of victim, medical record of victim, autopsy record of victim, and Air Force Office of Special Investigation's (OSI) Record of the Investigation (ROI), Brewster et al., 1998, p. 94] and developed 58 variables concerning the victim, perpetrator, family, or incident. The victims were 53% male and 47% female, 62% Caucasian and 38% African-American; most were the first or only child; more than half were between the 36th and 39th percentiles in weight and length for their age; and 58% died of traumatic head injuries while another 29% died of asphyxiation (Brewster et al., 1998, pp. 94–95). More than half of the babies had suffered abuse prior to the fatal incidents. The mean, median, and modal time of day of the incident were all between 11 a.m. and 12:17 p.m. — approximately lunch time for the infants.

The perpetrator was most often the baby's father, mid-20s in age, more often in the Air Force than not (77%), and provoked in 58% of the incidents by the infant's crying (Brewster et al., 1998, p. 97). Unlike the perpetrators in many other studies, 97% of the parents in this study were married and living with spouses and children at the time of the infants' deaths. Several had been abused themselves as children or had been seen clinically for spouse or child abuse. The fatal incident usually occurred "in the perpetrator's home (71%) when the perpetrator was left alone (86%) with the infant on the weekend (47%)" (Brewster et al., 1998, p. 100).

The fact that the victims were the first and only children in most of these cases suggests that the parents-perpetrators knew too little about child development and thus had unrealistic expectations regarding the infants' behaviors, a circumstance noted in many infanticide cases. Brewster et al. mentioned, however, that the Air Force has a Family Advocacy First Time Parents Prevention Program (for which two of the families in the sample were eligible), a resource that probably should have its audience expanded. In many cases, the parent or other caretaker was reared in what would be considered today an abusive home and thus had no other model for handling the day-to-day problems of babies such as soiled diapers, crying, not "understanding" the word "no," and so on. This is of course true in many non-Air Force cases of fatal child abuse as well.

Post-Partum Depression

Post-partum depression has been alleged in different times and places to be a cause of neonaticide, infanticide, and filicide. There *is* such a condition that arises a few weeks to a few months after delivery in perhaps 1 in 1000 or 2000 cases, and it has been used as a defense in cases where a mother has murdered her child. Depending upon the jurisdiction where a case is tried, it may need to be accompanied by evidence that the woman did not know right from wrong, i.e., was legally insane. This will be examined at greater length in the next chapter.

Munchausen Syndrome by Proxy

Munchausen Syndrome by Proxy (MBP) is a condition in which the parent alleges that the child is ill or injured in order to have the child tested and treated. The symptoms may have been created by the parent, typically the mother, in the form of over-administering medications, poisoning the child in barely detectable ways, causing numerous bruises or fractures, or otherwise abusing the child. The parent's need to elicit attention and sympathy from others because of the child's problems is a key aspect of this condition

(Artingstall, 1998; Kahan and Yorker, 1991). The child may also be suffering from genuine illness. In a number of cases, as noted elsewhere herein, the demise of multiple children in the same family originally attributed to SIDS has turned out to be due to MBP. This diagnosis is then converted to a defense argument when the parent is charged with murder.

Kay Biggs was convicted of second-degree murder and sentenced to life for smothering her two year old. She was a 19-year-old mother with marginal intelligence and a psychological profile which described her as immature, passive, and self-indulgent. She claimed she did not intend to kill her son, as she often smothered him and then revived him with CPR. She also burned the child and overdosed him with medication. These continual acts were her efforts to gain her husband's attentions (*People v. Biggs*, 1993). As with post-partum psychiatric problems, this will be examined more closely in the next chapter.

The Survivors

McKee and Shea (1998), in their study, mentioned the absence of research on sibling survivors of child homicide (in any of its forms). There is no question that the death of a sibling and subsequent incarceration of a parent for causing that death has to be traumatic for other children in the family. Are they placed in any kind of supportive relationship or left to flounder, perhaps to become mentally ill themselves? Should they be placed in foster care? In some cases, they have been so placed, which can be yet another traumatic event. Little attention, if any, has been given to other family members as well — parents of the homicidal parent, siblings of that parent. How do they deal with what the mother (or father) has done? Do they blame themselves for not foreseeing the tragedy, for not being alert to the individual's behaviors or feelings? Are they given any therapeutic support? It would seem that some kind of opportunity should be available for them to work out their interwoven feelings of anger, guilt, and depression. It may be that consideration of such therapeutic support should be included as one preventive measure of further child homicide, the subject of another chapter.

If These are the Causes …

It is readily apparent that the veracity of Wilcyznski's (1997a) list of motives for child homicide can be demonstrated easily. What is less apparent is how to prevent motives from being acted upon, how to handle the perpetrators within the legal system, and how to support the survivors of these tragedies. Education on parenting and child development is one possible avenue for prevention, and certainly psychotherapy is an appropriate course to follow for the survivors. These matters will be dealt with in a later chapter. The interaction of child homicide and the legal system, the natural outcome of the crime itself, is the center of focus in the next chapter. As will be seen, it is not easy to balance the questionable state of mind of the perpetrator with what may be perceived as a gender-discriminatory legal system.

Neonaticide, Infanticide, Filicide, and the Law

7

When a parent commits infanticide or filicide, it is much easier to accuse the parent of murder, for there is no denial that there was a living child, than it is to accuse the perpetrator of neonaticide, a crime that may not exist in a state's statutes or in the minds of legislators or jurists. However, what is murder? In many states, first-degree murder asserts that one person killed another willfully, deliberately, and with premeditation (Ford, 1996). In other states, there is a common law definition of murder as "the killing of another with malice aforethought," as distinguished from manslaughter, which involves unlawful killing without malice (Ford, 1996, p. 531).

What we will deal with here is the interaction of neonaticide and, to a lesser extent, infanticide and filicide and the law. Such interaction arouses many questions. What differences are there (or may there be) between those who commit neonaticide and those who abuse, neglect, or otherwise cause the death of a child older than newborn? Is there a self-defense that is plausible? Does one charge fit all cases? In what ways should the perpetrator(s) be punished if convicted of the crime?

The Insanity Defense(s)

In general, the insanity defense is based "on the belief that people who lack the ability to reason and exercise free choice should not be held criminally responsible for their conduct and that society is willing to excuse a person who is not culpable and did not make a meaningful choice" (Waldron, 1990, pp. 683–684). This does not mean that the act is condoned or seen as justified, only that this defendant may be excused because she did not know what she was doing and could not control her actions.

Although the ancient Romans recognized a state of *non compos mentis* or "no power of mind," it was not until 1843 that a statute was passed in England that acknowledged that sometimes a defendant really did not know what he was doing at the time of a crime. The M'Naghten rule stated that "at the time of the act, the accused was laboring under such defect of reason, from disease of the mind, as not to know the nature and quality of the act he was doing, or, if he did know it, that he did not know what he was doing was wrong" (Melton et al., 1987, p. 115). The concept of acting under an irresistible impulse was added in 1929. The M'Naghten rule was used as a defense in the U.S. until a new legal definition, the Durham rule, was enacted in 1954: "An accused is not criminally responsible if his unlawful act was the product of mental disease or mental defect." This was supplanted by the ALI/Brawner rule in the 1960s and 1972 which attempted to combine the earlier definitions, saying that a defendant is not responsible for his crime who, " … as a result of mental disease or defect [the Durham rule] lacked *substantial capacity* either to *appreciate* the criminality [wrongfulness — M'Naghten rule] of his conduct or to *conform his conduct* [irresistible impulse] to the requirements of the law." Finally, in the U.S., the Insanity Defense Reform Act of 1984 (IDRA of 1984) essentially returned to the M'Naghten rule by stating that "Insanity may be used as a defense *only* if the defendant was unable to understand the nature and wrongfulness of his/her acts." (This would be true in federal cases, but not necessarily in those tried under state homicide statutes which vary from state to state.) The American Psychiatric Association (1984) urged that the issue of mental capacity be retained as part of the insanity defense since those with severe mental defects could not *choose* to do wrong. However, the new law, which removed the volitional aspect of the earlier one, "placed the burden on the defendant to prove insanity by clear and convincing evidence rather than on the prosecution to disprove insanity" (Wrightsman, Nietzel, and Fortune, 1998, p. 310).

As Damme (1978) pointed out, "What is unique in the insanity defence for infanticide is its radical departure from the normal criminal insanity defence — the McNaghten Rules of 1843 … the standards set by the McNaghten case could not have been met by any of the women acquitted of child-killing because of temporary insanity" (pp. 14-15).

It *is* difficult to believe that even a 14 year old would not know that suffocating her newborn was wrong, *but* it could certainly be argued — and is, in some cases — that she would be in such a state of panic and distress when delivering the baby that she could not *appreciate* the wrongfulness of what she was doing. This would be more difficult, but not impossible, to argue on behalf of a defendant who was already a mother. Although many of these cases appear to be similar on the surface, there are often unique circumstances that outweigh, as it were, rational thinking at the time of the baby's birth. Clearly, these should be considered in determining the charge as well as the sentence if the defendant is found guilty.

Post-Partum Depression Vs. Post-Partum Psychosis

Other defenses for infanticide and filicide but not neonaticide include post-partum psychosis and post-partum depression. Post-partum psychosis is a highly controversial topic and has sparked heated debate within both the medical and legal communities. Women who have murdered their infants have used this defense successfully in some cases. There have been two different controversies about this presumption, however. Feminists criticized the notion of post-partum psychosis as an anti-female argument since this defense raises, like the PMS defense, an exclusively female defense which will abet sexism. They further argue, therefore, that continued use of this defense would lessen opportunities that women have gained over the past two decades. Legal experts have been worried that attempts to write laws which would provide automatic treatment guidelines for women who kill their children under the influence of post-partum illness would provide ways for defense attorneys to use this as a means of exonerating murderers (whether they were mentally ill or not). Other attorneys argued that present insanity and/or diminished capacity rules adequately protect sufferers of the condition (Schroeder, 1993). (Note: These arguments preceded the IDRA of 1984, but still raise legitimate concerns.)

Crying for no reason when there *is* reason for smiles, feeling depressed, and behaving as if the world is entirely too much to cope with are all symptoms of post-partum depression, a condition which may arise anywhere from a few days post-delivery to a few months or even a year later. "The exact cause of postpartum psychiatric illness is not clear; however, some researchers believe that it is a 'biopsychosocial' illness. This term implies that the illness is caused by the many bio-chemical, emotional, psychological, and social changes a woman experiences after childbirth" (Nelson, 1991, p. 95). "The widespread ignorance of postpartum disorders may be the reason why women suffering from postpartum disorders are not helped *before* an infanticide results. The lack of available medical attention for women suffering from postpartum disorders is a significant problem" (Reece, 1991, p. 748).

The condition is not listed separately in the *Diagnostic and Statistical Manual of Mental Disorders, Fourth Edition* (American Psychiatric Association, 1994) as it has not been in any of the prior volumes of this series because of difficulties in developing an appropriate nosology, although it is included under the heading of "Diagnostic Criteria for Psychotic Disorder Not Otherwise Specified" (Nieland and Roger, 1997). It may be that conflicts exist within the mental health community as to what constitutes post-partum depression, or if such a condition exists, which preclude any such inclusion. A key point, however, is that those who support the existence of such a condition tend to agree that it does not occur until "a few days post-delivery." This would negate its use as a defense for neonaticide, although it has been used in cases of infanticide at the trial court level. Katkin (1992) asserted that, "There are no appellate court decisions addressing the status of post-partum psychosis as a defense in infanticide cases" (p. 279), but that has changed in more recent years. On the other hand, if the symptoms interfere minimally with daily functioning, and are not brought to a professional's attention, lack of treatment at a crucial moment could have tragic results (Schroeder, 1993).

Williamson (1993) provides the highlights of the differences of opinion, but appears to favor Dalton's (1989) four-facet characterization of the condition: "maternity blues," "postnatal exhaustion," "postnatal depression," and "puerpural psychosis." (Comment: As an interesting side note, Dalton suggests that some of the "maternity" or "baby blues" can be attributed to the lack of support the new mother has as a result of early discharge from the hospital after delivery. As managed care has become more common in the U.S., and hospitals discharge new mothers after 24 to 48 hours in most cases, the absence of professional support is more obvious. Even the visit of a well-baby nurse at home the next day after discharge may not assuage the anxieties and blues of a new mother, especially a first-time one.) "Maternity blues," occurring just a few days to a few weeks after delivery and highly transient, can evoke sobs when the new mother is complimented on the name she chose for the infant, for example, or when the caller simply comments on "what a lovely day it is." The other conditions tend to have a later onset.

In a study comparing depression scores in post-partum and non-post-partum subjects in Yorkshire, Nieland and Roger (1997) found that the post-partum group had higher "Tension" and "Low self-esteem" scores whether or not they scored high on the depression scale. They suggested that, "Strategies aimed at bolstering or augmenting the self-esteem of women who are about to, or who have recently given birth, may therefore be effective in preventing or ameliorating post-partum symptoms" (p. 39). Whether there is a relationship between tension, self-esteem levels, and hormonal imbalance was not part of the study.

On the other hand, post-partum psychosis, which occurs in about 1 or 2 women per 1000 who give birth (Kaplan and Sadock, 1996; Morrison, 1995), is classified as a "Brief Psychotic Disorder." Dalton (1989) called this "puerpural psychosis" and estimated its frequency at 1 in 500 women who have given birth. Morrison (1995) says that it typically begins 4 weeks post-delivery, and the patient exhibits "at least one of the following that is not a culturally sanctioned response: Delusions, Hallucinations, Speech that is markedly disorganized, Behavior that is markedly disorganized or catatonic" (Morrison, 1995, p. 237). [Kaplan and Sadock (1996) suggest that it begins 2 to 3 days post-partum (p. 94).] The patient exhibits the symptom(s), which do(es) *not* stem from a mood or schizophrenia-related disorder, her general health, or intake of pharmacological substances, for 1 to 30 days, and she recovers completely. Whether this condition can serve to exculpate the new mother who has committed infanticide is arguable (and frequently argued).

Rather than being a specific diagnosis, it is regarded as a mental illness that happens to occur after the birth of a child.

The most severe (and rarest) form is psychosis, in which the woman does not know the difference between right and wrong, and this must be present if the post-partum depression defense is to succeed in many states (Lindsay, 1998b). Psychiatrist Doris Gunderson at the University of Colorado Health Sciences Center has described the patient as suddenly experiencing a marked drop in estrogen levels which can affect brain functioning and possibly hearing voices which tell her to kill her child (Lindsay, 1998a, 1998b).

British law recognizes that post-partum psychosis can contribute to infanticide and thus reduces both the charge and the penalty accordingly. It specifically refers to the stresses of giving birth and lactation as sources of post-partum psychosis if the child of this birth or breastfeeding is the victim. The Infanticide Acts of 1922 and 1938 reduced the charge from murder to manslaughter against the mother if she suffered from mental disturbance at the time (Kellet, 1992). Dalton (1989), as noted above, asserted that the condition could arise immediately after delivery or within 2 weeks of the birth, and that the symptoms could last for 20 years in some cases (Williamson, 1993). One of the symptoms Dalton cited was "threats to injure" the baby, but not necessarily the fact of infanticide. These conflicts among psychiatrists make it a small wonder that the courts are uncertain about the use of this defense. Indeed, the New South Wales Law Reform Commission (1997), stated that "it seems now to be generally doubted that there is any medical basis for the notion of 'lactational insanity.' Inclusion of lactation as a ground of mental disturbance within the infanticide provisions appears to have been based primarily on a desire to provide a medical justification for extending infanticide beyond the first few weeks of birth" (p. 114).

There are other considerations here. In one type of situation, relevant to cases where the mother harms or attempts to harm more than one child, Waldron (1990) suggested that a defense of post-partum psychosis can be appropriate the first time. However, if the woman becomes pregnant again but fails to seek medical advice or to take any precaution against a recurrence of the illness, "she should be liable for reckless homicide for her omission in taking steps to avoid a substantial and unjustifiable risk of which she was aware" (p. 693). Grossman (1990) pointed out that "women who suffer from postpartum psychosis once are at a significant risk of recurrence" (pp. 326–327). In one case that she cited, that of Sharon Comitz, medical records showed that she had a history of depression, particularly in association with the birth of her first child, but no one took precautions against her harming her next one (pp. 330–331; Maier-Katkin, 1991).

Grossman (1990), Nelson (1991), and Waldron (1990) have each suggested, in one way or another, that not enough attention is paid to the mental health of women during pregnancy or in the post-partum period. Many young women need to learn about the work and responsibilities of mother-hood as well as its joys, preferably before the babies arrive. Too often, post-partum depression or psychosis is handled as if it is not only a fairly common condition, but one that is self-limiting and does not require special psychi-atric or psychological care. Childbirth is a stressful life event, but additional emotional or social crises arising during or immediately after pregnancy may precipitate the development of post-partum illness. Often, experts note that there should be socio-communal assistance for new mothers (Schroeder, 1993). There are not only medical treatments, but also support groups avail-able for women with this condition, in addition to precautions that should be taken in the hospital and at home to avert harm to the infant. Grossman (1990) took the position that "the psychiatric community must learn more about postpartum disorders. Only when the medical and the psychological communities accept the legitimacy of the postpartum illnesses should the legal community determine whether postpartum psychosis is deserving of a role as a legitimate criminal defense" (p. 344). Part of her argument is that no one seems to be concerned about the child victims of these women — their mothers — so that something must be done to prevent further infan-ticides. Nelson (1991) added that the judiciary and the public should be educated about post-partum conditions and that research on causes and treatment should be encouraged.

Alternative Defenses

A related defense which has been applied to homicidal mothers is "Extreme Mental and Emotional Disorder" (EMED) and is included in the Model Penal Code 210.3(b) (American Law Institute, 1980). Typically this is based on internal, usually long-standing, stresses which lead the homicidal mother to some "reasonable excuse for the emotional disturbance" and subsequent homicide. This is a legal construct rather than a psychiatric or psychological one, and is used in several states to reduce the charge and/or penalty. Ford (1996) asserted that "If provocation need not be external and immediate under the EMED doctrine, then the identification of such internal and long standing emotional stresses may be employed to invoke this partial defense for some mothers who kill children" (p. 532). Such stresses might include dysfunctional or abusive families in their childhood. Susan Smith, who drowned her children, for example, had been abandoned herself — by her father who committed suicide when she was a child, by adult neighbors who knew that her stepfather abused her sexually, by her husband who committed adultery, and by her own lover. "She herself tried to commit suicide more than once" (Zibart, 1996, p. 177).

An alternative insanity defense could yield a verdict of "guilty but mentally ill" which generally requires that "1) the defendant is guilty of an offense, 2) was mentally ill when the offense was committed, but 3) the defendant was not legally insane at that time" (Sherman, 1981, p. 239). These defendants are typically not perceived as threats to the community at large as most murderers are. Thus there have been two possible verdicts resulting from use of the insanity defense: "guilty but mentally ill" (GBMI) and "not guilty by reason of insanity" (NGRI). In the first of these, the defendant is usually sent to a state or federal psychiatric hospital for treatment as well as incarceration. Should the individual recover from the mental illness, transfer to a regular prison would follow. In the NGRI cases, many defendants simply walk out of the courtroom to freedom. Although both of these verdicts have been the outcome in what we might call "regular" murder cases, they can also be applied to neonaticide and infanticide cases, particularly the NGRI verdict. In both verdicts there is no way to deny that the mother killed her newborn, merely that she was not "responsible" when she did so.

What seems not to have been used adequately is a defense of "diminished capacity," which would avoid the claim of insanity in cases of neonaticide. It might also cause the charge to be reduced from murder to manslaughter. As Barton (1998) has suggested, moreover, "the idea of diminished capacity provides jurors and judges with a medium somewhere between guilt and total innocence of the crime" (p. 618). Brusca (1990) had also expressed support for this defense where available evidence was insufficient to satisfy any of the standard insanity tests. It might even result in rehabilitative confinement rather than penal incarceration. Of all the defenses related to mental health (or illness), this would appear to be the one most closely fitting the rubric of therapeutic jurisprudence, i.e., making a legal judgment with awareness of its mental health implications, problems of sentencing, and offender rehabilitation (Winick, 1997).

Munchausen by Proxy (MBP) is another defense which may be mounted. As noted in Chapters 3 and 6, a few notable cases which had been thought to involve SIDS turned out to be MBP cases. The parent has then attempted to offer some version of an insanity defense to what is an unusual and, in these cases, fatal form of child abuse. Although the parent, almost always a biological mother (Yorker, 1995), actively induces the child's symptoms and/or death by asphyxiation, injection of medications to cause a variety of symptoms, or introduction of poison or infectious agents into the child's system, the courts have apparently been unwilling to believe that the parent's acts can be lethal (Kinscherff and Famularo, 1991). The illness of the child is certainly premeditated as that is what meets the parent's needs; proving that in a homicide charge may be more difficult. Indeed, Brady (1994) has suggested that the varied factors in each MBP case evoke so much complexity that the courts need to be creative in handling these matters.

In Defense of the Defendant

If postpartum depression or psychosis, or any similar defense, is going to be undertaken on behalf of the homicidal mother, there are several items of information that are critical for the defense attorney to have. A mental health professional familiar with the nature of these conditions should be used to: elicit information about the woman's personality both before and during pregnancy; find out about her early history, family (and later) environment, personality traits, religious beliefs, and approach to problems; and investigate her post-childbearing behavior in detail (Hickman and LeVine, 1992). A psychological or psychiatric examination occuring weeks or months after the crime may or may not be productive in terms of understanding what was going on in the defendant's mind at the time of the crime. It can, however, bring to light disorganized or schizophrenic thinking and other symptoms of mental illness which may have been a factor and should be considered in court. A study of homicidal women in Finland found that all of those who had committed neonaticide had personality disorders, and so they were judged not fully responsible for their acts (Putkonen et al., 1998).

The truth of the matter is that mothers who commit neonaticide face inconsistent charges across the country as well as inconsistent treatments if found guilty of crimes at any level. Rarely are they "sentenced" to psychiatric/psychological treatment or to education about sex and pregnancy to prevent recurrences. In the case of Lisa, despite the fact that the court asked the Commissioner of Corrections to place her "in the 'least threatening' correctional facility available and afford her psychological therapy, Lisa spent almost two months in maximum security until space became available in a minimum security wing. Her therapy consisted of a five minute contact with a social worker for five minutes per week" (Atkins et al., 1999, p. 31). So much for any realistic attempt to help a young woman who was anorexic, depressed, and suicidal, not to mention traumatized by her introduction to the criminal justice system.

There also appears to be inconsistent recognition of differences in the mother's mental state before and during the crime. This goes without saying that the crime is ever justified. However, the 15 year old who has been in denial throughout the pregnancy and continues her denial by attempting to literally flush away the "thing" that has emerged from her body is far less a criminal than the 15 year old or 30 year old who has told someone else of her pregnancy or who hides the newborn in a closet. *That* mother is aware of what is going on and, while she, as much as the girl in the previous example, needs psychotherapeutic help, she may also need a custodial sentence to make it very clear to her that what she did was wrong. Each case needs to be evaluated in its context of age, awareness of condition, and mental state of the accused. Stereotyped attribution of fault due to socio-economic level, race, or educational level is inappropriate.

Mothers who commit infanticide *may* be suffering from post-partum depression or psychosis and merit similar rehabilitative sentencing, or they may be guilty of manslaughter or homicide in the more usual sense and deserve sentencing to a women's prison. As Barton (1998) concluded, "The same murder by the same mother could receive different treatment depending on the jurisdiction's laws, particular jury, or even the beliefs of a particular judge" (p. 619). Such inequity should be impossible on principle.

Variations in Penalties

Judges can influence sentencing and many, indeed, do so. Two cases in which these differences are most notable (since most neonaticides are similar) are those of two young girls who had no criminal records and whose prior behaviors were adjudged to be exemplary. Twenty-year-old Meshell Buffin, living at home, denied pregnancy and gave birth secretly in the bathroom of her parent's home. Her newborn, discovered in a trash can, had severe head wounds and had been burned. She was indicted for second-degree murder, but in a plea bargain pleaded guilty to negligent homicide and was sentenced to 2 years. Seventeen-year-old Rebecca Hopfer denied and concealed her pregnancy from her parents (though she did admit it to a girlfriend). She, too, gave birth in the bathroom alone and disposed of the baby in garbage bags in a trash can in the garage. She was indicted for first-degree murder and gross abuse of a corpse (although unlike Buffin she did not burn her baby) and was convicted and sentenced to 15 years to life. It should be noted that psychiatric experts for both the defense and prosecution were in dispute (*State v. Buffin*, 1987; *State v. Hopfer*, 1996). Nineteen-year-old Barbara Jones gave birth alone in a bathroom and dropped her baby down an airshaft. She claimed that the baby was stillborn. She was convicted of murder and sentenced to 34 years in prison (although she, too, had no previous record as a teenager). The Court of Appeals denied a review of the evidence but suggested that her sentence deserved a review and noted that she had already served 9 years (*U.S. v. Washington*, 1993). There are also discrepancies among judges not just in sentencing but in evaluating the psychological factors in the mother's motivation. The result is that in similar cases some offenders are ordered into therapeutic care while others spend their time in prison. Andrea, a 17 year old, disposed of her newborn in a plastic bag in the schoolyard. She was tried as an adult, pleaded guilty to criminally negligent homicide, and sentenced to $1^1/_3$ to 4 years. When her case was appealed, the court granted her youthful offender status and remitted her case for re-sentencing. The evaluative psychiatric reports (both state and defense agreed) led to a recommendation for appropriate therapeutic care unavailable in prison. The defendant's punishment was reduced to time served and 5 years' probation in which she would receive necessary treatment (*People v. Andrea*, 1992). The reasons for this decision were stated:

> Because of the nature of the crime and the circumstances of its commission, we are persuaded that a period of probation with continued psychiatric counseling will be more helpful in rehabilitating this troubled young woman than will a return to incarceration. Because, as indicated in the presentence report, the much needed psychiatric care is not available to defendant in prison and it is conceded that she poses absolutely no threat to society, the only penal objectives to be served by imprisonment are retribution and deterrence. Here, the six months of prison time defendant has already served and the mental anguish visited upon her as a result of this tragic episode have had a markedly sobering effect. And, as society stands to gain so much from defendant, who is young, bright and has much to offer if her therapy is continued, and is in danger of losing so much if she is incarcerated, it is our view that a less restrictive deterrent is indicated than a return to incarceration.

Often many of these perpetrators are young adolescents who are often tried as adults, and that contributes to the variation of sentencing. The case of Sophia M. (14 years old), who had ripped the baby's umbilical cord with her hands, then abandoned the live baby in a shoebox in a field, and buried it a few days later, was tried in juvenile court. Expert testimony emphasized the defendant's immaturity. The judge, following the recommendations of the probation department, ordered that she stay in her mother's house, go to school and have therapy, and complete 100 hours of community service (*People v. Sophia M.,* 1987). In contrast, Diana Doss, age 15, whose case was discussed in Chapter 5, was sentenced to 20 years.

In the most recent cases occurring in the 1990s, the charges ranged from a misdemeanor ("abuse of corpse") in a 1996 Texas case to 19 charges of manslaughter and at least 46 indictments for murder, variously designated as homicide, murder one, or murder two. Some of the manslaughter cases began as murder cases, with plea bargaining as the basis for the less serious charge rather than an understanding of underlying psychological problems.

"It is clear that the lenient impulse in neonaticidal cases is integrally related to the ambivalence evoked in us by the horror of these women's experiences in childbirth. To insist that these women's actions be regarded and judged 'equally,' in some abstract sense, to the actions of men is as absurd as it is impossible" (Oberman, 1996, p. 84). Obviously this is a complex area, and certainly one not usually taught in law school or necessarily in any traditional curriculum. In Marlow's opinion (1998), judges should be able to do their own research on psychological issues such as those relevant to these cases so that they are in a better position to understand expert testimony and defense claims and to determine the most effective sentence in terms of the particular circumstances. This view concurs with that of Wexler and Winick (1991), who urge that the therapeutic impact, if any, of laws be considered.

In one article on neonaticide and infanticide (Hanson, 1997), it is interesting to note that in Texas, at least, there was a marked change in penalties for these crimes in the 1990s as compared to the mid-1980s. In 1986, according to Hanson, a mother who tried to kill all seven of her children, and succeeded in drowning two of them, received a sentence of 10 years' probation. In contrast, in four of five cases of neonaticide or infanticide tried between 1993 and January 1997, the murdering parent was given 1 or more life sentences (3 cases) or 50 years in prison (1 case).

In Oberman's two samples (1996), it can be seen that prosecutors and the courts were sometimes quite punitive: 12 of 49 infanticide trials resulted in a sentence with a minimum of 5 years in prison and going up to a life sentence, while 6 of the 47 neonaticidal mothers received prison sentences ranging in duration from 1 to 20 years in prison. Similarly, Moss (1988) reported Katkin's summary of outcomes in 15 cases of infanticide, over a 5-year period, where post-partum psychosis was the defense: "about half the women were found not guilty by reason of insanity, one-fourth received light sentences, such as probation, and one-fourth received long sentences" (Moss, 1988, p. 22).

By the time Grossman (1990) wrote, Katkin had found a few more cases, but the pattern was very similar to the earlier one. Others have also reported about a 50% conviction rate on charges that vary from involuntary manslaughter to first-degree murder, with sentences ranging from suspended sentences to life imprisonment (Nelson, 1991; Waldron, 1990), but there is some indication that all of these reports are based on the same cases.

As McKee and Shea (1998) pointed out, the crime is considered so terrible that sentences mandate prison or psychiatric hospitalization. That means that women receive their treatment in an institutional setting rather than within community-based programs. These women suffer difficulties adjusting to their families after conviction. This study also identified a group of victims who, like the filicidal women, also needed clinical services. "Seventy-eight percent of multichild families (24% in d'Orban's 1979 study) had sibling survivors who will likely require treatment for serious problems such as posttraumatic stress disorder or major depression. Published research on sibling survivors of filicidal parents, however, is nonexistent" (McKee and Shea, 1998, p. 686). Actually, we found one report where the 9-year-old son of a homicidal mother said he never wanted to see her again, but that *is* the only instance and certainly does not constitute "research."

Many of the cases we have tracked in the 1994 to 1999 period have yet to be resolved in the courts. Two cases occurred in 1990 but one was not settled until 1996, with the other in a second trial late in 1998; a third case occurred in 1994 but was appealed through 1997. In several of the 88 cases of neonaticide that we found, the charges were reduced from murder to manslaughter but, where a trial had taken place, the women aged 21 and older were more likely to be imprisoned than those who were younger. Whether this was because it was felt they should have "known better" or have been "more mature" is unclear, but it is possible that their acts were based more on biopsychosocial stresses than on hysterical denial which may have influenced juries or judges. It has been suggested that because "neonates may not be considered established members of their families and communities, perpetrators of neonatal deaths are expected to receive relatively lenient treatment from the legal system" (Crittenden and Craig, 1990, p. 205). The outcome of a case in the U.S. may depend on who is defining "lenient." Contrast this with the procedures in Britain and other countries.

Mackay (1993), reporting on 47 cases in Britain, of which 21 or 44.7% were neonaticide and an additional 24 were infanticide, found that the charge was generally reduced to manslaughter, with most of the female defendants, if convicted, placed on probation or referred for psychiatric help. Of the 13 male defendants, 12 of whom had previous criminal records, the 6 convicted for manslaughter were either imprisoned or, in 1 case, hospitalized with restrictions. Several of the 47 cases, especially among the neonaticides, were dismissed as the director of public prosecutions believed the cases did not serve the public interest, or that the perpetrator was not legally responsible for the act. The prosecutor was more lenient with females than males, as the 1938 Act criteria would favor such a bias, even though, as noted earlier, these alleged psychiatric outcomes of pregnancy and birth have been found unsound. On the other hand, the leniency may reflect a difference in victims, i.e., the victims of males were more likely infants or older pre-schoolers than neonates and vice versa for the females.

Similarly, Wilczynski and Morris (1993), also dealing with British cases, but in a range from neonaticide to filicide (N = 395) during the period 1982 to 1989, found that of the parents convicted, "Mothers were less likely than fathers to be convicted of murder or to be sentenced to imprisonment and were more likely to be given probation and psychiatric dispositions" (p. 35). The defense of infanticide, or even great stress, they indicated, tended to evoke sympathy and efforts at support for the women, but not for the "wicked" men. The perception of mothers as nurturing and caring leads others to "assume that a 'normal' woman could surely not have acted in such a way. She must have been 'mad' to kill her own child" (p. 36). The same comment about gender-related leniency related to the age of victim suggested above may be relevant here.

Indeed, a later study of Wilczynski's (1997b) is entitled "Mad or Bad?" She found in that study that twice as many women as men used psychiatric pleas when accused of filicide. Of those found guilty, the men more frequently received longer and more custodial sentences than the women. They were also less likely to receive psychiatric treatment than the women, even if it was evident that they needed such help. Wilczynski (1997b) found that filicidal women were more often viewed sympathetically than filicidal men, whose motives included spousal retaliation, jealousy, and discipline. She also found that the women were less likely to have committed violence prior to the case at hand, or to have been abusive, whereas the male offenders were more likely to have exhibited such behaviors in their pasts. The question to be resolved in her paper was whether the males and females should be treated similarly under the law when they had committed the same crime (filicide). In her view, the men should be treated less harshly, and given appropriate psychiatric treatment where warranted, although the women should not be treated more harshly.

Zingraff and Thomson (1984), on the other hand, cited research in which it had been suggested that the courts are more apt to sentence women harshly if their demeanors and behaviors do not conform to expected gender roles. Women, on the other hand, who do fit female stereotypical patterns are treated more sympathetically. This explanation sheds some light on research findings, at least for misdemeanors. Child abandonment and assualts, however, "seem directly to contradict gender role expectations for females and the sentence lengths women receive for these two offenses do tend to be longer than those received by their male counterparts, although only the abandonment differential is statistically significant" (p. 410). This negative view of women convicted for violent crimes who deviate from the maternal stereotype is supported by Edwards' study in Great Britain (1986). Coughlin (1994) similarly reported a negative relationship between gender stereotypes and sentencing.

Two American cases reflecting that negative relationship are those of Sheryl Ann Massip of Anaheim, California and Jamie L. Goodrum of Wisconsin. Massip, on her 24th birthday in April 1987, killed her 6-week-old son by running him over with the family station wagon after an unsuccessful attempt of throwing him, wrapped, in front of a passing car. That driver swerved and missed the "bundle." Massip was described as a "happy, healthy, nonviolent person who looked forward to motherhood" prior to Michael's birth. However, after the baby was born "she began feeling confused and worthless; and during the next six weeks could neither sleep nor eat. She began having suicidal thoughts, such as jumping off a building or out of a window. She also experienced hallucinations; voices were telling her the baby was in pain" (*People v. Massip*, 1990). Post-partum psychosis was used as a defense in this case, and a defense psychiatrist testified on her psychotic behavior. The jury did not agree and convicted her of second-degree murder.

In Goodrum's case (*People v. Goodrum*, 1989), she told police that her two sons, aged 14 months and 6 weeks, were kidnapped, and fabricated an elaborate story with a description of the car allegedly involved and of her being drugged by an assailant. Goodrum was on probation at the time. The police did not believe her story and called her probation agent, who ordered a probation hold. She was then picked up by the police. At first she maintained her story; later she confessed to killing the boys with a hammer. Goodrum was convicted on two counts of first-degree murder, with the jury finding that she was not suffering from a mental disease or defect. She appealed the decision based on a lack of psychiatric testing as had been recommended by an expert witness who testified on her behalf.

Are the Laws Anti-Female?

The arguments on post-partum psychosis and other biologically based defenses for females remind us of the arguments against having a female president of the U.S. (or prime minister of England), that her decisions would be subject to pre-menstrual — or post-menopausal — "whims." (Note: The British have overcome this argument as well.) Similarly, arguments on women murdering their babies which are based on lactation, the physical stress of childbirth, and similar causes, are seen as gender-biased.

In the absence of a federal law dealing with neonaticide and infanticide, and in accord with the 10th Amendment, we are confronted with at least 52 different sets of statutes dealing with such an event (50 states + Puerto Rico + District of Columbia). When a case arises, it also evokes arguments from anti-abortionists vs. pro-choice forces and from feminists of a variety of persuasions who perceive application of these laws as unfair, unreasonable, anti-female, or inadequate. In the case of neonaticide, the anti-abortionists see abortion and neonaticide as the same crime. Those who are pro-choice see no crime in abortion, generally permitted before the 24th week of pregnancy in most states, and tend to recognize (but not support) neonaticide as the solution a young woman may take who is religiously or otherwise opposed to abortion, but who panics at the time of delivery. In other words, the girl sees abortion as wrong — perhaps from a religious standpoint —

but for some reason, unclear to anyone, in her panic at the time of delivery does not see anything wrong with killing the baby. Infanticide, as we have previously noted, is a different crime, usually with motives different from those associated with neonaticide. Further, infanticide may be committed by someone other than the biological mother, whereas this is rarely true in cases of neonaticide. The recommendations of the New South Wales Law Reform Commission (1997) with respect to infanticide as a partial defense to murder provides helpful clarification of these questions.

The New South Wales Law Reform Commission (1997) acknowledged that the prosecution of women for the crime of infanticide as it has existed in the law has an unsound ideological basis, one with which many feminists would agree. "Women are given special treatment by way of a gender-specific law based on the notion that they are naturally susceptible to mental instability as a result of giving birth. Arguably, this conveys a conception of women as inherently unstable because of their biology" (p. 116). The Commission also pointed out that "No other crime is excused on the basis of social or economic necessity or adversity alone. To permit an exception to this general principle for women may benefit certain individuals but ultimately reinforces a view of women as especially weak and vulnerable because of their sex" (p. 123). Furthermore, the Commission voiced "concern that female offenders who do not fit easily into the stereotype of women as weak and frail victims of their biology may be condemned as 'bad mothers' and punished much more severely" (p. 117). A third consideration in the Commission's recommendation was that the offense (and defense) of infanticide was limited to the natural mothers of victims aged less than 12 months, which left out other groups of offenders such as fathers, adoptive mothers, foster parents, and other caretakers of infants. In fact, they noted that a large percentage of children (other than neonates) were victims of men in abuse-type killings (pp. 118–119), a fact frequently documented in the daily U.S. newspapers.

Opponents of the Commission's recommendation took the position that "by abolishing a specific defence which relates solely to women, particular attention to the special problems which women face is reduced and the individual's mental state is emphasised, rather than the social factors which contributed to that state" (New South Wales Law Reform Commission, 1997, pp. 122–123). Or, as Lentz (1989) put it, since post-partum psychosis is an exclusively female defense, it might promote sexism which is feared by many feminist groups because "regarding postpartum disorders as a defense will detract attention from other real events in women's lives and further the notion that women should not be accorded full responsibility for their actions" (p. 543). Similar arguments were advanced by Lansdowne (1990): "The offence of infanticide ... is a sex specific offence, that can only be committed by women, in fact only by mothers, which is additional to the general defences of disturbed mental state, insanity and, in New South Wales and England, diminished responsibility" (p. 41). Lansdowne further raised feminist objection to its status as a "specific homicide offence" in New South Wales, Victoria, and Tasmania. As we have seen, however, men as well as women can commit infanticide (and filicide); it is not a "sex specific offense," although neonaticide is (and may be the more appropriate term which should have been used by Lansdowne).

Looking Backward and Ahead

At this point, it is clear that children are endangered by their parents or caretakers for a variety of reasons, and that those reasons may or may not provide adequate defenses in court when child homicide occurs. It is also apparent that there are questions of gender discrimination involved in the law, at least in the U.S., which have not only biological aspects but also political and other ramifications and implications. Those political and religious arguments will be discussed in the next chapter, as their proponents (and opponents) can influence state and federal legislation which ultimately bears on the ways in which prevention measures, unwanted pregnancies, and prosecution of perpetrators are handled.

Choice and Reproduction: Political and Other Arguments

8

Among the alternative methods of preventing or dealing with unwanted and undesirable pregnancies have been the use of contraceptives and, if that failed, abortion. However, sex education is often needed to provide the information on how and when to use such alternatives. Contraception and abortion are practices that have provoked massive debate in our society. The disagreements involve not only moral and religious values, but also political issues and the status of women. The rhetoric that has encompassed the controversy conceals a public discourse that is not necessarily based on logic, but rather on a series of firmly held beliefs. Many arguments have employed words such as homicide, murder, child-killing, and infanticide or neonaticide as synonymous with abortion. Mary Glendon (1991) observed cogently that the way in which we name things and imagine them may be decisive for the way we feel and act with respect to them. If this is so, the dialogue over the issue of abortion reveals very passionate and powerful attitudes.

The language, symbol, analogy, and metaphor constantly evoked in various literary forms have also appeared in political verbiage and journalistic articles. The debates that have enveloped our communities, past and present, also used the lingual devices of infanticide to arouse emotional responses and reduce the level of rational discourse. The political divisiveness centered around the problems of neonaticide and infanticide encompass gender relationships, abortion, euthanasia, legal standards, and sex education. The rhetoric of abortion has often been heated and exaggerated as it concealed the hidden agenda of its proponents. Pro-life advocates regard those who disagree with them as "potential murderers;" pro-choice advocates view their opponents as violators of women's fundamental rights. The inability to arrive at any compromise or moral consensus in the dialogue on abortion has led instead to partisanship, fanaticism, and intolerance in language and even behavior.

At the heart of the debate is the definition of, "what is a child?" When does life begin? Does personhood begin at conception? At the end of the first trimester? At birth? A week or a month or a year after birth? Not only does the boundary differ by culture, including religion, but disputes rage among biologists, philosophers, ethicists, pro-choice proponents, right-to-lifers, and others. Even if we could define the exact moment when life begins, the underlying issues and cultural disagreements would prevent either compromise or any widespread acceptance of abortion. The problem of defining when life begins did not exist in the past. Present-day technological and medical developments that allow the early identification of pregnancy and permit fetal viability earlier than ever have altered perceptions of pregnancy and abortion. Moreover, amniocentesis and other intra-uterine testing have raised issues over the abortion or treatment of future babies found to be disabled.

The Abortion Controversy

Abortion was acceptable until the mid-19th century. Common law in the U.S. and Great Britain allowed abortion until "quickening" or the feeling of life. Before that, a woman was "irregular" in her menstrual cycle, and potions, herbs, vigorous exercise, and other strategies were used to bring on her period. Most abortions that occurred before then were helped by midwives practicing folklore methods which usually brought on spontaneous abortions, but no records were kept and so we know very little about this. As the 19th century progressed, there was more knowledge about how abortion was accomplished and much evidence to indicate that it was practiced by both the desperate poor and the well-to-do (Condit, 1990; Fuchs, 1992; Mohr, 1978).

Not until the middle of the 19th century, when medicine became the province of the male medical establishment, did abortion begin to acquire meaning, measurement, and state regulation. Physicians claimed that abortion and birth control were selfish actions which imperiled the family and the social order. Physicians did not seek to end abortion completely, only to control it. They wanted laws that permitted the doctor to decide if the woman needed an abortion for health reasons. They were not concerned about the "personhood" of the fetus. "In classifying abortion as both a criminal offense and a health problem, pregnancy and its consequences were increasingly subject to state and medical intervention" (Ginsburg, 1989, p. 24).

Religious Views

One of the most ardent proponents of anti-abortion laws in the past and present has been the Catholic Church which perceives life as beginning at the fertilization of the egg. However, in the distant past that was not always so. Christian thought under Augustine claimed that the soul was not present until quickening. By the 13th century, the church revised this point of view by adopting Aristotle's position: the presence of the soul did not appear until 40 days after conception for a male and 80 days after for a female. It was not until the end of the 17th century that the Catholic Church took its stand against abortion at any time (Rothman, 1989).

Abortion is now defined by the long-held church commitment to the notion that the fetus is a full human person from the moment of fertilization and therefore abortion is homicide. That means that even the possible death of the mother is insufficient reason to permit abortion. The only permissible exception is that of the unintended abortion if surgery is performed on the mother in life-threatening situations such as a cancerous uterus or an ectopic pregnancy (Noonan, 1970; Petchesky, 1981).

In contrast, the Jewish position, similar to the Protestant one, opposes "abortion on demand" as was noted earlier in Chapter 4. Jewish law declares that an existing human life must be protected over that of a potential life. For Jews, the fetus is not yet a human being, but has the potential for life. Therefore, if the mother's life or health is threatened, her needs are paramount and an abortion would be permitted.

The differing religious positions on abortion require a degree of tolerance that has not been forthcoming in political debates. The reasons often lie in the fact that the disputants have other hidden agendas masked by strident rhetoric.

The old disputes about contraception were gradually resolved by growing concerns over unrestrained population growth, and by the appearance of the birth control pill in 1960. The Supreme Court decision, *Griswold v. Connecticut*, in 1965, invoked the right of privacy which ended legal arguments over contraception and prepared the way for the pro-choice campaign for abortion rights which culminated in the *Roe v. Wade* decision in 1973 (Reagan, 1997; Tribe, 1990). As earlier cultural demands for sexual freedom came to fruition during this period, social and religious conservatives became alarmed at what they perceived as pernicious changes in American behavior and morality. The Catholic Church had opposed contraception and abortion on religious grounds, but then the Protestant evangelicals also embraced an anti-abortion position despite the fact that they had no prior history of such a position in their movement. Their leadership responded to feminism and the growing number of teenage pregnancies and abortions even within their own communities by sacralizing the abortion issue, equating it to sexual sinning in order to reemphasize Christian values of patriarchy, sacrificial motherhood, and sexual purity (Harding, 1990).

Language and Imagery

The pro-life faction has characterized abortion rationally as neonaticide. This provocative imagery has selected two perceptions: one that abortion is indeed neonaticide, and the other that it is equally as pernicious as the homicide of a newborn baby. By lumping the two actions together, the symbolism of the phraseology evokes a strong revulsion for abortion.

Visual aids used by pro-life propagandists enhance the impact of their arguments. The portrayal of actual fetuses evokes strong emotional reactions. "Any graphic depiction of an innocent sacrificial victim appeals to Christian themes deeply embedded in our culture" (Berger and Berger, 1984, p. 74). These pictures emphasize that the fetus is a developing child rather than its characterization by pro-choice people as just a piece of tissue (Wilson, 1994). Newman (1996) argues that in all of these representations the fetus is shown as intact while the woman's body appears inert and fragmented. "The effect is that the observer is encouraged to identify with the fetus rather than the woman who carries it — accepting the former as an autonomous and rights-bearing individual, while denying the latter any subjectivity, sympathy, and individuality, and hence any plausible claim to rights of her own" (Newman, 1996, p. 8). In contrast, pro-choice imagery is not as effective. Their pictures are symbols: the coat hangar to recall the risks of death in illegal abortion and the Statue of Liberty to symbolize the woman as downtrodden and threatened by those who would deny her reproductive freedom (Condit, 1990).

Pro-life advocates want to establish an environment that enhances the special and unique female characteristics of pregnancy and motherhood. For some, abortion saps the vitality of the family and vitiates the father's obligation to sustain his family financially. Thus hidden in some of the programs of the pro-life factions is also an agenda of banning sex education and contraception exclusive of sexual abstinence. Implicit in the pro-life dialogue is also a cultural code for the evils of our society: materialism. Therefore, according to the pro-life position, women who undergo pregnancies and deliveries in the face of adversity and obstacles are heroic and truly feminine, while those women who choose to abort are unnatural, weak, and unfeminine (not to mention selfish and immoral).

The use of this imagery in the partial birth abortion debate proved how effectively language can be used to garner support for a position by many who are pro-life. Further characterizing the procedure as murder akin to that of a living infant, one writer claimed that "doctors who performed this procedure (whatever their motive) are the American successors to Mengele, who performed medical experiments in Nazi Germany and who was an abortionist" (Bethell, 1988, pp. 22–23). Pro-life literature that shows photographs of the discarded bodies of concentration camp victims, and then, next to those, photographs of fetuses stuffed into plastic garbage bags for disposal, has offended many. Metaphoric allusions that compare abortion to the Holocaust have been cited by the religious right in their arguments (Isser, 1997). Numerous individuals perceive the equating of abortion with the victims of the Nazi Holocaust as both unseemly and a distortion of the debates. It seems very wrong to them to appropriate Jewish suffering for the propagation of views about abortion. They raise the question: does not comparing "abortions with the horror of the Holocaust deprive Nazism of moral significance and debase Jewish history by exploiting it for sectarian Christian goals?" (Mensch and Freeman, 1991, p. 935).

However, pro-choice proponents have used language in a similar fashion. The word *abortion* has been used in two ways. There are induced abortions and spontaneous abortions. One is caused by medical intervention and the other is a consequence of a bad pregnancy. Is the spontaneous abortion then an act of murder? Is it, too, neonaticide? Since spontaneous abortions occur very frequently, is nature a murderer? Modern medical research has shown that a newly fertilized egg has a small chance of coming to term. Pro-choice proponents stress that since the egg can be so easily destroyed by nature, it can be replaced by another one. The importance of the zygote (as they label the developing egg to distinguish it from the more developed fetus) rests upon the proper care which can bring it to full development. "The responsibility is to a fetus that will become one's child but not necessarily to this particular fetus. The use of similar language in both instances distorts and devalues the basic arguments and makes a middle ground more difficult to achieve" (Greenwood, 1994, p. 499). The use of ultrasound pictures in the early first trimester, a technique unknown 30 years ago, only reinforces their belief. The case of Sherri Finkbine, a woman pregnant with a fetus disabled by the drug thalidomide, has been particularly emphasized (Condit, 1990).

Furthermore, feminist women see their bodies as a part of their individuality, and they deny what they perceive as subjection to the decisions and regulation of others, including their male partners. They see any regulation as an infringement of liberty and individuality — a cardinal belief in our American society. Control over the womb is central to the notion of female identity and the woman's role in American society. Thus the arguments over abortion can be applied as well to the issues of contraception, amniocentesis, surrogate motherhood, and *in vitro* fertilization. These issues become very significant for young women when they face unwanted pregnancies, seek help for avoidance of motherhood, or search for fertility assistance. As they turn to counseling or proposals that could bring both comfort and aid, they discover that the agencies are involved in acrimonious controversies over gender roles and how they should behave in their unhappy circumstances.

On the other hand, for people who are strongly pro-choice, the imagery of the language equating neonaticide and abortion produces a different perception. Since the proponent of choice conceives of the fetus as potentially capable of human life but not yet a person, the equating of the life of an infant and that of a fetus is immoral. They see such language and judgment of homicide as a denial of the baby's humanity and a lessened respect for human life. In this case, the vivid imagery produced by pro-life adherents has widened the chasm between the two groups.

Part of the early struggles of the women's suffrage movement in America was to use the vote in order to have more control over their private lives. "The constitutional claim of choice in the personal, private world is thus even more important to women than the claim to equal citizenship. Male power over women's sexuality and maternity has restricted women to a passive role, permitting them to control conception and childbirth only through a strategy of denial" (Karst, 1984, p. 452). Furthermore, they envision the intensity of the pro-life language as proof of their opponents' desire to maintain a continuing control of women. By resisting laws that permit women to take charge of their own bodies, especially those laws with emphasis on their control of reproductive rights, pro-life positions are deemed destructive to equality and autonomy for women (Hernandez-Truyol, 1997). Ginsburg (1989) argued "that both symbolically and experientially the definition of female gender identity and the domestic domain have focused more and more on questions regarding reproduction and its relationship to nurturance" (p. 213).

Pro-choice proponents also view legal safe abortion as an essential aspect of protecting women from the problems associated with childbearing. "It is a basic condition enabling heterosexually active women to have the power to control whether, when, and with whom they will have children" (Ginsburg, 1989, p. 7).

In the Courts

After much protest and agitation, pro-choice forces were able to achieve the victory of *Roe v. Wade* (1973) which permitted abortion in the first trimester. Subsequently, state courts have wrestled with permitting abortion in later trimesters to save the mother's health and to allow teenagers to have abortions without parental consent (Harris, 1978). Restrictions have been required in some states, such as Pennsylvania and Missouri, like a waiting period or notification of a parent (or judicial approval in lieu of such notification). "Of the first 1300 Massachusetts abortion cases involving petitions to bypass parental consent, courts found the adolescent to be mature in 90% of all cases and in all but five of the remaining cases, held that abortion was in her best interest" (Rhode, 1992, p. 125). In New Jersey, the ACLU filed suit against a law due to be effective in September 1999 that would require doctors to notify a minor's parent 48 hours before performing an abortion or obtain a "judicial bypass" (Martello, 1999). The ACLU "says the law is unconstitutional because it would infringe on minors' rights to privacy and treat minor teens who seek abortions differently than those who carry their pregnancies to term" (Martello, 1999).

The arguments over such regulations rest in part on when life begins (or indeed, what is being considered "life") and when the fetus is viable. The *Casey* decision of the U.S. Supreme Court (*Planned Parenthood*, 1992) rejected the trimester framework of *Roe*; it reaffirmed the state's legitimate interest in "the protection of potential life;" and it explicitly held that even though a woman alone must choose whether to abort before the fetus is viable, the state is not prohibited "from taking steps to ensure that this choice is thoughtful and informed" (Wilson, 1994, p. 22).

In *Doe v. Bolton* (1973), the Supreme Court ruled that Georgia's require-ment of approval of an abortion by a hospital medical committee or other physician violated the privacy of the doctor and patient. However, in *Webster v. Reproductive Health Services* (1989), the court upheld a Missouri law that:

- Prohibited performance of abortions by public employees and in-state-financed facilities.
- "Upheld a provision that required physicians to determine whether an 'unborn child' is viable, if the physician has reason to believe its gestational age is 20 weeks or more" (Cleary, 1991, p. 54). (Note that the wording is "unborn *child*.")

A bare majority of the justices reaffirmed *Roe* but changed its meaning and application. Speaking through Justice Sandra Day O'Connor, the Supreme Court reasserted that a woman has a "constitutional liberty" to "some freedom to terminate her pregnancy." However, the state could now place restrictions on this right, even when the fetus is not yet viable, provided those restrictions do not impose an "undue burden" on its exercise. The *Casey* decision acknowl-edged that the state could exercise some degree of regulation of abortion (Poland, 1997). The Supreme Court's reasoning for these decisions also reflected a new philosophic leaning. The original *Roe* ruling had been based on the right to privacy, but feminist jurisprudence began to attack this concept, insisting that the abortion rights should be based on a criterion of sexual equality. They claimed that in the past contraception and abortion restrictions were enacted for the explicit purpose of enforcing separate spheres of behavior for the sexes and to engender subordination of women. Mackinnon (1989) argued that "giving women control over sexual access to their bodies and adequate support of pregnancies and care of children extends sex equality. In other words, forced maternity is a practice of sex inequality" (p. 117).

The U.S. Supreme Court has begun to move in this direction. In the rulings in the *Casey* decision, the Supreme Court narrowly upheld privacy rights, but also went on to declare that the "state was obliged to respect a pregnant woman's decision about abortion because her suffering is too intimate and personal for the State to insist … upon its own version of the woman's role, however dominant that role has been in the course of our history and our culture … " (Allen, 1992, p. 686).

Does Fetus = Person?

These issues have continued to cause disagreement and difficulties in interpretation and legislation. For instance, a key problem that arises from the rhetorical arguments of abortion is the one of "the fetus is a person" ideology. If that concept is legally adopted, the next step is to protect it even *in utero* (Tribe, 1990).

The woman's autonomy is then challenged in the workplace, clinics, and courts (Rhoden, 1988). The employer could both legally and morally bar women from jobs where there may be hazards to her present or future reproductivity. The excuse of hazards to the fetus gives employers the right to exclude women from equal employment opportunity, but also allows employers to ignore harmful agents in the workplace which may hurt the male's potential for fertility (Becker, 1986). For example, the case of *International Union U.A.W. v. Johnson Controls* (1991) centered around a ruling by the company banning women of childbearing age from certain jobs, contending that they were too risky for future pregnancies. The court rejected that ruling, calling the order gender biased and saying that the same jobs could injure male fertility as well. In medicine, the fetus could be the patient and the pregnant woman simply its "environment." In legal cases, the husband or male partner could assert that these issues are paramount in debates over women's rights and her quest for equality.

Amazing technological and medical developments have enabled physicians to treat and cure fetal defects *in utero*. This power may help parents who desire healthy babies, but do the procedures then become the entering wedge for the medical profession and social workers to impose their programs of prenatal care, or to stop abortions, or to supervise the lifestyles of prospective mothers under the rubric of avoiding child abuse (Bowes and Selegstad, 1981)? What can and does happen is that, depending upon the ideology of the medical personnel, doctors can discredit or annul the pregnant woman's right of decision in medical treatment. If the woman is merely a "vessel" for the unborn, then the rights of the fetus can prevail over her health and wishes. "Women are put into an impossible dilemma. If the damaged fetus can be treated, does that mean it must be? Is the woman guilty of 'neglect' if she refuses and complicit in denying her own autonomy if she doesn't?" (Petchesky, 1990, p. 358).

In matters of equal decision over abortion, do male partners have certain rights over the pregnancies? If the relationship is loving, caring, intimate, and based on mutual trust, the male should share, especially if he is supportive of the female. In contrast, paternal rights claims can also rest on the premise that the fetus has independent rights, and the father has a traditional proprietary right in the partner's body and its progeny. (Wives and children have not been viewed as *property* in family law for more than 50 years. That does not mean, however, that practice necessarily follows in step.)

The nature of laws, therefore, involving the status of family, the role of society, the role of welfare, and, indeed, the regulation of women's lives, becomes a part of passionate political debate. If the fetus is a separate being, the government may define how a woman lives and how she cares for herself. Her life can be rigidly regulated. Petchesky (1990) claims that "men have reduced the pregnant woman to the status of maternal environment, a passive spectator in her own pregnancy" (p. 240). In addition, this view, according to Sunstein (1992), "is often closely identified with the understanding ... that sexual activity should be exclusively for purposes of reproduction" (p. 30). Some pro-lifers allege that the easy availability of abortion would encourage sexual promiscuity and activity for non-reproductive purposes. Their opponents believe, on the contrary, that sexual freedom is important for both men and women, and that that freedom includes the right to have an abortion as well as to engage in non-reproductive sexuality. Indeed, a large part of Sunstein's argument rests on the issue of sex role stereotyping and sexual discrimination. Forcing a woman to continue her pregnancy by law, it is argued, dictates roles that differ for men and women and make women second-class citizens, which is, itself, unconstitutional and against several laws passed in recent decades.

As the issue is debated not only in the press and other media, it has also entered the legal and political arenas. Various states have enacted legislation, or the courts have ruled in appeal decisions, on the question of whether a fetus is a child. In South Carolina, for example, Cornelia Whitner was accused of child abuse because she took drugs during her pregnancy. In 1992, she pled guilty to criminal child neglect because her baby was born with cocaine metabolites in the baby's system as a result of her ingestion of crack cocaine during her pregnancy. Subsequent appeals brought the case to the South Carolina Supreme Court in 1997 where her conviction was upheld. This court ruled that provisions about child abuse and endangerment in the 1985 South Carolina Children's Code applied to a fetus, for, they wrote, "We hold the word 'child' as used in that statute includes viable fetuses" (*Whitner v. State of South Carolina*, 1997, p. 27). In a second case in South Carolina, that of Talitha Renee Garrick, the mother-to-be was also found guilty of killing her unborn fetus and sentenced to a prison term, but it was subsequently changed to probation (Copeland, 1997). "South Carolina is the only state where a pregnant woman can be sent to prison for potentially harming a viable fetus" (Anon., 1998, p. 24). (Note: South Carolina was joined by Wisconsin later in 1998.)

The *Whitner* case (1997) is one of several conflicting decisions cited by the Supreme Court of Wisconsin, which was also wrestling with the question of what was meant by the word "child" in the state's CHIPS (Child In Need of Protection or Services) statute. In the instant case, Angela M. W. was pregnant and using cocaine. Lower courts had ruled that the "child," i.e., the fetus, was in need of protective custody because of the mother's drug use, and the petitioner argued that if the child was placed in protective custody that would violate her (the mother's) rights to equal protection and due process (*Angela M.W. v. Kruzicki*, 1995). The Wisconsin Supreme Court, in a divided decision, reversed the lower courts and ruled that a fetus was not a child under the relevant statute. However, that would not have been the decision if the case had been heard in mid-1998 instead of 3 years earlier, as a bill was passed by the Wisconsin legislature in 1998 which defined a fetus as a human being from the moment of fertilization (Herbert, 1998). Relevant to this problem of drug-addicted pregnant women is a call to several states to enact legislation that would oblige the woman to complete a drug reha-bilitation program or lose their parental rights (Zitella, 1996).

In Florida, the Florida Supreme Court ruled that a pregnant woman could not be charged with murder or manslaughter for shooting herself in the abdomen to kill her fetus. (News in Brief, 1997). The 19-year-old woman charged had been turned away from an abortion clinic for lack of funds. She was single, unemployed, and already the mother of a toddler. The Florida court "pointed out that American and English common law confers immu-nity on pregnant women who cause injury or death to their fetuses, although a third party may be prosecuted" (Anon., 1998, p. 24).

For a third view, the Pennsylvania legislature passed a fetal homicide bill in 1997 that would make it a crime "to kill an *unborn child* through an assault on the mother." The bill in no way affected the state's abortion laws (Capitol Report, 1997, p. 9). This would appear to parallel the Florida law rather than the South Carolina law. However, in a case involving an accident caused by a drunken driver, a Pennsylvania Superior Court "ruled that a viable fetus is considered a person under the state's criminal code and that criminal actions that injure or kill a fetus can be prosecuted" (Henson, 1999).

Feminists have found in this issue questions that relate to their functions and roles in society. This discussion had its roots in the feminist movement at the end of the 19th century. The key factors in the feminists' search for autonomy rested on the conflicts between personhood and the societal requirement that the female could be fulfilled only in marriage and motherhood. Neonaticide, infanticide, filicide, and abandonment have been, as both literature and history have taught us, a persistent problem plaguing governments although they were perceived largely as female crimes. The issue for feminists has been not only that women have been stereotyped and pushed by community mores into subordinate and defined roles, but that the policies of legislators (mostly male) can legally bind and control women, making their lives rigidly regulated.

The ongoing quarrels also involve "morning after" pills, birth control, and RU-486. Pro-life advocates claim that these are the "slippery slope" to infant euthanasia, teen illegitimacy, and, in general, moral debauchery. On the other side, pro-choice groups characterize any attempt at regulation or limits on education as the "slippery slope" to denial of civil rights, invasion of privacy, and the restoration of patriarchy (Roberts, 1993). The majority of Americans have embraced *Roe v. Wade* because they desire to have the option of abortion, but at the same time they want it only as a last resort and thus are willing to permit some state regulations upon the procedure. In practice, the American public has adopted a workable compromise, but to the ardent believers on both sides of the issue these pragmatic methods of handling a sensitive moral cause is seen as dangerous precedent. The vitriolic language and the deep cleavages of cultural and moral beliefs have poisoned the ability to solve the many social problems attached to family planning and adolescent development. In so doing, there is a high risk of rhetoric overriding reason.

Proponents of anti-abortion or "right to life" legislation are entitled to their views. They overstep the boundaries of church-state separation in the Constitution and respect for the rights of others, however, when they seek to impose their views on everyone else. As we have already indicated, most religions are opposed to abortion, but some permit it on a limited range of grounds such as rape, incest, or danger to the physical or mental health of the mother. If a member of one of the latter faiths, or if an atheist for that matter, seeks an abortion on such a legitimate basis, it is not the business or right of pro-lifers to prohibit it through legislation. Further, if the right to an abortion exists "in rape or incest cases, the only realistic way to protect that right seems to be to create a general right to abortion" (Sunstein, 1992, p. 40).

Euthanasia and Infanticide

Medical science, through the test of amniocentesis and the use of ultrasound, can provide women with information on whether they will have babies with serious defects. That raises new issues: women who learn that their fetuses

are defective may elect to have an abortion, and pro-life advocates characterize those abortions as "fetal euthanasia" (Ramsey, 1970). The latter found
an ally among those who see these abortions as an expression of dislike of
and prejudice against the disabled. In contrast, both doctors and patients
who support early testing and the consequent decisions of the parents have
done so because they feel that the family should decide whether they are
willing to accept the commitment for the care of such children. Calmer voices
which have been drowned in the polemical outrage of both sides have suggested that perhaps abortion in these cases should be restricted only to those
conditions incompatible with life, such as Tay-Sachs disease. Or, perhaps,
that women who are prepared to act on the basis of the tests' results must at
least learn more about what is involved in caring for children with disabilities
before they are allowed to end their pregnancies (Rhoden, 1988).

To Treat or Not to Treat

Many newborns whose congenital abnormalities are horrific are not being
treated so as to spare them and their families the hardships of continuing
therapies, pain, disability, and emotional havoc (Zajac, 1989). If and when a
child is born with terrible illness and incurable defects which would hamper
any normal development, what should be the policy of the parents? The issue
is fraught with the same indeterminancy of language and the same distortions
observed in the abortion debates. Is the denial of medical or surgical procedures infanticide, as claimed by those who believe that all measures should
be employed to save every infant? (Koop, 1989). In the past, midwives often
did let severely impaired infants die, and in many places, these babies were
destroyed (Hontela and Reddon, 1996).

Death for sick infants, accompanied by parental participation, can be
accomplished by withdrawing or withholding medical treatment or by
administering lethal overdosage for eugenic or humanitarian reasons. This
is a more common problem than has generally been believed. Until recently,
children would have died because nothing could be done for them, but now
they survive, especially if they are treated at a hospital with specialized intensive care units (Lund, 1985; Rhoden, 1988). The cases of many newborns are
complex, with few available answers. For instance, there are babies who are
born alive, but who have such massive problems that they will die no matter
what is done for them. In those cases, there is little argument that they should
be left untreated. In other cases, babies born with minor problems should
certainly be treated and kept alive. Cases that are more difficult to assess,
such as extremely premature births, Down's syndrome, and spina bifida, lead
to questioning of parents' and physicians' judgments.

In 1973, a study in a New Haven hospital revealed that in an 18-month
period 14% of the 299 infant deaths were related to withholding treatment.

As more knowledge of these practices occurred, more objections were raised to what had been considered a private matter to be decided between the parents and physician (Maciejczyk, 1983). The debate gained momentum with the publicity arising from the "Baby Doe" case in 1982. A Down's syndrome infant, known only as "Infant Doe," needed surgery to correct a blocked esophagus and thereby allow food to reach her stomach. The parents refused consent to the surgery and also withheld food and water from the child. The infant died 6 days later. National media attention touched off debate about decisions made in neonatal intensive care cases. The widespread public interest caused the Department of Health and Human Services to issue regulations designed to require hospitals to provide medically indicated treatment to handicapped infants. The rulings were immediately challenged in the courts. Several states then enacted legislation concerning withholding treatment from defective infants. Before the Baby Doe case, the practice of withholding treatment had received little or no publicity; afterward, more and more cases were heard in the courts. When judges were confronted with these medical decisions, they found competing rights and interests, with some courts granting *a priori* parental rights and others granting priority to the defective infant's right to life (Maciejczyk, 1983).

Legislative and Judicial Responses

The problem has continued, however, because the issues are so complex, ambiguous, and difficult to define that neither state nor federal legislation has responded to the challenges of ill babies, and court rulings in individual cases have been contradictory and sometimes misleading. The controversy remains heated but unresolved. Parents and physicians who decided whether or not to treat the infants were neither consistent in their judgments, nor were the ethical or moral beliefs universally acceptable. Indeed, there was dissension about what laws were even applicable (Evans, 1989).

The state always makes the value of life a basic, integral concept and therefore the common law concept of *parens patriae* vests the state with guardianship power over disabled individuals which allows intervention to preserve their physical and mental well-being. In the case of sickly infants, the state must also consider the allocation of scarce medical resources. The state's *parens patriae* power has frequently been invoked to limit parental authority in cases of parental neglect or abuse, and extends over a wide range to limit parental freedom and authority in things affecting a child's welfare (Maciejczyk, 1983). But parents also have intrinsic rights and interests, for they bear the ultimate responsibility for the care and treatment of their children, and traditionally, they have the authority to make decisions concerning their children's welfare. In the case of Baby K in 1994, for example, the courts ruled that the treatment of an encephalic infant at the parents' request must be honored by the hospital despite the apparent futility of such help (Poland, 1997).

Eugenics, Mercy-Killing, and Euthanasia

Modern debates over abortion and the right to (let) die are not new and are not the result of new technologies. Eugenics played a large role in American debates in the past, often encompassing race, immigration, and health policies, including who was fit to live (Pernick, 1996). However, the Nazi programs of racial purity during the 1930s and 1940s made the issue totally unsavory, for the Nazis did not practice mercy-killing, but a form of mass annihilation of infants, children, and adults who they thought were physically and mentally ill or inferior. Such eugenics became forevermore unacceptable. Recall the primitive form of eugenics practiced in primitive societies, and in Greece and Rome, by exposing or killing deformed or so-called weak babies, and the shift to no justification for killing as Jewish, and then Christian, practices became more widespread. The controversy has been intensified by debates over Dutch legislation and Dr. Kevorkian's campaign to permit assisted suicides, or mercy-killing as in Oregon's legislation. In contrast, there are those who declare that "the deliberate killing — because that is what it is — of a newborn whether by act of omission or a deliberate procedure that deprives the child of life is infanticide" (Koop, 1989, p. 101).

Debates in the medical and bioethical establishments re-emerged: how aggressive should the treatment be for such babies? Do we just let them die? Do we give them some treatment to ease the pain, but let them die, etc.? Some physicians feel that their decisions made with the parents' consent should be private and respected. Most of the cases of ill newborns are complex, and doctors are often motivated by what they consider to be the needs to relieve the parents and the infants' siblings from seemingly crushing burdens (Koop, 1989).

The most acrimonious debates have occurred over the views of Peter Singer, a widely respected philosopher, notably on "animal rights," and on the necessity of the affluent peoples of the earth to help the starving. Basing his ethical conceptions upon utilitarian philosophical principles rather than traditional morality, he has aroused emotional responses to his views that advocate both abortion and euthanasia. Singer's reputation stems from his book *Animal Liberation* (1975), in which he argued that humans were not special or essentially different from animals and, therefore, should not enjoy special rights. He asserted that newborns are not yet self-conscious beings aware of themselves as distinct entities. A day-old infant has no desires or feelings. If it is morally right to shoot a badly injured or sick animal if it is in pain and has no hope of recovery, then it is equally right to kill an incurably sick infant. It is only our misplaced respect for the doctrine of the sanctity of human life which prevents us from seeing that what is obviously wrong to do to a horse is equally wrong to do to a defective infant (Singer, 1979).

Singer's view provoked opposition because it seemed to many an excursion into moral relativity and a denial of the Christian-Judaic tradition of the sanctity of life (Jamieson, 1999). To others, the arguments were reminiscent of those used in Nazi Germany to justify their mass killings (Burleigh, 1994).

The Parental Positions

Those people who object to abortion motivated by knowledge that the fetus would be born with a disability maintain that this type of abortion, unlike most others, is not a private event. Therefore, many pro-life proponents advocate restricting access to the diagnostic technologies that provide women with information about their fetuses. That raises new issues. Children need to be wanted, desired, and cherished. The family undertakes the unending chores and demands of children — feeding, support, love, and discipline. Parents cannot relinquish their decision to raise a child when he or she has colic or an extreme case of the "terrible two's," or when he becomes a rotten adolescent.

Opponents of criminalization of infant euthanasia (or abortion) believe that the fetus is not a person, or at least it is not yet a member of the family. The family should be able to decide when they want a baby and accept their commitment once the child is conceived (Greenwood, 1994). Whatever their reasons for either abortion or withholding care, they are attempting to say that they could not handle this problem and that the child might suffer in their care. They passionately believe that a child should be a commitment of love undertaken willingly by the family. The family that assumes responsibility for an infant with disabilities undertakes a monumental task. The demands on the mother may be overwhelming, the emotional drain on the marriage and the other siblings in a family may be heavy, and the financial costs may be staggering. There is little community support in this situation, especially for poorer families. These are only some of the reasons to avoid the birth of a baby with disabilities, and people who make such decisions should not be judged by one criterion (Buchanan, 1996).

On the other hand, there are others who are even more passionate about caring for the infant no matter what his condition may be. As Koop wrote, "I believe that our patients, no matter how young or small they are, should receive the same consideration and expert help that would be considered normal in an adult. Just because he is small, just because he cannot speak for himself, this is no reason to regard him as expendable" (1989, p. 101). Some affirm that, if euthanasia were permitted, parents would be denied the rewards and satisfaction of working for the rehabilitation of their children.

In their view this care could lead only to the growth of the family in compassion, character, deeper understanding, and stronger affectionate bonds (Evans, 1989).

Despite the belief by some that suffering and care for children strengthens character and the family, evidence indicates that many family members do suffer chronic anxieties, guilt, and depression (Fost, 1981; Gustafson, 1973; Stinson and Stinson, 1981). The decisions to withhold treatment, reduce care, or do everything possible necessitates agreements by both the family and physicians. To achieve this is sometimes difficult. Physicians play a central role in the diagnosis of baby defects, and they may question individual cases of parental refusal to authorize medical care by referring the case to state child welfare agencies as a form of child neglect. Strong disagreements can develop between the common law right of family autonomy and medical personnel insistence on enforcement of state child neglect laws (Knepper, 1994).

Those proponents of the primacy of parental decisionmaking with respect to treatment decisions often do not take into account that many families are incapable of assuming such responsibility. The parents of an impaired infant may be teenagers. They may be unmarried, raising questions about parenthood, itself, particularly if the father wishes to enforce his rights. Some families may be dysfunctional, have a single mother, be a blended family, be unmarried co-habitors, or perhaps the parents may be drug addicted, illiterate, or abusive. That complicates the situation, for if care is to be provided for these babies, who in such a family will assume the responsibility for a sickly infant who requires more care, more love, and more financial resources than these dysfunctional parents can provide?

Closing Thoughts ...

Despite these diverse opinions, most people are uncomfortable with the actual murder of sick infants. The withholding of treatment, on the other hand, is complicated and requires more analysis than that of ideology. Certainly communities need to be sympathetic when parents, for economic and other reasons, desire to withhold care for infants with severe disabilities, for there is little support for either the parents or the disabled themselves. But even if we could accept infant euthanasia, we should never forget that infants are full human beings and should not be considered either as expendable or having lesser value. There is an intrinsic moral principle that all human life is sacred; therefore, mercy-killing should never be acceptable. Treatment for the very defective infant is another matter; there are some cases in which it might be permissible, even in the infant's best interests, to withdraw or withhold care (Post, 1990).

Just as the abortion issue has been concerned with morality, theology, and differing cultural values and traditions, the topic of sex education as one of the methods of dealing with teenage pregnancies has become the center of heated political controversies. The pertinence, utility, and even the need for such programs will be discussed in the next chapter.

Child Homicide: Preventive Measures

9

As enlightened as we may think we have become as we enter the 21st century, a society that focuses on punishment rather than prevention has learned little from the past. It is doubtful that we will ever eradicate the abuse and murder of children totally, but we have a moral and professional obligation to do what we can to prevent these crimes.

As we have shown, children are killed most often because of the problems of people who are supposedly adult enough to know better. Our emphasis in prior chapters has been on neonaticide; our emphasis here is the prevention of neonaticide, beginning with the prevention of pregnancy, and the somewhat related crimes of infanticide and filicide. The latter crimes are frequently related to child abuse, which may occur in the form of outright neglect as well as physical assaults. The U.S. Advisory Board on Child Abuse and Neglect noted an increase in the reported cases during the period from 1985 to 1993 (Bethea, 1999), and is one of many agencies and groups calling for more extensive and intensive efforts at primary prevention of child abuse on both the societal and familial levels. Primary prevention involves, among other ingredients, a healthy injection of education.

Prevention of Neonaticide

There are two major approaches to combating the problem of neonaticide. One is to prevent pregnancy, especially among girls in their teens. A strong voice for this option is that of Oberman (1996), as noted earlier. As the National Center for Health Statistics has reported, the birth rate for teenagers has been declining steadily since 1994 (Ventura et al., 1999b). Whether we are addressing teens or older women, however, prevention of pregnancy is a major key to reducing the number of births of unwanted babies. The other possible approach is to insure prenatal care when pregnancy does occur so that the prospective mother and the fetus not only have appropriate medical care, but also the social and psychological support that both eliminates denial and makes her aware of her options.

"In terms of prevention … it seems critical to ensure that every pregnant mother is attended during childbirth … both the public and medical personnel need to be alerted to the danger and to provide support to new mothers who may be experiencing post-partum depression" (Crittenden and Craig, 1990, pp. 212–213). Programs aimed at preventing pregnancy are termed *primary*; those working with teens (or older women) who are already pregnant or parenting are considered to be *secondary* programs. There will probably always be a problem with prenatal care and continuing support where the woman is in a state of denial about being pregnant, but the proposed programs can at least reduce the number of cases in that category. Again, according to the federal statistics, in 1997, first trimester prenatal care improved for the eighth consecutive year (Ventura et al., 1999a).

In many cases that we found, the girl or young woman had had medical attention while pregnant, but *not* for the pregnancy, because she denied the pregnancy to herself and described any symptoms to her doctor as menstrual "irregularities." Wissow (1998) has suggested that doctors be more careful in their examinations and use tactful questioning and pregnancy tests to detect pregnancy. (Note: In this era of managed care, there may be more need for justification of pregnancy tests than mere suspicion on the doctor's part if the cost of the test is to be reimbursed.) They can refer the patient, if pregnant, for appropriate prenatal care and support services. They may also need to reassure some of their patients of confidentiality, i.e., they will not tell the girl's parents of her pregnancy unless she agrees. (This flies in the face of legislation that has been passed that requires parents to be notified if their underage daughter seeks an abortion, but even those laws permit exceptions where such notification may endanger the girl.)

Sex Education

Society, confronted by changing sexual mores, teen pregnancies, and more never-married mothers, seeks ways to influence the prevalent youth culture. One of the ways suggested is to increase sexual education for the whole community, but make it particularly directed toward the young and available in the public schools. The issue is whether there should be sex education in the schools at all and if there should be, what it should include. Liberals have wanted to develop new curricula to include contraception information which would encourage young people to take proper precautions not only to avoid possible pregnancy, but also to prevent the growing menaces of venereal disease and AIDS. Conservative Christian groups have opposed sex education which promoted knowledge of contraception as well as giving information on homosexuality. They feared that the full discussions of sexual information would encourage pre-marital sexual relationships. Many, however, do advocate the teaching of abstinence only.

Although debate remains passionate over programs to influence teen behavior, many state legislators seem to favor some kind of sex education in schools. Most states have provided a basic form of instruction on disease prevention and contraception as well as stressing abstinence education. In 1996, 22 bills were introduced on school-based sex education. One half would have increased parental involvement or insisted on emphasizing abstinence until marriage; the other half would expand existing programs. In Florida, AIDS education activities were supported, with details of the programs specified. Massachusetts law insisted that students have parental permission to attend sex education classes, while Rhode Island passed laws that allowed parental review of curricula and materials and also permitted parents to remove their children from these classes (Sollum, 1997). In Colorado in 1996, conservatives attempted, but failed, to amend the state constitution by a law that would have given parents the right "to direct and control the upbringing, education, values and discipline of their children" (Donovan, 1997, p. 187).

A large number of parents expressed concerns that schools cannot present sex without including values and since teachers could not be neutral, the curriculum should center on biology rather than attempt to regulate teen behavior. They claimed that parents, churches, and other community groups should assume the responsibility of educating children in more morally directed teenage pregnancy prevention. What should be emphasized, they asserted, was that pre-marital sex was wrong and abstinence was the only permissible behavior. As one writer suggested, "Unless sex education addresses values, ethics, morality, deferment of gratification, and goals, it is incomplete and potentially dangerous" (MacDonald, 1987, p. 384).

The existence of sex education in schools has led to research on how effective such teaching is, whatever its content. As in the case of arguments over what should be taught, debates range widely. One of the proposed solutions to reducing the number of unwanted pregnancies has been to introduce sex education and contraception information into the curriculum starting in the junior high school. Evidence available to Stout and Rivara (1989) indicated that the traditional sex education programs in junior and senior high schools had little or no impact upon adolescent sexual activity. Most studies emphasize that there is a lack of evidence that "sex education classes, condom distribution programs or exposure to pregnant and parenting classmates promotes sexual activity ... " (Stevens-Simon and Kaplan, 1998, p. 1206).

Yet, impelled by ideological bias, many studies report more or less success depending upon their point of view. One excellent study is an example of these inconsistencies. The authors reflected the commonly held opinion that the effect of sex education at best was problematic, citing test reports which demonstrated less change than hoped. Then another author continued by noting that most Americans feel that sex education should begin at home, but also believe that it should be taught at school, and that the programs should stress sexual restraint, promote family values such as fidelity and commitment in marriage. They concluded that "it appears that sex education programs that promote abstinence can be effective in producing a positive attitude change toward abstinence ... " (Olsen et al., 1991, p. 640). In contrast, in an equally valid study, the authors claimed that "abstinence only" education, though seemingly successful, had major drawbacks. They found that studies show that convincing, strong inculcation of the necessity of sexual abstinence before marriage inhibited conversation about safe sex. It created "an atmosphere in which teenagers are emotionally incapable of using the knowledge they acquire in the classroom to make the kinds of conscious decisions about their behavior to avoid pregnancy" (Stevens-Simon and Kaplan, 1998, p. 1206).

Mauldon and Luker (1996) claimed that contraceptive education was successful. If contraceptive education occurs in the same year that a teenager becomes sexually active, the odds of any method and/or condom use are increased by 70 to 80%, and the odds of pill use are more than doubled (p. 19). In direct contradiction, Maynard and Rangarajan (1994) said that enhanced family planning information and counseling for first-time teen mothers did little or nothing to stop subsequent pregnancies.

Other reports adopted a more dispassionate view. One cited 23 studies that discussed the most successful of these programs. They noted that "not all sex and AIDS education programs had significant effects on adolescent sexual risk-taking behavior, but specific programs did delay the initiation of intercourse, reduce the frequency of intercourse, reduce the number of sexual partners, or increase the use of condoms or other contraceptives" (Kirby et al., 1994, p. 339). Later research from California (Kirby et al., 1997) echoed these sentiments, while a condom distribution program in Philadelphia also produced results that showed there was not an increase in the level of sexual activity among young people (Furstenberg et al., 1997). But both studies indicated that there was not a statistically significant increased use of con-traceptives, either.

What has been shown in these studies is that some programs are more effective than others, and effort is needed to discover, distill, and use the more effective curricula. So long as the debates are mired in ideological and cultural conflicts, however, the necessary pursuit of the best means to teach our children more careful and meaningful sexual behavior will not take place.

Pregnancy Prevention

Prevention of pregnancy begins with information. Vance (1985) urged sex education in a family context from kindergarten through grade 12, using precise language to avoid misconceptions. For those who think that kindergarten is too early to mention such concepts, it might be informative to watch the television programs these little ones observe and see what sexual content is conveyed in them. In one study (Ward, 1995), it was found that more than one in four interactions in primetime programs watched by young viewers had statements related to sexuality, with more such content in the programs aimed at adolescents rather than young children (which does not mean that younger children do not see these programs). Hogue (1997) pointed out that while explicit sexuality is on television and film screens, contraceptive ads are not allowed and the consequences of unprotected sex are rarely presented. This is an inappropriate imbalance.

One example of Vance's approach is seen in a long-term study in Seattle. A 12-year study conducted in Seattle's most crime-ridden neighborhoods worked with children in grades one through six and sought to "foster an interest in school and learning among children and to enhance their self-esteem … " (Brody, 1999). The findings at follow-up when the subjects were age 18 showed that, compared to peers who had not been in the intervention program, the subjects were "13 percent less likely to engage in sexual inter-course, 19 percent less likely to have had multiple sex partners and 35 percent less likely to have caused a pregnancy or to have become pregnant" (Brody, 1999). Not only were the youngsters taught problem-solving skills beginning in first grade, but they were also taught how to say "no" and still retain their friends. In addition, parenting programs were offered and more than 40% of parents of the subjects participated in this aspect of the intervention project. With the resulting enhanced self-esteem, improved parenting at home, and enhanced skills, there was apparently less need on the part of many of the participating youngsters to find "love" or acceptance through sexual activity.

The programs sponsored by the 1996 Welfare Reform bill were princi-pally of the primary type, but were based on an "abstinence-only" philosophy and were not permitted to provide information about contraception (Wurf, 1997). Similarly, in late 1998, an amendment to the Health and Human Services bill then in Congress would have mandated that all Title X clinics (established in 1970 to reduce unintended pregnancy among low-income women) require minors to obtain parental consent before receiving contra-ceptives — or abortion-related services (Russell, 1998). Although such an approach may mirror some religious and idealistic views, it does not conform either to other religious (and non-religious) practices or to contemporary reality. Some parents (and others) allege that if contraceptive information is included, this is tantamount to telling adolescents that their sexual activity is expected and approved. Similarly, anti-abortionists are loudly opposed to abortion even being mentioned as part of sex education. For the youths, the necessary admission of sexual activity needed to gain the consent may be more than they are willing to do; they would rather risk pregnancies than tell their parents what they do. Indeed, it is taking this risk that has too often resulted in neonaticide.

Participants in the 1999 Teen Pregnancy Prevention Conference held at Pennsylvania State University in November 1999 discussed education programs that began as early as age nine, and that involved both boys and girls (not necessarily together) and their parents. [Note: Age nine is *not* too early to begin this instruction. The National Vital Statistics Report lists the number of babies born to mothers aged 10 to 14 years (Martin et al., 1999), although the figures reported on decreases in adolescent pregnancies refer to the 15- to 19-year age group and do not mention the younger girls.] Some of the programs offered in Pennsylvania involve working with diverse communities and encouraging community support for pregnancy prevention programs. At least one middle school program stresses training in parenting, although others include facets of parenting skills. Abstinence is a principal focus of several programs, but others explore the pleasurable as well as painful aspects of sexual feelings. This means that self-respect as well as respect for others is also taught in some of the workshops.

Several abstinence programs are described by Napier (1997), who is obviously against sex education programs that include contraceptive information with its implication that "teens will be teens." One such program, sponsored by To Our Children's Future With Health, Inc., a Philadelphia group, provides a variety of programs to pre-teens, teenagers, and parents. Supported by both state and federal funds, the program pays stipends to the pre-adolescent participants, and for some, that is sufficient reason to attend (Raghavan, 1998). Another Philadelphia study, however, reported in the *Journal of the American Medical Association*, divided sixth- and seventh-graders into three groups, each of which received 8 hours of health education. "One focused on abstinence; one concentrated on condom use; and a control group addressed avoiding non-sexual diseases" (Jemmott, Jemmott, and Fong, 1998). The researchers found that after 6 months and again after 12 months, more of the abstinence group students were having sex than condom-group students, and more of them were having unprotected sex. An Institute of Medicine study found that abstinence-only sex education did not delay the onset of sexual intercourse (Hogue, 1997).

On the other hand, Weckerle and Wolfe (1998) cited programs introduced at the elementary and middle school levels that try to teach relationship skills and provide information about dating. As they commented, "It is disturbing that teenagers appear to be poorly informed concerning what constitutes normative dating behavior" (p. 355), and also appear to be at risk for dating violence. Their program tries to identify (and ultimately to reduce) the risk factors, which include family background, psychological adjustment, and personal resources.

A handbook addressed to adolescent girls, and written in language that they can understand, together with its discussion guide (Mathes and Irby, 1993), provides an informative basis for pregnant teens in terms of what is happening within their bodies, what care they need, and what happens at delivery. It also has several very useful chapters on the baby's development during pregnancy and post-natally so that the young mother knows what to expect. Perhaps tucked *between* these two sections deliberately, there are two chapters that focus on choices to be made with respect to becoming or remaining pregnant and sexually transmitted diseases. The chapter on choices includes information ranging from abstinence to prescriptions, but opens with a concept too often overlooked: "Thinking ahead." The chapter on diseases brings to the forefront risks in this aspect of sexual activity which adolescents too often ignore, much to their later distress.

Pathway/Senderos, a neighborhood-based teen pregnancy prevention program in New Britain, Connecticut (Pearlman and Bilodeau, 1999), is a replication of a very successful youth development/teen pregnancy prevention program begun in Harlem in the 1980s (Carrera and Dempsey, 1988). Participants are recruited during the sixth grade "and they attend the center 5 days each week year-round and remain in the program until they graduate from high school. The sole criterion for remaining in the program is avoiding pregnancy. However, if a female participant does become pregnant, or a male participant impregnates anyone, she or he is then referred to the appropriate community agency for young parents" (Pearlman and Bilodeau, 1999, p. 93). Collaboration between academic psychologists and the community-based workers seeks to intervene in the poverty/school dropout/teen parenting cycle prevalent in a "deteriorating Spanish-speaking area" in New Britain. The program, which uses a case management approach, is based on "a philosophy that connects academic failure and continuing poverty to teen pregnancy, and academic success, including college, to a vision of future opportunity" (Pearlman and Bilodeau, 1999, p. 93). The doctoral students and their professors who are involved contribute information, resources, and time to the program while also learning of the real community needs and problems involved in working with these disadvantaged youths.

In another program that uses slightly older peers to provide education about safe sex practices, young medical students in Australia are sent back to their former schools to teach adolescents before they become sexually active (Short, 1998). The program, in operation since 1992, has been so successful that its sponsors in Melbourne have been invited by the Chinese Ministry of Health to work with medical schools in Beijing and Shanghai to try to develop something similar in those cities.

Just looking at the issue of sex education from the standpoint of providing adequate and appropriate information to young people, it is apparent that this is not being done in most schools. Indeed, it is not being provided adequately even at home. The result is that adolescents, and children even younger, are surrounded by sexual stimuli but lack adequate information to deal with it. For example, how many mothers tell their pre-teen daughters much about their maturing bodies beyond the details of menstruation? How many say to a daughter, "It's *your* body. *You* are responsible for its care. It is up to *you* to see that it is not violated."? There is at least one magazine addressed to teenagers, *Teen Voices*, published in Boston, that has published a series of articles on teen pregnancy containing the thoughts of pregnant teenagers ("So You're Going to be a Mother … " 1999). How well it reaches the appropriate target audience is unknown.

Stoiber, Anderson, and Schowalter (1998) have indicated several items of misinformation held by adolescents relevant to sexuality, and urge the use of small group counseling-type programs to provide not only correct information, but also support to teenagers in this area. They also point out that the best prevention programs reach youngsters *before* they become sexually active; such programs promote abstinence, provide information about sexually-transmitted diseases, and improve decisionmaking skills, among other themes. "It should be noted that frank discussions about sex often do not occur in classroom settings or occur too late, after adolescents have already become sexually active" (p. 285).

Planned Parenthood's TIPS (Teen Information and Peer Services) program trains teens to be resources for their high school peers. They can discuss pregnancy as well as birth control, sexually transmitted diseases, and abstaining from sex (Brown, 1997; Minton, 1998). The Girls, Inc. organization, which seeks to help girls reach their potential, also sponsors a number of programs to provide this type of information to young girls.

Not only girls have to be taught though. The Mother-Son Health Promotion Project being conducted in several Philadelphia public housing projects has as one of its goals to educate mothers so that they can teach their sons and influence their sexual behavior (Dubin, 1998). Emphasis in this area is on both sexually transmitted diseases and the use of condoms. On the other hand, where adolescent boys have already become fathers, they also need intervention programs. "Four aims of intervention groups for adolescent fathers are supported in the literature: (1) social support, (2) vocational/career development, (3) parent/child relationship, and (4) prevention of subsequent conceptions" (Stoiber, Anderson, and Schowalter, 1998, p. 295).

Corcoran, Franklin, and Bell (1997) asked 105 teenagers participating in adolescent pregnancy education programs in Texas what they thought should be included in the programs. These males (22%) and females (78%), ranging in age from 11 to 22 years (86% aged 14 to 18), and largely from lower income families, answered a variety of questions, often with embarrassment.

Questions concerning the use or avoidance of birth control led to some answers that indicated that young people rejected birth control because of the lack of spontaneity, embarrassment at buying birth control, fear of parents finding out, anxiety about side effects of medical methods, or belief that pregnancy will not happen to them (invincibility). Youngsters' responses to why they have babies indicated that they desired or needed love, or they wished to keep the male partner. For some, babies are "accidents," while others wanted either attention from or popularity with peers.

When queried on "all the reasons you can think of for teens becoming pregnant *when they don't want to be*," young people cited the lack of knowledge about or misuse of contraceptives, or peer pressure. Then they were asked, in view of their knowledge, what advice they would give to a teen who did not want to become pregnant. The teens had a variety of suggestions to offer peers to reduce their vulnerability to pressures to have sex, and to increase sources of information available.

Other questions were asked of teens already pregnant or parenting, beginning with "How many of you had planned to get pregnant when you did?" (Corcoran, Franklin, and Bell, 1997, p. 373). Many commented that they had not been prepared for the rigors of pregnancy, or the lack of sleep and isolation from others once the baby arrived. These comments demonstrate the need for information such as that contained in the Mathes and Irby handbook (1993).

Secondary Prevention

Bluestein and Starling (1994) recommended that physicians who see teenagers who may be pregnant should exercise supportive communications skills in order to encourage the girls to continue prenatal care for their own benefit and that of their babies. Obviously, the patient must trust the doctor and the doctor must reassure the patient that their discussions are confidential unless the patient gives permission to disclose them. Then the doctor must exercise patience "as repeated explanations and suggestions may be needed, depending on levels of anxiety and immaturity" (p. 141). Consideration of the girl's psychosocial developmental stage is important as this affected to some degree the reasons she engaged in sexual relations and the ways in which she perceives the pregnancy and future child. Bluestein and Starling (1994) emphasized that the doctor must remain nonjudgmental throughout, but at the same time explore all possible options with the patient, helping her to think about the consequences of her decision in terms of her education, job plans, and family life.

In a study of 70 patients delivered at a Cleveland hospital in 1978 who had no prenatal care, 20 out of 43 cited internal barriers for not having prenatal care: depression, denial of pregnancy, fear of doctors, unplanned pregnancy; 10 out of 43 cited external barriers: financial problems, no transportation, no child care, inability to obtain clinic appointment, clinic wait too long; and 13 out of 43 said they had no problems with the pregnancy or no special reason for not seeking prenatal care (Joyce et al., 1983). These researchers concluded that while hospitalized women received good prenatal care and were prepared for future pregnancies, those women who denied their pregnancies or did not seek care remained at risk for the future. "In order to reduce the incidence of 'no care' deliveries, community outreach and marketing strategies to reach the patient population who do not seek care are necessary in addition to hospital-based approaches" (pp. 94–95).

Other studies that cite barriers to prenatal care including long waits at clinics, short time with the medical personnel, and communications difficulties, especially for non-English-speaking patients, are cited by Oropesa et al. (1999). They also found, in their study of 1255 mothers from the Puerto Rican Maternal and Infant Health Survey, that prenatal care was less likely when the pregnancy was an unwanted one.

Another program aimed at pregnant adolescents, but also at those who are parenting, is the Chance to Grow Project (Donnelly and Davis-Berman, 1994). The pregnant teenagers were exposed to full counseling and case-management services aimed in part at improving their decisionmaking skills and behaviors that would enable them to cope with or to prevent future crises. A follow-up study 2 years later showed positive results. The "catch" here, as in other programs, is to see the adolescents *while* they are pregnant. As Wissow (1998) pointed out, increased efforts are needed to identify those adolescents who hide their pregnancies so that they can be provided with prenatal care. An alternative would be to introduce techniques taught in the Project to students as early as age ten, with perhaps annual reinforcement of the concepts, rather than waiting until they are pregnant. The techniques used include a decisionmaking balance sheet, stress inoculation, and role playing.

In Baltimore, the city school system established the Paquin School in 1966 to make a positive change in the lives of childbearing adolescents (Boyer-Patrick, 1999). A magnet school that draws from beyond the city limits, Paquin also has a school-based clinic providing counseling services from clinical social workers and psychiatrists. In addition to academic (grades 6 to 12) and counseling services, the school has an on-site day care facility, vocational and back-to-school re-entry programs, plus a program aimed at young fathers and grandparents. Boyer-Patrick found, in the responses to his survey at the school (answered anonymously), that only 4% of the sample (N = 110) felt that they would not be able to complete high school due to parenting responsibilities. More than one third of the group believed they would be able to complete college, and almost one quarter thought that they would be able to complete an advanced professional degree; these figures, as

Boyer-Patrick noted, were seen despite the fact that many of the girls lived in homes where their parents had not completed high school, let alone college. Perhaps more important was his finding that they did not stay in therapy unless they had previously been willing to discuss their pregnancies with close friends or significant adults. He concluded that an atmosphere of trust had to be developed if the professional counseling was going to be effective — an important point if special programs are truly going to help these adolescents.

Needless to say, not all prospective mothers are adolescents, nor are all of them substance abusers of one kind or another. Those women who *are* drug addicts, however, place the babies they carry at considerable risk of brain damage, organ damage, seizures, respiratory disorders, and behavioral symptoms. The Medical University of South Carolina in Charleston established a program in which pregnant women who tested positive for cocaine use were given a choice: they could enter a rehabilitation program at the hospital to become drug-free or they might be arrested and serve jail time (Zitella, 1996). Hospital personnel did extensive drug counseling, as well as urging of the pregnant patients to participate in the rehabilitation program for their benefit (no arrests) and so that they would give birth to healthy babies. There were successes with this approach, but it was stopped because the federal government perceived it as discriminatory (most of the participants were poor non-whites) and threatened to withdraw funding from the medical school (Zitella, 1996). Zitella's proposal that cocaine-addicted mothers participate in such a program or lose parental rights may be perceived in the same way, but she does have a valid point — if parents don't take responsibility for their children's well-being, then government is forced to care for them — at great expense socially as well as financially.

Preventing Infanticide and Filicide

In the cases of infanticide and filicide, clearly there needs to be prevention as well. Parents must be shown the value and effectiveness of alternative disciplinary strategies. "Classes in behavior management and parent-child communication should be made available to all parents at no charge; school children should be taught similar concepts and skills. The media, especially television, should be used to convey attitudes and information and to model appropriate disciplinary procedures" (Crittenden and Craig, 1990, p. 213). Parenting education, i.e., the realities of infant and child development among other matters, is critical for adolescent parents, perhaps especially the fathers, but it is also important for chronologically, if not emotionally, more mature parents. There might then be fewer abusive over-reactions to wet diapers, infant cries, and similar normal situations which too often result in homicide. These classes, too, might begin, and be required, at fourth or fifth grade level, emphasizing the 24-hour responsibility of parenting, the total commitment needed by babies, and the fact that parents "give" more to babies than they "get" back, at least for many months or even years. Other needs for adolescent parents, typically, include taking control of their sexual activity, learning how to set goals and to move toward their attainment, and how to follow through on their plans and commitments.

One program for adolescent mother groups is outlined in terms of session-by-session objectives, with samples of specific activities, for which only the session titles are cited here:

> Session One: Memories as Motivation for Being the Best Possible Parent.
> Session Two: Communication Competence.
> Session Three: Exploring Communication Patterns.
> Session Four: Sexual Refusal and Pregnancy Prevention.
> Session Five: Reflective Decision Making Applied to Sexual Situations and Parent Situations.
> Session Six: Feeling Nurtured.
> Session Seven: Understanding Love, Friendship, and Sexuality.
> Session Eight: Goal Setting and Future Planning.
> Session Nine: Constructing Career Pathways.
> Session Ten: Staying on Track (Stoiber, Anderson, and Schowalter, 1998, pp. 299–300).

Another type of program, involving home visits by nurses and even trained non-nurses, has been found to be very helpful to unmarried single mothers in terms of avoiding welfare dependence, child abuse, involvement with drugs, or trouble with the law (Olds et al., 1998). The support begins when a female is pregnant with her first child and continues until the child is 2 years old, and includes advice on child-rearing and life skills as well as medical matters. For a program that cost less than $3,000 per year per mother, the results, followed for 15 years, seem highly cost-effective both in their positive results for the families involved and in savings for welfare programs.

In some communities, such as Burlington, Vermont and Glenside, Pennsylvania, there are residential "family centers" for young mothers where parenting, life skill, and therapeutic classes are offered in addition to regular high school education. The combination of support, instruction, and therapy provides benefits to the mother, child, and thereby society, as well as in social and economic costs (Berman, 1999).

Confirmation of the value of intensive care in infancy and early childhood comes from the follow-up studies of programs such as High/Scope at Perry

Preschool in Ypsilanti, Michigan (almost 30 years of follow-up studies) and the Frank Porter Graham Child Development Center at the University of North Carolina at Chapel Hill, where more than 100 subjects first seen as toddlers were evaluated at age 21 (Waggoner, 1999). Benefits to the mothers as well as the children were found in terms of education and employment status. A cost-benefit analysis of the High/Scope program "showed that for every $1 spent on child care, taxpayers saved $7, mainly from costs to crime victims" (Waggoner, 1999). In addition, one might expect savings from the lack of need for welfare payments, extended medical care to babies born to drug-addicted or malnourished mothers, and extended schooling in the form of repeated grades.

Other Alternatives

If the girl or young woman can admit her pregnancy to herself and to someone who can help her, then she need not be placed in the position of feeling that there is no alternative to neonaticide. If she and her boyfriend or husband can admit that they do not know how to parent and seek help, then infanticide and filicide might also be reduced. In the case of pregnancy, adoption is a very constructive alternative. To avert child abuse or neglect, the foster care system *may* be helpful to the child, at least until the parent learns how to parent effectively.

Adoption

Historically, adoption was a largely satisfactory alternative to teenage or unmarried motherhood, and certainly to neonaticide and infanticide. Whether the neonate was left where he was certain to be found and cared for, or the pregnant woman was cared for in a Salvation Army or other program and the newborn placed for adoption, the new baby had a fighting chance at a good life. In some other cases, especially where the mother was quite young and had little support, she might turn to adoption when she found infant care overwhelming. The benefits to the child and to the receiving caretakers who achieved their much-desired status as parents, were generally strongly positive.

There are potential problems today, however, that were less common in the past. One is obviously substance abuse before or during pregnancy and its effects on the fetus. Another is exposure to unhealthy factors in the environment and to diseases such as AIDS, which were unknown decades ago. The possibility of a girl or young woman reneging on her decision for placement, or of becoming too intrusive in an "open adoption" situation, also plays a role in domestic neonatal adoptions. [Having heard of one too many upset adoptions in this country, or being faced with a years' long wait for a placement via a social services agency, many prospective adoptive parents are looking elsewhere. Overseas adoptions have their potential problems as well, though, including the difficulty of adopting a very young healthy baby (Schwartz, 2000).]

Foster Home Placement

A major function of welfare agencies across the U.S. is the protection of children from abuse. When, as the result of someone's call, they find actual abuse or child endangerment, the agency typically removes the child from the home and places the youngster in a foster home. This can prevent infanticide or filicide for as long as the child is in a safe foster setting. Meanwhile, at least in theory, the potentially abusive parent can be helped with psychotherapy and parenting education. A parent sensitive to her own emotional difficulties might even request the temporary foster placement on her own while she seeks to straighten out the difficulties in her life. There is concern today, however, that some foster home placements continue too long for the welfare of the children involved, and a number of states have moved to make such placements permanent via adoption if the parents have not been rehabilitated within a 2- or 3-year period. In addition, social workers with too heavy a caseload may not be effective in their supervisory visits to homes where there has been a history of child abuse or neglect.

Summarizing the Alternatives

It is important for people in our society to recognize that we cannot solve all problems regarding neonaticide, infanticide, and filicide, nor can we prevent teenage pregnancy completely. It is also important to recognize that there are certain realities that cannot be ignored: youths and adults alike will engage in sexual relations without being aware of, or ignoring if they are aware, the possible consequences or the preventive alternatives to these consequences. There is no reason why parents cannot teach abstinence at home while the school conveys information available in the larger society such as the use of contraceptive measures to avoid pregnancy and sexually transmitted diseases. Therefore, a rapprochement must be reached in terms of what is included in sex education, as prevention is far less costly in human lives as well as dollars than paying the welfare, psychotherapy, and penal bills after the fact.

Concluding Thoughts and Recommendations 10

"Society is often only concerned with treating, or prosecuting, the mother after she has hurt or killed her child; what is more important is protecting her before she has a chance to do so" (Schroeder, 1993, p. 292). The better and more rational approach is to educate young people and sensitize their teachers, social workers, and medical professionals to their sexual and psychological needs.

Reviewing the historical, literary, and multicultural aspects of neonaticide, infanticide, and filicide, as has been done here, provides a context for crimes that some people may think are new bases for today's headlines. Clearly, this is not the case. Motives have not changed appreciably over the centuries either, although we may be more aware of their variety today. What *has* changed in some jurisdictions is the way in which the perpetrators of these crimes, especially neonaticide, are regarded by the law. There is also greater awareness, in some quarters, of the need for changing society's perspective as Schroeder, just quoted, has suggested, although we would add lawyers, legislators, and judges to his target audience.

Provide Information

It is already evident that a focus on preventing unwanted pregnancy is needed, especially among teenagers, although women in their 20s and older may also be in need of appropriate information. That should be made available through multiple outlets, from medical offices to schools to recreation centers. Public service announcements on radio and television, around the clock, should make women aware of where they can get help and information. In addition, factual information about the joys and irritants of infant and child development needs to be available to all who interact with children of any age. Education should have, therefore, a very high position on the priority list of eliminating, or at least reducing, crimes against children.

That not everyone will be reached or, if reached, will pay attention to this information is a given. There will still be neonaticides, infanticides, and filicides, but if *one* child's life is saved, if *one* adult is kept from committing homicide and another intervenes to prevent fatal child abuse, the effort will be worthwhile. Ultimately, the ripple effect will occur and more children and adults will be spared tragic ends.

Therapeutic Rehabilitation

In the present, however, we are confronted with hundreds of child homicides each year. The uneven treatment across the U.S. of mothers who commit neonaticide, with an emphasis on punishment, needs to be restructured. That the young woman has committed a crime is not disputed; the way(s) in which she "pays" for her act must be re-evaluated. Great Britain and other sectors of the U.K. recognize that these women are typically not "threats to society," who need punishment in prison, but rather that they need mental health therapy and rehabilitative education as well. They can be confined, if necessary, and receive treatment in psychiatric hospitals instead of prison, and participate in community service projects as part of their sentences — perhaps teaching younger girls how to prevent pregnancy, or if pregnant how important it is to have prenatal care, what alternatives there are to neonaticide, or how to be good mothers if that is their choice.

For mothers who commit neonaticide, infanticide, or filicide, there is a great need to bring together the efforts of those who work in the fields of psychology, law, and public policy in the interdisciplinary arena known as "therapeutic jurisprudence." This approach goes beyond mental health law per se, and "seeks to focus attention on an often neglected ingredient in the calculus necessary for performing a sensible policy analysis of mental health law and practice — the therapeutic dimension … " (Wexler and Winick, 1991, p. 979).

Of the three broad categories of child homicide with which we have been concerned, neonaticide appears to be the one where therapeutic rehabilitation should be introduced first as a major component of any sentence determined by the court. Fazio and Comito (1999) have asserted that those who have committed neonaticide, especially teenagers in this group, are the criminal offenders most amenable to rehabilitation. Further, they typically are not repeat offenders, nor do they pose a threat to society. In the view of these lawyers, "… neonaticide is not a premeditated homicide; it is a compulsive and rash act that occurs immediately after birth when the girl confronts what she has denied for nine months" (p. 3167).

We would not say that the crime occurred as a result of physiological changes in the female during pregnancy or immediately following delivery; that creates an inferiority in females that is untrue. More appropriately in most of the neonaticide cases, we would say that the new mothers suffered from "diminished capacity" to appreciate the wrongfulness of what they were doing because of a host of other sources of emotional upset at the time of delivery and immediately following. The girl is rarely a threat to society in the way a child abuser is, or those guilty of other violent crimes, and so should be helped to understand *what* she did and *why* she did it so as to prevent a recurrence. This would ultimately benefit society more than the typical incarceration where rehabilitation is a minor concern if it is offered at all.

When mothers become conscious of their imprudent actions and sincerely regret their behavior, their remorse will be punishment enough. So, is it necessary "for the state to impose the longest or most severe penalties when she, herself, is her own worst punishing agent? ... Generally, society considers random, repeated, and cold-blooded killers as the most dangerous to society. How much does a murdering mother's profile conform to this description?" (Ford, 1996, p. 529).

Some of the neonaticides, more than one-third of those we located, were committed by women aged 21 years and older. Assuming that these women were of at least average intelligence, they should certainly have been conscious of their pregnancies, aware that pre-natal care was needed for themselves if not for the babies-to-come, and also aware of the fact that there were alternatives to raising the children which did not involve murder. Although these "older" women should have known better than the adolescents, they may well have had some of the same emotional conflicts and psychological problems that the younger women had, and today may be equally in need of psychotherapy if they are to be restored to society as contributors rather than parasites or pariahs.

It is tragic that a mother feels she cannot afford (economically) to have another child, but then she has to think ahead of the consequences if she has sexual relations without using contraceptive measures, whatever her reason for doing so may be. Indeed, teaching that there may be multiple options which require making a choice among them and that decisionmaking has consequences, should be integral parts of elementary, middle, and senior high school education. It would most likely have positive effects in many areas of life, not just in this one.

Infanticide and filicide are crimes quite different from neonaticide in motive as well as method. Fathers or father-figures are more frequently involved in these crimes than in neonaticide. There is no argument that they should be handled somewhat differently at the time of sentencing as their motives and emotional states are usually quite different from that of the mothers. In some cases, impatience with normal infant or child behavior, such as crying or soiling, is involved. What is very much needed here, as a preventive measure, is parenting education, i.e., knowledge of the realities of infant and child development. This should be recommended for pregnancy prevention, beginning in the early school years for both boys and girls as the age of becoming a parent seems to occur earlier as the years pass. It should certainly be available in women's prisons, and ideally in men's as well, even though this is after the fact; it may prevent a recurrence if the prisoner is ever released.

In other cases, malice is at the root of the crime, whether it's anger and a desire for revenge with respect to the other parent or some other reason. In an ideal world, becoming mature would include learning how to handle disappointments and anger in constructive ways; unfortunately, we cannot reach everyone in our real world. Where some form of malice is the motive, clearly punishment is appropriate; therapy could be rehabilitative in some cases. Some homicidal mothers may be sociopathic and are more dangerous to society than other perpetrators of the same crime. Whether they can be helped by counseling or therapy varies with the specific nature of their mental illness. A third source of child homicide is Munchausen Syndrome by Proxy, which, like neonaticide, calls for psychotherapy as part of the sentence. A recent study by a professor of psychiatry at Johns Hopkins University has indicated that almost 300,000 prisoners across the country who have committed violence are mentally ill and in need of psychotherapy (Butterfield, 1999). Many of these have been guilty of child homicide.

Homicidal mothers are generally at the bottom of the pecking order in women's prisons (Coulombis, 1998), and this may be true for homicidal fathers as well. Apart from any physical harm that might befall them as a result of this, the emotional impact of so much negative attention can only create more psychological problems than the girls or women had when they committed the crimes. These may lead to suicide attempts, self-hatred which immobilizes them in non-prison relationships, or full-blown psychosis. Support groups for these women have been founded in some prisons (France, 1997; Kaplan, 1988), attempting to reduce the most negative feelings and foster more positive aspects of their beings.

The Role of Therapeutic Jurisprudence

The variations in laws around the nation, let alone differences in perspective and knowledge among members of the judiciary, too often do not permit jurisprudence to function in a therapeutic or prudent manner in terms of what is best for the individual and society. It would be helpful if legislators learned about the ways in which neonaticide, infanticide, and filicide can differ from more "traditional" homicides, and enacted statutes that recognized these differences from both the prosecutorial and punitive perspectives.

Judges should be aware of the mental health views regarding the stresses of pregnancy, post-partum depression, and even the changes impending parenthood bring. Marlow (1998), among others, as we have noted earlier, has argued that judges should be able to undertake their own research in an effort to better understand the complex issues with which they are confronted rather than be dependent on the arguments presented at the bar. Indeed, Wexler (1997) has proposed a sub-field of *comparative* therapeutic jurisprudence that would actually encourage judges to learn how other countries deal with a particular offense, which might be particularly beneficial when dealing with neonaticide, as well as infanticide and filicide. If the judiciary were more aware of both the mental health aspects of these crimes and the ways in which they are handled in various countries, their instructions to juries as well as their applications of sentencing guidelines might be more constructive to the women's futures.

The goal of sentencing should also be considered. Philosophically, we might ask what is accomplished by prolonged incarceration? Is sentencing to be primarily, perhaps solely, punitive? Is it to be retribution by a vengeful society? Is it to be a deterrent to others? Or, is the aim to return the individual to society as a contributor rather than as a threat to the community? "Incarcerating one girl for this act will not result in deterring another girl from committing neonaticide; if one does not plan for an act to occur, one cannot be deterred from such [an] act" (Fazio and Comito, 1999, p. 3167). The therapeutic/rehabilitative goal, particularly with the neonaticidal mother and one who committed infanticide, benefits the community ultimately in that the individual will no longer represent a danger to herself or others and may, in the long term, mean that fewer prisons will have to be built. In the case of infanticides and filicides which have motives less related to intense and irrational emotionality, there should certainly be incarceration of the guilty in most cases, but there should also be mandatory rehabilitative counseling or psychotherapy of the perpetrators as a condition of probation, parole, or ultimate release from prison. If the individual has learned only how to cope with prison and fellow prisoners, nothing has been accomplished in terms of teaching him or her how to be a better person in the family and in society.

In addition to considering the benefits of applying therapeutic jurisprudence, the critical importance and value of teaching many life skills from early childhood on, including the facts that there are choices to be made and consequences of those choices, and facts about sex, pregnancy, and parenting, should be apparent. Virtually everyone agrees that one has to learn how to drive before obtaining a driver's license, for example, but we have no such mandate for the far more important role as parent. Perhaps it is time that we did.

Appendix A: Neonaticide Cases by State*: Year, Age of the Accused, Charge, and Outcome (N = 86)

Year	Age	Charge	Outcome**
		Arizona	
1997	19	Murder 1 negotiated to negligent homicide	1 year (out days to work) + 3 years probation + 500 hours community service + fines
		Arkansas	
1995	17	Murder 1	?
1998	19	Negligent homicide and abuse of corpse	Prosecution asking for 6 years
		California	
1995	27	Murder 1	15 years to life
1995	36	Murder 2	15 years to life
			Therapy recommended in prison
1996	21	Murder 2	25 years to life
1997	20	Murder 1	?
1997	19	Murder	?
1997	22	Suspicion of murder — pleaded to involuntary manslaughter	14 years
1997	20	Murder 1 + assault of minor convicted of murder 2	25 years to life
1998	22	Murder 2 — convicted of involuntary manslaughter	?
1998	20	Murder	?
1998	19	Murder — suffocation of newborn	?
		Colorado	
1996	40	Suspicion of murder 1	5 years
1997	17	Murder 1, child abuse, and criminal negligent child abuse	2 years [Note: girl was mildly retarded]
1998	14	No charges as of 4/98	
		Connecticut	
1997	27	Murder/capital felony	?
1998	?	Murder/capital felony	? [Trial set for 2/99]
		Delaware	
1996	18	Murder 1 — pleaded guilty to manslaughter (7/98)	21/2 years + 5 years probation and 300 hours community service
	18	Manslaughter (boyfriend)	2 years + 6 years probation + 300 hours community service

157

Year	Age	Charge	Outcome**
		Florida	
1996	23/24	Murder 1 + child abuse pleaded no contest to murder 2	21 years without parole
1997	24	Murder 1	15 years — on appeal
1999	16	Decomposing body of neonate found in backpack	"Mother" being questioned
		Georgia	
1999	20	No charges as of 4/1/99	
		Illinois	
1990	30	First-degree murder	58 years Retrial on appeal 12/98; found guilty
1996	15	First-degree murder	Allegedly admitted 10/99
1996	40	Murder 2 — pleaded guilty	15 years to life
1996	19	Murder — guilty of involuntary manslaughter	4 years
1996	19	Murder 1 — pleaded guilty to involuntary manslaughter and concealment of a homicide	30 months probation + 500 hours community service + **psychotherapy** + full-time work/school
1997	29	Murder 1	?
1997	20	Murder 1 — plea to involuntary manslaughter rejected	1¹/₂ years + 2¹/₂ years intensive probation + **counseling** + community service
1998	22	Not notifying coroner of a death	90 days + 2 years "intense probation" + 90 hours community service + **counseling**
		Iowa	
1997	31	Murder 1–2 counts; pleaded guilty to "killing a viable fetus aborted live"	2 consecutive 25-year terms
		Kentucky	
1998	28	Murder + abuse of corpse + tampering with evidence in death of an infant	?
		Louisiana	
1995	32	Murder 1 — pleaded to manslaughter	45 years
1995	17	Murder 2	Life (mandatory)
		Maryland	
1998	16	Murder 2 and child abuse; pleaded guilty	20 years (12 years suspended)

Year	Age	Charge	Outcome**
		Massachusetts	
1997	18	Murder 1	? (illegal immigrant)
1997	19	Murder	?
1999	16	Grand jury called	?
		Michigan	
1994	17	Involuntary manslaughter (plea in 1997)	5 years probation + 2000 hours community service
1996	18	Murder 2	?
		Minnesota	
1999	17	?[1/13/99]	
		Nevada	
1998	18	Murder 2 and child abuse	?
		New Hampshire	
1999	17	Negligent homicide	$3^1/_2$ to 7 years suspended
		New Jersey	
1996	31	Pleaded guilty to manslaughter (8/98)	7 years
1997	17	Pleaded to manslaughter	4 years — paroled after 10 months
1997	18	Murder — pleaded guilty to aggravated manslaughter	15 years
1997	16	Aggravated manslaughter	Not guilty (by judge) — 5/98
1998	16	Aggravated manslaughter	
1999	?	Aggravated manslaughter — pleaded guilty	?
		New Mexico	
1999	22	Child abuse leading to death; tampering with evidence	?
		New York	
1990	20	Criminally negligent homicide	1 to $1^3/_4$ years Appeal; case decided 12/96
1994	23?	Manslaughter	8 months + 5 years probation (to be served in England)
1996	19	Murder 2 negotiated to manslaughter 2	5 years probation + community service + **psychotherapy program**
1997	21	Murder 2	Free on bail (9/98)
1997	38	Murder	?
1997	15	Murder	?
1998	15	"Unlawful disposal of body"	?
1999	20	Probable murder 2	?
1999	20+	Homicide? Miscarriage?	?

Year	Age	Charge	Outcome**
		North Carolina	
1997	20	Murder 1 — pleaded to murder 2	10 years
		Ohio	
1994	17	Murder	15 years to life
1997	17	Murder; found guilty of involuntary manslaughter and abuse of corpse	8 years appeal 1/99 — in community college retrial — 4/99
1998	less than 18	Involuntary manslaughter	Probably 2 years in juvenile facility
1998	16	Delinquency by reason of murder; child endangerment; pleaded guilty to delinquency by involuntary manslaughter	?
		Oklahoma	
1995	17	Murder 2 ("Alford" plea)	10 years + 10 years suspended sentence with mandatory pregnancy test every 90 days
		Oregon	
1997	26	Murder by abuse	
		Pennsylvania	
1994	18	First-degree murder	Life
1994	17	Drowned newborn	Life
1995	24	Third-degree murder	?
1999	18	Criminal homicide	?
1999	14	Criminal homicide	?
		South Carolina	
1995	25	Involuntary manslaughter	3 years — suspended to 3 years probation
		Tennessee	
1995	17	Murder 1/facilitating murder	10 years (found to be under husband's total control)
	22	Murder 1 (husband)	Life
		Texas	
1996	24	Misdemeanor and abuse of corpse	1 year?
1997	18	Murder	10 years + 10 years probation
1998	14	Capital murder — pleaded to "injury to a child"	3 years in juvenile correctional facility
1998	17	"Injury to a child"	?
1999	17	Under investigation	?

Year	Age	Charge	Outcome**
		Utah	
1998	22	Third-degree felony child abuse	1 year in **treatment program**
		Virginia	
1999	25	Involuntary manslaughter and felony child neglect	Faces 10 years on each charge
1999	24	Murder	?
		Washington	
1998	19	Murder 2 — suffocation of newborn	?
		West Virginia	
1995	21	Voluntary Manslaughter	3 to 15 years
		Wisconsin	
1998	13	Murder 1 and hiding a corpse Guilty of first-degree reckless homicide (had been raped)	(possibly 7 years in juvenile)
1998	30	Homicide — pleaded guilty	30 years

* Arranging the cases by state enables the reader to see the intrastate as well as interstate differences in charges and sentences.

** We logged every case of neonaticide that we found, but were frequently unable to find out the outcome of the cases, partly because of delays and appeals of trials, and partly because our sources (both newspapers and on-line) did not report the outcomes. It was not possible to travel to every site to examine local records. In each case, we have included as much data as was published regarding age of the accused, charges (and changes to charges), and sentences where this was available. In cases where psychotherapy or counseling has been part of the sentence, that has been put in bold print.

Appendix B: Sample of Infanticide and Filicide Cases*

1. Marie Noe	20–40	1949–1968	PA	Accused of suffocating 8 out of 10 children — Munchausen by proxy — other 2 children died of natural causes. Arrested 8/98 and accused of murders.
2. Teresa Torres	23	January 1994	NJ	Killed 4-month-old daughter during bout of depression. Charged with aggravated manslaughter. Trial 7/1–7/2/98.
3. Susan Smith	23	November 1994	SC	Drowned 2 sons in her car. Found guilty of murder — sentenced to life.
4. Selina Anderson	?	1995	LA	Smothered 17-month-old daughter — murder 2. May have killed 4-month-old in 1992 and 19-day-old in 1994.
5. Elizabeth Rosa	25	November 1996	NJ	Suffocated 3¹/₂-month old son — "fussy." Mother smoked crack cocaine that a.m. Pleaded guilty to aggravated manslaughter and could get 40 years.
6. Andrea Blue, RN	35	March 1997	PA	Fed 4-month-old son formula laced with cocaine.
Donald Ford, MD	39			Charged with murder; conspiracy, and drug violations (9/98).
7. Charlene Wise	36	August 1997	PA	Starved 5-year-old daughter to death in basement; also endangered 8-year-old son — both as punishment. Found guilty of third-degree murder, child endangerment, and concealing a corpse. **Maximum of 28–56 years** — blamed drugs.

8. Renee Beth Smith	20	September 1997	HI	Suffocated 9-week-old daughter — husband in Navy, left for 14-week course in Texas the day after baby's birth. Charged with murder 1 (federal court). **Pleaded guilty to Murder** (to avoid "incarceration without possibilities") — may have some therapy in sentence.
9. Susan Mitchell Billy G. Mitchell	37 45	October 1997	KY	Starved 2-year-old son but had paid-up insurance on 3 children at $60K each — all malnourished. Charged with murder.
10. Nancy J. Montealbano	45	October 1997	PA	Beat 3-year-old adopted daughter to death for knocking over potty. Charged with murder 3/aggravated assault/ endangering welfare.
11. Carla Lockwood	34	October 1997	NY	Starvation death of 4-year-old daughter. Pleaded guilty to murder 2. **15 years.** Mother of 10, including twins (age 7 months).
12. Barbara Brown Ricky Brown Janette Ables	? ? ?	December 1997	WV	Arson death of 5 children to collect on homeowner's insurance policy. Charged with arson/maybe murder.
13. Jason LeeRoy Hunt Tina Reinmann	25 22	March 1998	OK	Slapped, choked, and threw 3-year-old daughter of his live-in girlfriend because she wet her diaper. Both charged with murder 1 (mother was aware he was abusive).
14. Bethe Feltman	32	April 1998	CO	Strangled 3-year-old son and suffocated 3-month-old daughter. Charged with murder. Defense is postpartum depression (had been hospitalized prior to murders).

15. Sharon Alley	29	May 1998	VA	Killed 8-month-old daughter. Charged with murder 1. Claimed NGRI — postpartum depression/psychosis — (under treatment). Pleaded guilty to murder 2 and felony child abuse. **Sentenced to 36 years (1/24/99) — 9 year-old son never wants to see her again.**
16. James H. Proctor, Jr.	23	November 1998	PA	Killed 10-week-old daughter for crying too long. Charged with murder 1 — death penalty sought.
17. Daywaren Stewart	23	December 1998	GA	Murder and cruelty to children in shaking death of 2-month-old daughter.
18. Dina Abdelhaq	34	January 1999	IL	Suffocated 7-week-old daughter to collect $200K life insurance to support gambling. Convicted of insurance fraud — federal court.
19. Marilyn Lemak	41	March 1999	IL	Suffocated 3 children and attempted suicide. Had been depressed since birth of youngest 3 years earlier — in the midst of a divorce. Court-appointed psychiatrist declared her unfit to stand trial on murder 1 (*USA Today,* 5/6/99, p. 10A).
20. Alejandro DeJesus	c.50	March 1999	PA	Estranged husband, denied custody of 6-year-old, shot her and 22-year-old son + 2 other boys. Committed suicide — wife had had restraining order — escaped shooting.

For 20 cases ...

Age	20–29	30+	U.K.
Male	2	3	1
Female	9	8	2

* Each of these cases was highly publicized in the news media and was included to illustrate the variety of backgrounds and motives involved in child homicides.

References

ABC News (July 7, 1997) ABC Good Morning America, Transcript #97070711-j01.

Accused baby-killer avoids death penalty (May 20, 1998) *Honolulu Star-Bulletin*, p. 1.

Adler, N.E. (1984) Contraception and unwanted pregnancy, *Behav. Med. Update*, 5(4), 28–34.

Adler, N.E. (1992) Unwanted pregnancy and abortion: definitional and research issues, *J. of Soc. Issues*, 48, 19–35.

Adler, N.E., Smith, L.B., and Tschann, J.M. (1998) Abortion among adolescents, in *The New Civil War: The Psychology, Culture, and Politics of Abortion*, Beckman, L.J. and Harvey, S.M., Eds., American Psychological Association, Washington, D.C., 285–298.

Alexander, R.D. (1987) *The Biology of Moral Systems*, A. de Gruyter, Hawthorne, N.Y.

Allen, A.L. (1992) Autonomy's magic wand: abortion and constitutional interpretation, *Boston Univ. Law Rev*, 72, 683–698.

Alley, H. (1993) George Eliot and the ambiguity of murder, *Stud. in the Novel*, 25(1), 59–75.

American Law Institute (1980) *Model Penal Code and Commentaries: Official Draft and Revised Comments*, American Law Institute, Philadelphia.

American Psychiatric Association (1980) *Diagnostic and Statistical Manual of Mental Disorders, Third Edition*, American Psychiatric Association, Washington, D.C.

American Psychiatric Association (1984) *Issues in Forensic Psychiatry*, American Psychiatric Association, Washington, D.C.

American Psychiatric Association (1987) *Diagnostic and Statistical Manual of Mental Disorders, Third Edition, Revised*, American Psychiatric Association, Washington, D.C.

American Psychiatric Association (1994) *Diagnostic and Statistical Manual of Mental Disorders, Fourth Edition*, American Psychiatric Association, Washington, D.C.

Amighi, J.K. (1990) Some thoughts on the cross-cultural study of maternal warmth and detachment, *Pre- and Peri-Natal Psychol.*, 5(2), 131–146.

Angela M.W. v. Kruzicki, WI 95-2480-W (1995) .

Anon. (1988) Note: maternal rights and fetal wrongs: the case against the criminalization of "fetal abuse," *Harv. Law Rev.*, 101, 994–1012.

Anon. (January 10, 1998) Abortion: when a fetus is a person, *The Economist*, 346, 24.

Arnoldi, K. (1999) *The Amazing "True" Story of a Teen-age Single Mom*, Hyperion, New York.

Artingstall, K. (1998) *Practical Aspects of Munchausen by Proxy and Munchausen Syndrome Investigation*, CRC Press, Boca Raton, FL.

Ashe, M. (1992) The "bad mother" in law and literature: a problem of representation, *Hastings Law J.*, 43, 1017–1037.

Associated Press (May 18, 1997a) Newborn is found alive in shallow grave, *The New York Times*, p. A15.

Associated Press (October 22, 1997b) Baby is left in box; mother is 12, note says, *The New York Times*, p. A16.

Associated Press (December 9, 1998) Teen hopes to avoid deportation in rape, *Ann Arbor News*.

Associated Press (January 9, 1999) Man is given life term in boy's AIDS infection, *The New York Times*, p. A12.

Atkins, E., Grimes, J.P., Joseph, G.W., and Liebman, J. (1999) Denial of pregnancy and neonaticide during adolescence: forensic and clinical issues, *Am. J. of Forensic Psychol.*, 17(1), 5–33.

Ball, H.L. and Hill, C.M. (1996) Reevaluating "twin infanticide," *Curr. Anthropol.*, 37(5), 856–863.

Barlow, S.A. (1989) Stereotype and reversal in Euripides' *Medea*, *Greece and Rome*, 36(2), 158–171.

Barlow, S.H. and Clayton, C.J. (1996) When mothers murder: understanding infanticide by females, in *Lethal Violence 2000: A Sourcebook on Fatal Domestic, Acquaintance and Stranger Aggression*, Hall, H.V., Ed., Pacific Institute for the Study of Conflict and Aggression, Kamuela, HI, 203–229.

Barton, B. (1998) Comment: when murdering hands rock the cradle: an overview of America's incoherent treatment of infanticidal mothers, *South. Methodist Univ. Law Rev.*, 51, 591–619.

Becker, M.E. (1986) From *Muller v. Oregon* to fetal vulnerability practices, *Univ. of Chicago Law Rev.*, 53, 1219–1273.

Behlmer, G.K. (1979) Deadly motherhood: infanticide and medical opinion in mid-Victorian England, *J. of the History of Med.*, 34(4), 403–427.

Bell, F. and Robins, E. (1901; reprint, 1991) *Alan's wife*, in *New Woman Plays*, Fitzsimmons, L. and Gardner, V., Eds., Methuen Drama, Portsmouth, NH.

Bendix, R. and Zumwalt, R.L. (1995) *Folklore Interpreted: Essays in Honor of Alan Dundes*, Garland Publishing, New York.

Bennett, H. (1922) The exposure of infants in Ancient Rome, *The Classical J.*, 23, 341–351.

Benoit, M.B. (1997) The role of psychological factors on teenagers who become parents out-of-wedlock, *Child. and Youth Serv. Rev.*, 19, 401–413.

Berger, P. and Berger, B. (1984) *The War Over the Family: Capturing the Middle Ground*, Anchor Press, Garden City, NY.

Berman, N. (1999) personal communication.

Bethea, L. (1999) Primary prevention of child abuse, *Am. Fam. Physician*, 59, 1577–1585.

Bethell, T. (1988) A heinous procedure, *The American Spectator*, 31(4), 20–24.

Bluestein, D. and Rutledge, C.M. (1992) Determinants of delayed pregnancy testing among adolescents, *J. of Fam. Pract.*, 35, 406–410.

Bluestein, D. and Starling, M.E. (1994) Helping pregnant teenagers, *West. J. of Med.*, 161(2), 140–143.

Bond, E. (1965) Saved, in *Bond: A Study of His Plays*, Hays, M. and Roberts, P., Eds., Eyre Methuen, London.

Bonnet, C. (1993) Adoption at birth: prevention against abandonment or neonaticide, *Child Abuse and Neglect*, 17, 501–513.

Bookwalter, B.E. (1998) Note: throwing the bath water out with the baby: wrongful exclusion of expert testimony on neonaticide syndrome, *Boston Univ. Law Rev.*, 78, 1185–1210.

Boswell, J. (1988) *The Kindness of Strangers: The Abandonment of Children in Western Europe from Late Antiquity to the Renaissance*, Pantheon, New York.

Bourget, D. and Bradford, J.M.W. (1990) Homicidal parents, *Can. J. of Psychiatr.*, 35, 233–238.

Bourget, D. and Labelle, A. (1992) Homicide, infanticide, filicide, *Psychiatr. Clin. of North America*, 15(3), 661–673.

Bowes, W.A. and Selegstad, B., Jr. (1981) Fetal versus maternal rights: medical and legal perspectives, *Obstetr. and Gynecol.*, 58, 209–214.

Boyer-Patrick, J. (1999) Use of counseling by pregnant or postpartum teens, *Psychiatr. Times*, 16(9).

Brady, M.M. (1994) Munchausen syndrome by proxy: how should we weigh our options?, *Law and Psychol. Rev.*, 18, 361–375.

Brenton, H. (1996) Can you refuse the bargain of a lifetime?, *New Statesman*, 9(420), 38–39.

Brewer, C. (August 29, 1994) With sex and kids, men get off the hook, *Dayton Daily News*, p. 6A.

Brewster, A.L., Nelson, J.P., Hymel, K.P., Colby, D.R., Lucas, D.R., McCanne, T.R., and Milner, J.S. (1998) Victim, perpetrator, family, and incident characteristics of 32 infant maltreatment deaths in the United States Air Force, *Child Abuse and Neglect*, 22(2), 91–101.

Brezinka, C., Huter, O., Biebl, W., and Kinzl, J. (1994) Denial of pregnancy: obstetrical aspects, *J. of Psychosomatic Obstet. and Gynecol.*, 15, 1–8.

Bridis, T. (October 3, 1997) Kentucky parents are charged in toddler's starvation death, *The Philadelphia Inquirer*, p. A3.

Brienza, J. (1997) When the bough breaks: can justice be served in neonaticide cases?, *Trial*, 33(12), 13–17.

Broder, S. (1988) Child care or child neglect? Baby farming in late nineteenth-century Philadelphia, *Gender and Soc.*, 2(2), 128–148.

Brody, J.E. (February 10, 1998) Genetic ties may be factor in violence in stepfamilies, *The New York Times*, pp. F1, F4.

Brody, J.E. (March 15, 1999) Earlier work with children steers them from crime, *The New York Times*, p. A16.

Brown, P. (November 5, 1997) Hidden pregnancies: girls bearing bad secrets, *Newsday (New York)*, p. A50.

Brozovsky, M. and Falit, H. (1971) Neonaticide: clinical and psychodynamic considerations, *J. of Am. Acad. of Child Psychiatr.*, 10, 673–683.

Brusca, A.D. (1990) Postpartum psychosis is a way out for murdering moms, *Hofstra Law Rev.*, 18, 1133–1170.

Bryant, T.L. (1990) *Oya-ko Shinju:* death at the center of the heart, *UCLA Pacific Basin Law J.*, 8(1), 1–31.

Buchanan, A. (1996) Choosing who will be disabled: genetic intervention and the morality of inclusion, *Soc. Philos. and Policy*, 13, 18–46.

Burden of Proof (July 9, 1998) CNN Television.

Burke, B. (1984) Infanticide: why does it happen in monkeys, mice, and men?, *Science*, 5, 26–31.

Burleigh, M. (1994) Return to the planet of the apes? Peter Singer controversy in Germany, *Hist. Today*, 44(10), 6–10.

Buss, M. (1999) *Evolutionary Psychology: The New Science*, Allyn and Bacon, Boston.

Butterfield, F. (July 12, 1999) Prisons brim with mentally ill, study finds, *The New York Times*, p. A10.

Callahan, R. (June 28, 1999) Father says he suffocated son in revenge, *The Philadelphia Inquirer*, p. A2.

Campion, J. F., Cravens, J. M., and Covan, F. (1988) A study of filicidal men, *Am. J. of Psychiatr.*, 145, 1141–1144.

Capital Report (September 29, 1997) *Pennsylvania Law Weekly*, p. 9.

Carr, C. (1991) *The Angel of Darkness*, Random House, New York.

Carr-Saunders, A.M. (1922) *The Population Problem: A Study in Human Evolution*, Clarendon Press, Oxford, England.

Carrera, M. (1997) My secret life, Pact, an Adoption Alliance, Pact Press, 28–30.

Carrera, M. and Dempsey, P. (1988, January/February) Restructuring public policies priorities on teen pregnancy: a holistic approach to teen development and teen services, *SIECUS Rep.*, 6–9.

Cavaliere, F. (1995, August) Parents killing kids: a nation's shame, *APA Monitor*, p.34.

Chandra, A., Abma, J., Maza, P., and Bachrach, C. (1999) Adoption, adoption seeking, and relinquishment for adoption in the United States, *Advance Data from Vital and Health Statistics,* 306, National Center for Health Statistics, Hyattsville, MD.

Chase, J. (January 27, 1999) Accused mom stole jewelry, witness says theft, baby's death linked to gambling, *Chicago Tribune,* p. 4.

Chen, D. (June 18, 1998) Insanity defense may be used in retrial of Palatine woman, *Chicago Tribune,* p. 7A.

Christoffel, K.K. (1984) Homicide in childhood: a public health problem in need of attention, *Am. J. of Public Health,* 74, 68–70.

Cleary, M.F. (1991) From Roe to Webster: psychiatric, legal and social aspects of abortion, *Am. J. of Forensic Psychol.,* 9(1), 51–63.

Cohen, M. (1993) Empowering the sister: female rescue and authorial resistance in *The Heart of Midlothian, Coll. Lit.,* 20(2), 58–69.

Cole, J. (1996) A sudden and terrible revelation: motherhood and infant mortality in France, 1858–1874, *J. of Fam. Hist.,* 21(4), 410–445.

Coley, R.L. and Chase-Lansdale, P.L. (1998) Adolescent pregnancy and parenthood: recent evidence and future directions, *Am. Psychol.,* 53, 152–166.

Commonwealth v. Campbell, 580 A2d 868 (Pa. Super. 1990), cited from 1991, *Juvenile and Fam. Law Digest,* 116–118.

Committee on Psychiatry and Law (Group for the Advancement of Psychiatry) (1969) The right to abortion: a psychiatric view, *GAP Rep.,* 7(75), 197–227.

Condit, C.M. (1990) *Decoding Abortion Rhetoric,* University of Illinois Press, Urbana, IL.

Copeland, L. (December 5, 1997) S.C. woman guilty in death of unborn child, *The Philadelphia Inquirer,* p. A3.

Corcoran, J. (1998) Consequences of adolescent pregnancy/parenting: a review of the literature, *Soc. Work in Health Care,* 27(2), 49–67.

Corcoran, J., Franklin, C., and Bell, H. (1997) Pregnancy prevention from the teen perspective, *Child and Adolescent Soc. Work J.,* 14, 365–382.

Cornell, L.L. (1996) Infanticide in early modern Japan? Demography, culture, and population growth, *J. of Asian Stud.,* 55(1), 22–50.

Cordes v. State, 54 Tex. Crim. 204, 112 S.W. 943 (1908).

Costen, J. (1995) *Sleep, My Child, Forever,* Penguin Books, New York.

Coughlin, A.M. (1994) Excusing women, *California Law Rev.,* 82, 1–93.

Coulombis, A. (November 23, 1998) Bearing weight of a scarlet letter, *Philadelphia Inquirer,* pp. 1, 5.

Crimmins, S., Langley, S., Brownstein, H.H., and Spunt, B.J. (1997) Convicted women who have killed children: a self-psychology perspective, *J. of Interpersonal Violence,* 12(1), 49–69.

Crittenden, P.M. and Craig, S.E. (1990) Developmental trends in the nature of child homicide, *J. of Interpersonal Violence*, 5, 202–216.

Crouch, S. (1987) Aunt Medea, *New Republic*, 197, 1538–1543.

Cummings, P., Theis, M.K., Mueller, B.A., and Rivara, F.P. (1994) Infant injury death in Washington State: 1981 through 1990, *Arch. of Pediatr. and Adolescent Med.*, 148, 1021–1026.

Cushman, L.F., Kalmuss, D., and Namerow, P.B. (1993) Placing an infant for adoption: the experiences of young birthmothers, *Soc. Work*, 38, 264–272.

Cutrona, C.E., Hessling, R.M., Bacon, P.L., and Russell, D.W. (1998) Predictors and correlates of continuing involvement with the baby's father among adolescent mothers, *J. of Fam. Psychol.*, 12, 369–387.

Dalton, K. (1989) *Depression After Childbirth*, Oxford University Press, New York.

Daly, M. and Wilson, M. (1984) A sociobiological analysis of human infanticide, in *Infanticide: Comparative and Evolutionary Perspectives*, Hausfater, G. and Hrdy, S.B., Eds., Aldine, New York, 487–502.

Daly, M. and Wilson, M. (1988) Evolutionary social psychology and family homicide, *Science*, 242, 510–524.

Damme, C. (1978) Infanticide: the worth of an infant under the law, *Med. Hist.*, 22, 1–24.

Darnton, R. (1985) *The Great Cat Massacre and Other Episodes in French Cultural History*, Vintage Books, New York.

Daubert v. Merrell Dow Pharmaceuticals, Inc., 509 U.S. 579 (1993), 125 L.Ed. 2d 469, 113 S.Ct. 2786.

David, H.P. (1992) Born unwanted: long-term developmental effects of denied abortion, *J. of Soc. Issues*, 48(3), 163–181.

Davies, D.S. (1937) Child-killing in English law, *Mod. Law Rev.*, 1, 203–221.

Dawkins, R. (1976) *The Selfish Gene*, Oxford University Press, New York.

Demb, J. (1991) Abortion in inner-city adolescents, *Fam. Syst. Med.*, 9, 93–102.

DePalma, A. (Dec. 1, 1997) Father's killing of Canadian girl: mercy or murder, *The New York Times*, p. A3.

Dickemann, M. (1975) Demographic consequences of infanticide in man, *Ann. Rev. of Ecol. and Syst.*, 6, 1007–1037.

Dickemann, M. (1979) Female infanticide, reproductive strategies and social stratification: a preliminary model, in *Evolutionary Biology and Human Behavior: An Anthropological Perspective*, Chagnon, N.A. and Irons, W.I., Eds., Duxbury Press, North Scituate, MA, 321–368.

Doe v. Bolton, 410 U.S. 179 (1973).

Doege, D. (November 19, 1998) Mother pleads guilty in newborn's death; charge reduced to reckless homicide, *Milwaukee Journal Sentinel*, p. 3.

Donnelly, B.W. and Davis-Berman, J. (1994) A review of the Chance to Grow Project: a care project for pregnant and parenting adolescents, *Child and Adolescent Soc. Work J.*, 11, 493–506.

Donovan, P. (1997) The Colorado Parental Rights amendment: how and why it failed. *Fam. Plann. Perspect.*, 29(4), 187–190.

Donsky, P. (May 23, 1997) Prosecutors mull lesser charges against mother in baby's burial, *The Tennessean*, p. 2B.

Donzelot, J. (1979) *The Policing of Families* (Hurley, R., transl.), Pantheon Books, New York.

d'Orbán, P.T. (1979) Women who kill their children, *Br. J. of Psychiatr.*, 560–571.

Dribben, M. (July 16, 1998) Sexism slanted Del. baby case, *The Philadelphia Inquirer*, p. R1.

Dubin, M. (May 11, 1998) Serious mother-son talk, *The Philadelphia Inquirer*, pp. F1, F4.

Durham, W.H. (1990) Advances in evolutionary cultural theory, *Ann. Rev. of Anthropol.*, 19, 187–210.

Eau Claire teen admits reckless homicide charge in baby's death (September 26, 1998) *Star Tribune (Minneapolis)*, p. 3B.

Ebrahim, A.F.M. (1991) *Abortion, Birth Control and Surrogate Parenting: An Islamic Perspective*, American Trust Co, Indianapolis, IN.

Editorial (February 26, 1998) Side arguments obscure appeal for Hopfer, *Dayton Daily News*, p. 1A.

Editorial Roundup (June 15, 1998) *Idaho Statesman*, p. 7A.

Edwards, S. (1981) *Female Sexuality and the Law*, Martin Robertson, Oxford, England.

Edwards, S.S.M. (1986) Neither bad nor mad: the female violent offender reassessed, *Women's Stud. Int. Forum*, 9(1), 79–87.

Ehrenreich, B. (January, 1998) Where have all the babies gone?, *Life*, 21, 68–76.

Eliot, G. (1859; reprint, 1981) *Adam Bede*, Signet Books, New York.

Ellsworth, P.C.T. (June 7, 1998) North and south: different standards around the world, *The New York Times*, p. 16 WK.

Emerick, S.J., Foster, L.R., and Campbell, D.T. (1986) Risk factors for traumatic infant death in Oregon, 1973 to 1982, *Pediatrics*, 77, 518–522.

Euripides (431 B.C.; reprint, 1938). *Medea* (Coleridge, E.P., transl.), in *The Complete Greek Drama, Vol. I*, Oates, W.J. and O'Neill, E., Jr., Eds., Random House, New York, 723–762.

Evans, D. (1989) The psychological impact of disability and illness on medical treatment decisionmaking, *Issues in Law and Med.*, 5(3) 277–299.

Fazio, C. and Comito, J.L. (1999) Note: rethinking the tough sentencing of teenage neonaticide in the United States, *Fordham Law Rev.*, 67, 3109–3168.

Fimbres, G. (September 22, 1998) Living hell: a local psychiatrist will show the differences between heartless baby-killers and girls who don't understand they are having a baby, *Tucson Citizen*, p. 1B.

Finnegan, P., McKinstry, E., and Robinson, G.E. (1982) Denial of pregnancy and childbirth, *Can. J. of Psychiatr.*, 27, 672–674.

Firstman, R. and Talan, J. (1997) *The Death of Innocents*, Bantam Books, New York.

Fitzsimmons, L. and Gardner, V. (1991) *New Woman Plays*, Methuen Drama, Portsmouth, NH.

Folkenberg, J. (May, 1985) Teen pregnancy: who opts for adoption?, *Psychol. Today*, 16.

Forbes, T.R. (1986) Deadly parents: child homicide in eighteenth- and nineteenth-century England, *J. of the Hist. of Med.*, 41, 175–199.

Ford, J. (1996) Note: Susan Smith and other homicidal mothers — in search of the punishment that fits the crime, *Yeshiva Univ. Cardozo Women's Law J.*, 3, 521–548.

Fost, N. (1981) Counseling families who have a child with a severe congenital anomaly, *Pediatrics*, 67, 321–324.

Fox-Genovese, E. (1988) *Within the Plantation Household: Black and White Women of the Old South*, University of North Carolina Press, Chapel Hill, NC.

France, D. (1997) Why was disposal the only thought that occurred to them?, *New Woman*, 27(9), 124–125, 144–145.

Francus, M. (1997) Monstrous mothers, monstrous societies: infanticide and the rule of law in restoration and eighteenth-century England, *Eighteenth-Century Life*, 21(2), 133–156.

Fried, S. (April, 1998) Cradle to grave, *Philadelphia Magazine*, 56–63, 98–116.

Friedman, L.M. (1991) Crimes of mobility, *Stanford Law Rev.*, 43, 637–658.

Frye v. United States, 54 App. D.C. 46 (1923), 293 F. 1013.

Fuchs R. (1984) *Abandoned Children: Foundlings and Child Welfare in Nineteenth-Century France*, State University of New York Press, Albany, NY.

Fuchs, R. (1992) *Poor and Pregnant in Paris: Strategies for Survival in the Nineteenth Century*, Rutgers University Press, New Brunswick, NJ.

Furstenberg, F.F., Geitz, L.M., Teitler, J.O., and Weiss, C.C. (1997) Does condom availability make a difference? An evaluation of Philadelphia's Health Resource Centers, *Fam. Plann. Perspect.*, 29(3), 123–127.

Gartner, R. (1991) Family structure, welfare spending, and child homicide in developed democracies, *J. of Marriage and the Fam.*, 53, 231–240.

Gavitt, P. (1994) Perche non avea chi la ghovernasse: cultural values, family resources and abandonment in the Florence of Lorenzo d'Medici, 1467–85, in *Poor Women and Children in the European Past*, Henderson, J. and Wall, R., Eds., Routledge, New York, 65–94.

Gelles, R.J. (1996) *The Book of David: How Preserving Families Can Cost Children's Lives*, Basic Books, New York.

Gelles, R.J. (1997) *Intimate Violence in Families*, 3rd ed., Sage, Thousand Oaks, CA.

Geraghty, M. (September 12, 1997) Hidden pregnancies and babies' deaths raise painful questions for colleges, *The Chron. of Higher Educ.*, 44, p. A49–A50.

Geronimus, A.T. (1987) On teenage childbearing and neonatal mortality in the United States, *Population and Dev. Rev.*, 13, 245–280.

Gibbons, T.J., Jr. (April 1, 1998) Couple questioned in 3-decade-old string of baby deaths, *The Philadelphia Inquirer*, p. R1.

Gillis, J.R. (1983) Servants, sexual relations and the risks of illegitimacy in London, 1801–1900, in *Sex and Class in Women's History*, Newton, J.L., Ed., Routledge and Kegan Paul, London, 114–146.

Ginsburg, F.D. (1989) *Contested Lives: The Abortion Debate in an American Community*, University of California Press, Berkeley, CA.

Glendon, M.A. (1991) *Rights Talk*, Free Press, New York.

Goethe, J.W. Von (1808; reprint, 1950) *Faust* (Taylor, B., transl.), Modern Library, New York.

Goodnough, A. and Weber, B. (July 2, 1997) The picture of ordinary, *The New York Times*, pp. B1, B6.

Gottlieb, C.N. (1996) Filicide: a strategic approach, *Psychol. — A J. of Hum. Behav.*, 33(3), 40–42.

Gould, S.J. (1980) Sociobiology and human nature: a postpanglossian vision, in *Sociobiology Examined*, Montague, A.E., Ed., Oxford University Press, New York, 283–290.

Granzberg, G. (1973) Twin infanticide   a cross cultural test of a materialistic explanation, *Ethos*, 1(4), 405–412.

Graves, R. (1988) *The Greek Myths*, Moyer Bell, Ltd., Mt. Kisco, NY.

Green, C.M. (1990) Neonaticide and hysterical denial of pregnancy, *Obstet. and Gynecol. Surv.*, 45(8), 534–535.

Green, C.M. and Manohar, S.V. (1990) Neonaticide and hysterical denial of pregnancy, *Br. J. of Psychiatr.*, 156, 121–123.

Green, E.C. (1999) Infanticide and infant abandonment in the new South: Richmond, Virginia, 1865–1915, *J. of Fam. Hist.*, 24(2), 187–211.

Greenwood, D.J.H. (1994) Review essay: beyond Dworkin's dominions; investments. Memberships, the tree of life and abortion, *Tex. Law Rev.*, 72, 471–630.

Grim, W.E. (1988) *The Faust Legend in Music and Literature*, The Edwin Mellen Press, Lewiston, NY.

Griswold v. Connecticut, 381 U.S. 479 (1965).

Grossman, J.L. (1990) Postpartum psychosis — a defense to criminal responsibility or just another gimmick?, *Univ. of Detroit Law Rev.*, 67, 311–344.

Gustafson, J.M. (1973) Mongolism, parental desires, and the right to life, *Perspect. in Biol. and Med.*, 16, 529–557.

Hall, H.V. (1999) personal communication.

Hanley, R. (June 25, 1997) New Jersey charges woman, 18, with killing baby born at prom, *The New York Times*, pp. A1, B4.

Hanley, S.B. (1983) A high standard of living in nineteenth century Japan, *J. of Econ. Hist.*, 43(1), 183–192.

Hanson, E. (January 30, 1997) Infanticide cases still evoke shock, horror in jaded public, *Houston Chronicle*, p. A21.

Harding, S. (1990) If I should die before I wake: Jerry Falwell's pro-life gospel, in *Uncertain Terms: Negotiating Gender in American Culture*, Ginsberg, F. and Tsing, A., Eds., Beacon Press, Boston, 76–98.

Harris, M. (1977) *Cannibals and Kings: The Origin of Cultures*, Random House, New York.

Hay, M. and Roberts, P. (1980) *Bond: A Study of His Plays*, Eyre Methuen, London.

Heimmel, J.P. (September 13, 1993) Defenses: personality disorder may satisfy mental disease or defect needed for diminished capacity defense, *New Jersey Lawyer*, 19.

Henriques, U.R.Q. (July, 1967) Bastardy and the new Poor Law., *Past and Present*, 37, 103–129.

Henshaw, S.K. (1997) Teenage abortion and pregnancy statistics by state, 1992, *Fam. Plann. Perspect.*, 29(3), 115–122.

Henson, R. (April 9, 1999) Pa. court rules fetus is a person, *The Philadelphia Inquirer*, pp. B1, B6.

Herbert, B. (June 14, 1998) In America: hidden agendas, *The Philadelphia Inquirer*, p. WK15.

Hernandez-Truyol, B.E. (1997) Conceptualizing violence: present and future developments in international law: panel 1: human rights and civil wrongs at home and abroad; old problems and new paradigms; sex, culture, and rights: a reconceptualization of violence for the twenty-first century, *Albany Law Rev.*, 60, 607–634.

Hesketh, T. and Zhu, W.X. (1997) The one child family policy: the good, the bad, and the ugly; health in China, part 3, *Br. Med. J.*, 314, 1685–1692.

Hickman, S.A. and LeVine, D.L. (1992) Postpartum disorders and the law, in *Postpartum Psychiatric Illness: A Picture Puzzle*, Hamilton, J.A. and Harberger, P.N., Eds., University of Pennsylvania Press, Philadelphia, 282–295.

Higginbotham, A.R. (1989) Sin of the age: infanticide and illegitimacy in Victorian London, *Victorian Stud.*, 32(3), 319–337.

Hoffer, P.C. and Hull, N.E.H. (1981) *Murdering Mothers: Infanticide in England and New England 1558–1803*, New York University Press, New York.

Hogue, C.J.R. (1997) Missing the boat on pregnancy prevention, *Issues in Sci. and Technol.*, 13(4), 41–46.

Holden, C.E., Burland, A.S., and Lemmen, C.A. (1996) Insanity and filicide: women who murder their children, *New Directions for Ment. Health Serv.*, 69, 25–34.

Hontela, S. and Reddon, J.R. (1996) Infanticide of defective newborns: an old midwife's story, *Psychol. Rep.*, 793(2), 1275–1278.

Hornblower, S. (1983) *The Greek World, 479–323 BC*, Methuen, London.

Hrdy, S.B. (1984) When the bough breaks: there may be method in the madness of infanticide, *Sciences*, 24(2), 45–50.

Hrdy, S.B. (1992) Fitness tradeoffs in the history and evolution of delegated mothering with special reference to wet-nursing, abandonment, and infanticide, *Ethol. and Sociobiol.*, 13, 409–442.

Hufton, O.H. (1974) *The Poor of Eighteenth-Century France 1750–1789*, Clarenden Press, Oxford, England.

Hughes, J. (1987) *The Fatal Shore: A History of Transportation of Convicts to Australia, 1787–1868*, Harvill Press, London.

Hughes, R.A. (1990) Psychological perspectives on infanticide in a faith healing sect, *Psychotherapy*, 27(1), 107–115.

Hull, T.H. (1990) Recent trends in sex ratios at birth in China, *Population and Dev. Rev.*, 16(1), 63–83.

Iffy, L. and Jakobovits, A. (1992) Infanticide: new medical considerations, *Med. and Law*, 11, 269–274.

Illick, J.E. (1974) Child-rearing in seventeenth century England and America, in *A History of Childhood*, DeMause, L., Ed., Psychohistory Press, New York, 303–351.

Illinois Report (August 8, 1998) *State Journal Register (Springfield, IL)*, p. 7.

Insanity Defense Reform Act of 1984, Pub. L. No. 98-473, 18 U.S.C.§17.

International Union U.A.W. v. Johnson Controls, 111 S. Ct. 1196 (1991).

Isser, E.R. (1997) *Stages of Annihilation*, Associated University Presses, Cranbury, NJ.

Jackson, M. (1996) *New-Born Child Murder: Women, Illegitimacy and the Courts in Eighteenth-Century England*, Manchester University Press, Manchester, England.

Jamieson, D., Ed. (1999) *Singer and His Critics*, Blackwell, Malden, MA.

Jemmott, J.B., III, Jemmott, L.S., and Fong, G.T. (1998) Abstinence and safer sex: HIV risk-reduction interventions for African American adolescents: a randomized controlled trial, *J. of the Am. Med. Assoc.*, 279, 1529–1536.

Jimmerson, J. (1990) Female infanticide in China: an examination of cultural and legal norms, *UCLA Pacific Law Basin J.*, 8, 47–79.

Johansson, S. and Nygren, O. (1991) The missing girls of China: a new demographic account, *Population and Dev. Rev.*, 17(1), 35–51.

John Josef v. State, 34 Tex. Crim. 446 (1895).

Jones, C.M. (1993) *Sula* and *Beloved*: images of Cain in the novels of Toni Morrison, *Afr. Am. Rev.*, 27, 615–626.

Jones, O.D. (1997) Evolutionary analysis in law: an introduction and application to child abuse, *N.C. Law Rev.*, 75, 1117–1180.

Joyce, K., Diffenbacher, G., Greene, J., and Sorokin, Y. (1983) Internal and external barriers to obtaining prenatal care, *Soc. Work in Health Care*, 9(2), 89–96.

Kahan, B. and Yorker, B.C. (1991) Munchausen Syndrome by Proxy: clinical review and legal issues, *Behav. Sci. and the Law*, 9, 73–83.

Kalmuss, D., Namerow, P.B., and Cushman, L.F. (1991) Adoption versus parenting among young pregnant women, *Fam. Plann. Perspect.*, 23, 17–23.

Kaplan, H.I. and Sadock, B.J. (1996) *Pocket Handbook of Clinical Psychiatry*, 2nd ed., Williams and Wilkins, Baltimore.

Kaplan, M.F. (1988) A peer support group for women in prison for the death of a child, *J. of Offender Counseling, Serv. and Rehabilitation*, 13(1), 5–13.

Karst, K.L. (1984) Woman's constitution, *Duke Law J.*, 447–508.

Katkin, D.M. (1992) Postpartum psychosis, infanticide, and criminal justice, in *Postpartum Psychiatric Illness: A Picture Puzzle*, Hamilton, J.A. and Harberger, P.N., Eds., University of Pennsylvania Press, Philadelphia, 275–281.

Kaye, N.S., Borenstein, N.M., and Donnelly, S.M. (1990) Families, murder, and insanity: a psychiatric review of paternal neonaticide, *J. of Forensic Sci.*, 35(1), 133–139.

Kellet, R.J. (1992) Infanticide and child destruction — the historical, legal and pathological aspects, *Forensic Sci. Int.*, 53, 1–18.

Kellum, B.A. (1973) Infanticide in England in the later Middle Ages, *Hist. of Childhood Q.*, 1(3), 367–388.

Kertzer, D.I. (1993) *Sacrificed for Honor: Italian Infant Abandonment and the Politics of Reproductive Control*, Beacon Press, New York.

Kingston, M.H. (1989) *Woman Warrior: Memoirs of a Girlhood Among Ghosts*, Vintage Books, New York.

Kinscherff, R. and Famularo, R. (1991) Extreme Munchausen Syndrome by Proxy: the case for termination of parental rights, *Juvenile and Fam. Court J.*, 40, 41–49.

Kirby, D., Korpi, M., Barth, R.P., and Cagampang, H.H. (1997) Impact of postponing sexual involvement curriculum among youth in California, *Fam. Plann. Perspect.*, 29(3), 100–108.

Kirby, D., Short, L., Collins, J., Rugg, D., Kolbe, L., Howsard, M., Miller, B., Sonenstein, F.A., and Zabin, L.S. (1994) School-based programs to reduce sexual risk behaviors: A review of effectiveness, *Public Health Rep.*, 109, 339–360.

Kirwin, B. (September 1997) The coed baby killer, *Cosmopolitan*, 272–275.

Knelman, J. (1998) Women murderers in Victorian Britain; popular press portrayal of women murderers during the Victorian era, *Hist. Today*, 48(8), 9–14.

Knepper, K. (1994) Withholding medical treatment from infants: when is it child neglect?, *Univ. of Louisville J. of Fam. Law*, 33, 1–53.

Kobbé, C.W. (1919; reprint, 1987) *The Definitive Kobbé Opera Book*, Earl of Harewood, Ed., Putnam, New York.

Koop, C.E. (1989) Life and death and the handicapped, *Issues in Law and Med.*, 5, 101–107.

Korbin, J.E. (1986) Childhood histories of women imprisoned for fatal child maltreatment, *Child Abuse and Neglect*, 10, 331–338.

Kord, S. (1993) Women as children, women as childkillers: infanticide in eighteenth-century Germany, *Eighteenth Century Stud.*, 26(3), 449–466.

Kouno, A. and Johnson, C.F. (1995) Child abuse and neglect in Japan: coin-operated locker babies, *Child Abuse and Neglect*, 19(1), 25–31.

Kunz, J. and Bahr, S.J. (1996) A profile of parental homicide against children, *J. of Fam. Violence*, 11, 347–362.

Lagaipa, S.J. (1990) Suffer the little children: the ancient practice of infanticide as a modern moral dilemma, *Issues in Compr. Pediatr. Nursing*, 13, 241–251.

Lane v. Commonwealth, 248, S.E. Va. (1978).

Lane, R. (1986) *Roots of Violence in Black Philadelphia, 1860–1900*, Harvard University Press, Cambridge, MA.

Langer, W.L. (1974) Infanticide: a historical survey, *Hist. of Childhood Q.*, 1, 353–366.

Lansdowne, R. (1990) Infanticide: psychiatrists in the plea bargaining process, *Monash Univ. Law Rev.*, 16(1), 41–63.

Leboutte, R. (1991) Offense against family order: infanticide in Belgium from the fifteenth through the early twentieth centuries, *J. of the Hist. of Sexuality*, 2(2), 159–185.

Ledwon, L. (1996) Maternity as a legal fiction: infanticide and Sir Walter Scott's *The Heart of Midlothian*, *Women's Rights Law Rep.*, 18(1), 1–16.

Lee, A.K. (1994a) Attitudes and prejudices toward infanticide: Carthage, Rome and today, *Archaeological Rev. from Cambridge*, 13(2), 65–79.

Lee, R. (1994b) Missing peace in Toni Morrison's *Sula* and *Beloved*, *Afr. Am. Rev.*, 29(4), 571–583.

Lentz, M.E. (1989) A postmortem of the post partum psychosis defense, *Capital Univ. Law Rev.*, 18, 525–544.

Lester, D. (1986) The relation of twin infanticide to status of women, societal agression, and material well-being, *J. of Social Psychol.*, 126(1), 57–59.

Leung, A.K.C. (1995) Relief institutions for children in nineteenth-century China, in *Chinese Views of Childhood*, Kinney, A.B., Ed., University of Hawai'i Press, Honolulu, 251–279.

Levene, A. (September 6, 1998) Italian dustbins bear a warning: "not for babies," *Chicago Tribune*, p. 8.

Lewin, T. (October 15, 1998) Youth pregnancy rate falls, report says, *The New York Times*, p. A27.

Lewis, C.F., Baranoski, M.V., Buchanan, J.A., and Benedek, E.P. (1998) Factors associated with weapon use in maternal filicide, *J. of Forensic Sci.*, 43, 613–618.

Li, L. (1991) Life and death in a Chinese famine: infanticide as a demographic consequence of the 1935 Yellow river flood, *Comp. Stud. in Soc. and Hist.*, 33(3), 466–510.

Lindsay, S. (April 26, 1998a) Depression exceeds "baby blues;" "voices" may tell mom she must kill children, *Rocky Mountain News (Denver)*, p. 32A.

Lindsay, S. (April 26, 1998b) Mom accused of killing kids may attempt rare defense, Postpartum depression is central to legal claim, *Rocky Mountain News (Denver)*, p. 5A.

Litchfield, R.B. and Gordon, D. (1980) Closing the "tour," *J. of Soc. Hist.*, 13, 458–472.

Loggins, K. (November 7, 1998) Appeals court affirms guilty verdict of father in murder of newborn son, *The Tennessean*, p. 6B.

Loyd, L. (August 6, 1998) Mother, now 69, charged with suffocating 8 babies, *The Philadelphia Inquirer*, pp. A1, A18.

Loyd, L. (March 10, 1999) Jury convicts mother who starved child, *The Philadelphia Inquirer*, p. R1.

Lumsden, C.J. and Wilson, E.O. (1983) *Promethean Fire: Reflections on the Origin of Mind*, Harvard University Press, Cambridge, MA.

Lund, N. (1985). Infanticide, physicians, and the law: the "Baby Doe" amendments to the Child Abuse Prevention and Treatment Act, *Am. J. of Law and Med.*, 11, 1–29.

MacDoman, M.F. and Atkinson, J.O. (1999) Infant mortality statistics from the 1997 period linked birth/infant death data set, *Nat. Vital Stat. Rep.*, 47(23), National Center for Health Statistics, Hyattsville, MD.

MacDonald, D.I. (1987) An approach to the problem of teenage pregnancy, *Public Health Rep.*, 102, 377–385.

Maciejczyk, J.M. (1983) Withholding treatment from defective infants, *Notre Dame Law Rev.*, 59, 21–30.

Mackay, R.D. (1993) The consequences of killing very young children, *Criminal Law Rev.*, 21–30.

Mackinnon, C.A. (1989) *Toward a Feminist Theory of the State,* Harvard University Press, Cambridge, MA.

Mahler, K. (1997) Young mothers who choose adoption may be regretful, but not usually depressed, *Fam. Plann. Perspect.*, 29(3), 146–147.

Maier-Katkin, D. (1991) Postpartum psychosis, infanticide and the law, *Crime, Law and Soc. Change*, 15, 109–123.

Mapanga, K.G. (1997) The perils of adolescent pregnancy, *World Health*, 50(2), 16–17.

Marks, M.N. and Kumar, R. (1993) Infanticide in England and Wales, *Med., Sci. and the Law*, 33(3), 329–339.

Marks, M.N. and Kumar, R. (1996) Infanticide in Scotland, *Med., Sci. and the Law*, 36, 299–305.

Marleau, J.D., Poulin, B., Webanck, T., Roy, R., and Laporte, L. (1999) Paternal filicide: a study of 10 men, *Can. J. of Psychiatr.*, 44, 57–63.

Marlow, G.D. (1998) From black robes to white lab coats: the ethical implications of a judge's *sua sponte, ex parte* acquisition of social and other scientific evidence during the decision-making process, *St. John's Law Rev.,* 72, 291–335.

Martello, T. (September 14, 1999) ACLU sues to block N. J. abortion law, *The Philadelphia Inquirer,* p. R5.

Martin, J.A., Smith, B.L., Mathews, T.J., and Ventura, S.J. (1999) Births and deaths: preliminary data for 1998, *Nat. Vital Stat. Rep.,* 47(25), National Center for Health Statistics, Hyattsville, MD.

Mary Harris v. State, 30 Tex. Ct. App. 549; 17 S.W. 1110 (1891).

Massaro, T.M. (1997) The meanings of shame: implications for legal reform. *Psychol., Public Policy, and the Law,* 3, 645–704.

Mathes, P.G. and Irby, B.J. (1993) *Teen Pregnancy and Parenting Handbook,* Research Press, Champaign, IL.

Mathis, D. (December 22, 1997) Rape in Brazil leads to ultimate child-abuse case, *The Orlando Sentinel,* p. A21.

Matsuoka, A. (November 7, 1997) Grand jury indicts mom for first-degree murder, *Honolulu Star-Bulletin,* p. 4.

Mauldon, J. and Luker, K. (1996) The effects of contraceptive education on method use at first intercourse, *Fam. Plann. Perspect.,* 28(1), 19–24, 41.

Maynard, R. and Rangarajan, A. (1994) Contraceptive use and repeat pregnancies among welfare-dependent teenage mothers, *Fam. Plann. Perspect.,* 26(5), 198–205.

Mays, S. (1993) Infanticide in Roman Britain, *Antiquity,* 67(257), 883–888.

McBride, T.M. (1976) *The Domestic Revolution: The Modernisation of Household Services in England and France (1820–1920),* Holmes and Meier, New York.

McCoy, C.R. (June 29, 1999) No jail in decades-old deaths, *The Philadelphia Inquirer,* pp. A1, A8.

McCullough, M. (March 6, 1998). Amy Grossberg passed polygraph tests, lawyers say, *The Philadelphia Inquirer,* pp. B1, B4.

McKee, G.R. and Shea, S.J. (1998) Maternal filicide: a cross-national comparison, *J. of Clin. Psychol.,* 54, 679–687.

McKee, L. (1984) Sex differentials in survivorship and the customary treatment of infants and children, *Med. Anthropol.,* 8(2), 91–108.

McQuaide, S. and Ehrenreich, J.H. (1998) Women in prison: approaches to understanding the lives of a forgotten population, *Affilia,* 13, 233–246.

Melton, G.B., Petrila, J., Poythress, N.G., and Slobogin, C. (1987) *Psychological Evaluations for the Courts: A Handbook for Mental Health Professionals and Lawyers,* Guilford, New York.

Mendlowicz, M.V., Rapaport, M.H., Mecler, K., Golshan, S., and Moraes, T.M. (1998) A case-control study on the socio-demographic characteristics of 53 neonaticidal mothers, *Int. J. of Law and Psychiatr.,* 21, 209–219.

Mensch, E. and Freeman, A. (1991) The politics of virtue: animals, theology, and abortion, *Georgia Law Rev.*, 25, 923–982.

Milden, R., Rosenthal, M., Winegardner, J., and Smith, D. (1985) Denial of pregnancy: an exploratory investigation, *J. of Psychosomatic Obstet. and Gynecol.*, 4, 255–261.

Miller, L.J. (1990) Psychotic denial of pregnancy: phenomenology and clinical management, *Hosp. and Community Psychiatr.*, 41, 1233–1237.

Minton, L. (June 14, 1998) "Oh, no, I can't get pregnant": teen parents talk about what they've learned, *Parade*, 16–17.

Minturn, L. and Stashak, J. (1982) Infanticide as a terminal abortion procedure, *Behav. Sci. Res.*, 17(1–2), 70–90.

Mitchell, E.K. and Davis, J.H. (1984) Spontaneous births into toilets, *J. of Forensic Sci.*, 29(2), 591–596.

Mohr, J.C. (1978) *Abortion in America: The Origins and Evolution of National Policy, 1800–1900*, Oxford University Press, New York.

Montague, A.E. (1980) Introduction, in Montague, A.E., Ed., *Sociobiology Examined*, Oxford University Press, New York, 3–15.

Morgan, C. (1995) Psychosocial variables associated with teenage pregnancy, *Adolescence*, 30, 277–289.

Morrison, J. (1995) *DSM-IV Made Easy: A Clinician's Guide to Diagnosis*, Guilford, New York.

Morrison, T. (1988) *Beloved*, Plume, New York.

Moss, D.C. (August 1, 1988) Postpartum psychosis defense, *ABA Journal*, p. 22.

Most, D. (1999) *Always in Our Hearts: The Story of Amy Grossberg, Brian Peterson, and the Baby they Didn't Want*, Record Books, Hackensack, NJ.

Munoz, R.A. (1985) Postpartum psychosis as a discrete entity, *J. of Clin. Psychiatr.*, 46, 182–184.

Murphy, P. (1994) Scott's disappointments: reading *The Heart of Midlothian, Mod. Philology*, 92(2), 179–198.

Myers v. Commonwealth 1780-92-1, WL389 748 (Va. Ct. App. 1994).

Nadeau, M. (1997) Parents killing children: a revised typology of filicide, paper presented at the Ann. Meeting of the American Psychological Association, Chicago, IL.

Napier, K. (1997) Chastity programs shatter sex-ed myths, *Policy Rev.*, 83, 12–15.

Neal, O.R. (1995) National issues: myths and moms: images of women and termination of parental rights, *Kansas J. of Law and Public Policy*, 5, 61–71.

Nelson, A.L. (1991). Postpartum psychosis: a new defense?, *Dickinson Law Rev.*, 95, 625–650.

New South Wales Law Reform Commission (1997) *Partial Defences to Murder: Provocation and Infanticide*, New South Wales Law Reform Commission, Sydney, Australia.

Newman, K. (1996) *Fetal Positions, Individualism, Science, Visuality,* Stanford University Press, Stanford, CA.

News in Brief (October 31, 1997) *The Philadelphia Inquirer,* p. A4.

Nieland, M.N.S. and Roger, D. (1997) Symptoms in post-partum and non-post-partum samples: implications for postnatal depression, *J. of Reprod. and Infant Psychol.,* 15, 31–42.

Noonan, J. (1970) An almost absolute value in history, in *The Morality of Abortion,* Noonan, J., Ed., Harvard University Press, Cambridge, MA, 55–63.

Oberman, M. (1996) Mothers who kill: coming to terms with modern American infanticide, *Am. Criminal Law Rev.,* 34(1), 1–110.

O'Donovan, K. (1984) The medicalisation of infanticide, *Criminal Law Rev.,* 259–264.

Ogle, R.S., Maier-Katkin, D., and Bernard, T.J. (1995) A theory of homicidal behavior among women, *Criminology,* 33(2), 173–193.

Ohio v. Hopfer, 112 OH App. 3d 521 (1996).

Olds, D., Henderson, C.R., Jr., Cole, R., Eckenrode, J., Kitzman, H., Luckey, D., Pettitt, L., Sidora, K., Morris, P., and Powers, J. (1998) Long-term effects of nurse home visitation on children's criminal and antisocial behavior: 15-year follow-up of a randomized controlled trial, *J. of the Am. Med. Assoc.* 280, 1238–1244.

Olsen, J.A., Weed, S.E., Ritz, G.M., and Jensen, L.C. (1991) The effects of three abstinence sex education programs on student attitudes toward sexual activity, *Adolescence,* 26, 631–641.

Oropesa, R.S., Landale, N.S., Inkley, M., and Gorman, B.K. (1999) Prenatal care among Puerto Ricans on the U. S. Mainland, paper presented at the Ann. Meeting of the American Sociological Association, Chicago, IL.

Overpeck, M.D., Brenner, R.A., Trumble, A.C., Tripiletti, L.B., and Berendes, H.W. (1998) Risk factors for infant homicide in the United States, *New England J. of Med.,* 339, 1211–1216.

Pact, an Adoption Alliance (1996) Overview of Pact, an Adoption Alliance, with questions and answers on adoption, *Is Adoption for You,* 1–11.

Parness, J.A. (1993) Pregnant dads: the crimes and other misconduct of expectant fathers, *Oregon Law Rev.,* 72, 901–918.

Pearlman, S.F. and Bilodeau, R. (1999) Academic-community collaboration in teen pregnancy prevention: new roles for professional psychologists, *Prof. Psychol.,* 30, 92–98.

People v. Andrea, FF 586, NYS 2d, NY App. Div. (1992).

People v. Apodaca, 76 CA App. 3rd 479; 1978 Cal. App. LEXIS 1145; 142 Cal Reptr.830.

People v. Avery, 88 IL App 3d 771; 410 NE 2d 1093 (1980).

People v. Biggs, 202 MI App. 450, 509 NW 2d 803 (1993).

People v. Campbell, 159 IL 9; 42 NE 123 (1895).

People v. Doss, 214 IL App. 3d 1051; 574 NE 2d 806 (1991).

People v. Ehler, 1-93-1518 274 IL App. 3rd 1026 (1990).

People v. Goodrum, 152 WI 2d 540, 449 NW 2d 41 (WI App. 1989).

People v. Keeler, 2 al. ed 619; 470 P. 2d 617 (1970). CA Rptr. 481; 40 LR 3d 420.

People v. Kirby, 223 MI 440; 194 NW (1923).

People v. Massip, 274 CA Rptr. 369, 798 p. 2d 1212 (1990).

People v. Sophia M. 234 CA Reptr. 698 (Cal. Ct. App. 1987).

People v. Wernick, 89 NY 2d 111; 674 NE 2d 322 (1996); 651 NYS 2d 392.

People v. Westfall, 198 CA App.; 18 CA Rptr. 3561 (1961).

Pernick, M.S. (1996) *The Black Stork: Eugenics and the Death of "Defective" Babies in American Medicine and Motion Pictures Since 1915*, Oxford University Press, New York.

Petchesky, R.P. (1981) Antiabortion, antifeminism, and the rise of the New Right, *Feminist Stud.*, 7, 206–246.

Petchesky, R.P. (1990) *Abortion and Woman's Choice: The State, Sexuality, and Reproductive Freedom*, Northeastern University Press, Boston.

Piers, M.W. (1978) *Infanticide*, W. W. Norton, New York.

Pinholster, G. (1995) Multiple "SIDS" case ruled murder, *Science,* 268, 494.

Pinker, S. (November 2, 1997a) Why they kill their newborns, *The New York Times Magazine*, pp. 52–54.

Pinker, S. (1997b) *How the Mind Works*, W. W. Norton, New York.

Pipher, M. (1994) *Reviving Ophelia: Saving the Selves of Adolescent Girls*, Ballantine Books, New York.

Planned Parenthood of Southeastern Pennsylvania, et al., v. Robert P. Casey, et al., 505 U.S. 833; 112 S. Ct. 2791 (1992).

Poland, S.C. (1997) Landmark legal cases in bioethics, *Kennedy Inst. of Ethics J.*, 7(2), 191–209.

Pomeroy, S.B. (1993) Infanticide in Hellenistic Greece, in *Images of Women in Antiquity,* Cameron, A. and Kuhrt, A., Eds., Wayne State University Press, Detroit, 207–219.

Posner, R. (1998) Lecture: Oliver Wendell Holmes lectures. The problematics of moral and legal theory, *Harv. Law Rev.*, 111, 1637–1709.

Post, S.G. (1990) Infanticide and geronticide, *Ageing and Soc.*, 10, 317–328.

Prince v. Commonwealth of Massachusetts, 321 U.S. at 166 (1944).

Puit, G. (March 16, 1998) Experts offer reasons why teens kill their babies, *Las Vegas Rev.-J.*, p. 1A.

Putkonen, H., Collander, J., Honkasalo, M.L., and Lonnqvist, J. (1998) Finnish female homicide offenders, 1982–92, *J. of Forensic Psychiatr.*, 9, 672–684.

Quadagno, J.S. (1979) Paradigms in evolutionary theory: the sociobiological model of natural selection, *Am. Sociol. Rev.*, 44, 100–109.

Raghavan, S. (May 31, 1998) Seminar tells teens in Phila. why to say no to sex, *The Philadelphia Inquirer*, p. B2.

Ramsey, P. (1970) Reference points in deciding about abortion, in *The Morality of Abortion*, Noonan, J., Ed., Harvard University Press, Cambridge, MA, 60–89.

Ransel, D.L. (1988) *Mothers of Misery: Child Abandonment in Russia*, Princeton University Press, Princeton, NJ.

Ratner, R.A. (1985) A case of child abandonment — reflections on criminal responsibility in adolescence, *Bull. of the Am. Acad. of Psychiatr. and Law*, 13, 291–301.

Reagan, L.J. (1997) *When Abortion Was a Crime: Women, Medicine and Law in the United States, 1867–1973*, University of California Press, Berkeley, CA.

Reece, L.E. (1991) Mothers who kill: postpartum disorders and criminal infanticide, *UCLA Law Rev.*, 38, 699–757.

Reid, M.C. (1997) The case of *Medea* — a view of fetal-maternal conflict, *J. of Med. Ethics*, 23(1), 19–25.

Resnick, M.D. (1992) Adolescent pregnancy options, *J. of Sch. Health*, 62, 298–303.

Resnick, P. (1970) Murder of the newborn: a psychiatric review of neonaticide, *Am. J. of Psychiatr.*, 126, 1414–1420.

Reuters. (December 14, 1997) Girl, 11, asks judge for abortion, *The Philadelphia Inquirer*, p. A20.

Rhode, D.L. (1992) Politics and pregnancy: adolescent mothers and public policy, *South. Calif. Rev. of Law and Women's Stud.*, 1, 99–132.

Rhoden, N.K. (1988) Litigating life and death, *Harv. Law Rev.*, 102, 375–442.

Richter, J.S. (1998) Infanticide, child abandonment, and abortion in Imperial Germany, *J. of Interdisciplinary Hist.*, 28(4), 511–551.

Riet, D. (1986) Infanticide et société au XVIIIe siècle, Bruits publics et rumeurs dans la communauté, *Ethnologie Française Nouvelle Série*, 18(4), 402–406.

Roberts, D.E. (1993) Motherhood and crime, *Iowa Law Rev.*, 79, 95–141.

Robinson, B.E. (1988) Teenage pregnancy from the father's perspective, *Am. J. of Orthopsychiatr.*, 58(1), 46–51.

Roe v. Wade, 410 U.S. 113 (1973).

Rose, L. (1986) *The Massacre of the Innocents: Infanticide in Britain 1800–1939*, Routledge and Kegan Paul, London.

Rothman, B.K. (1989) *Recreating Motherhood. Ideology and Technology in a Patriarchal Society*, W. W. Norton, New York.

Rothstein, M. (May 2, 1998) Now a warm welcome instead of a cold bath for a Harvard biologist, *The New York Times*, pp. B9, B11.

Rowe, G.S. (1991) Infanticide, its judicial resolution and criminal code revision in early Pennsylvania, *Proc. of the Am. Philos. Soc.*, 135(2), 200–232.

Ruble, R. (February 21, 1999) Number of abandoned babies rises, *Tulsa World*, p. 25.

Rue, V.M. (1985) Death by design of handicapped newborns: the family's role and response, *Issues in Law and Med.,* 1(3), 201–225.

Ruggiero, K. (1992) Honor, maternity, and the disciplining of women: infanticide in late nineteenth-century Buenos Aires, *Hispanic Am. Hist. Rev.,* 72(3), 353–373.

Russell, E. (October 14, 1998) Fox, Planned Parenthood at odds over vote on Title X amendment, *Jenkintown Times-Chronicle — Glenside News (Pennsylvania),* p. 19.

Ryan, J. (December 6, 1998) Freedom of choice, *San Francisco Chronicle,* p. 1.

Sadoff, R.L. (1995) Mothers who kill their children, *Psychiatr. Ann.,* 25, 601–605.

Salter, J. (April 24, 1998) Man accused of giving AIDS to son, *The Philadelphia Inquirer,* p. A2.

Sanger, C. (November 20, 1997) Pregnant teens hide behind denial, *Newsday (New York),* p. A49.

Sanger, C. (June 23, 1999) A humiliating choice, *The Philadelphia Inquirer,* p. A19.

Sauer, R. (1974) Attitudes to abortion in America, 1800–1973, *Population Stud.,* 28(1), 53–67.

Sauer, R. (1978) Infanticide and abortion in nineteenth-century Britain, *Population Stud.: A J. of Demography,* 32(1), 81–93.

Saunders, E. (1989) Neonaticides following "secret" pregnancies in seven case reports, *Public Health Rep.,* 104(4), 368–372.

Scheper-Hughes, N. (1989, October) The human strategy: death without weeping, *Nat. Hist.,* 8–16.

Schmall, L. (1996) Forgiving Guin Garcia: women, the death penalty and commutation, *Wis. Women's Law J.,* 11, 283–326.

Schroeder, T.L. (1993) Postpartum psychosis as a defense for murder?, *Western State Univ. Law Rev.,* 21, 267–293.

Schulte, R. (1984) Infanticide in rural Bavaria in the nineteenth century, in *Interest and Emotion: Essays in the Study of Family and Kinship,* Medick, H. and Sabean, W., Eds., Cambridge University Press, Cambridge, England, 77–102.

Schultz, M. (1991) The blood libel: a motif in the history of childhood, in *The Blood Libel Legend. A Casebook in Anti-Semitic Folklore,* Dundes, A., Ed., University of Wisconsin Press, Madison, WI, 273–303.

Schwartz, L.L. (2000) Adoption: parents who choose children and their options, in *Handbook of Couple and Family Forensics,* Kaslow, F.W., Ed., John Wiley, New York, 23–42.

Scott, W. (1830; reprint, 1994) *The Heart of Midlothian,* Penguin Books, New York.

Scrimshaw, S.C.M. (1978) Infant mortality and behavior in the regulation of family size, *Population and Dev. Rev.,* 4(3), 383–403.

Sharp, D. (December 12, 1997) 3 parents held in fatal fire in W. Va., *The Philadelphia Inquirer,* p. A40.

Shedd v. State, 178 GA 653 173 SE 847 GA (1934).

Sherman, S.L. (1981) Note and comment: guilty but mentally ill: a retreat from the insanity defense, *Am. J. of Law and Med.*, 7, 237–264.

Short, R. (1998) Teaching safe sex in school, *Int. J. of Gynecol. and Obstet.*, 63, S147–S150.

Shorter, E. (1975) *The Making of the Modern Family*, Basic Books, New York.

Showalter, E. (1980) Victorian women and insanity, *Victorian Stud.*, 23, 157–180.

Siegel, C.D., Graves, P., Maloney, K., Norris, J.M., Calonge, B.N., and Lezotte, D. (1996) Mortality from intentional and unintentional injury among infants of young mothers in Colorado, 1986 to 1992, *Arch. of Pediatr. and Adolescent Med.*, 150, 1077–1083.

Silva, J.A., Leong, G.B., Dassori, A., Ferrari, M.M., Weinstock, R., and Yamamoto, J. (1998) A comprehensive typology for the biopsychosociocultural evaluation of child-killing behavior, *J. of Forensic Sci.*, 43, 1112–1118.

Silverman, R.A. and Kennedy, L.W. (1988) Women who kill their children, *Violence and Victims*, 3(2), 113–127.

Simpson, C. (February 12, 1999) Woman guilty of killing baby for insurance, *Chicago Sun-Times*, p. 9.

Singer, P. (1975) *Animal Liberation: A New Ethic for Our Treatment of Animals*, Random House, New York.

Singer, P. (1979) *Practical Ethics*, Cambridge University Press, Cambridge, MA.

Singer, P. (1981) *The Expanding Circle: Ethics and Sociobiology*, Farrar, Strauss, and Giroux, New York.

Singleton v. State, 33 AL App. 536; 35 So. 2d 375 (1948).

Smithey, M. (1998) Infant homicide: victim/offender relationship and causes of death, *J. of Fam. Violence*, 13, 285–297.

So you're going to be a mother (1999) *Teen Voices*, 8(1), 23–29.

Sobol, M.P. and Daly, K.J. (1992) The adoption alternative for pregnant adolescents: decision making, consequences, and policy implications, *J. Soc. Issues*, 48, 143–161.

Solinger, R. (1990) The girl nobody loved: psychological explanations for white single pregnancy in the pre-*Roe v. Wade Thomas* era, 1945–1965, *Frontiers*, 11(2/3), 45–54.

Solinger, R. (1992) Race and "value": black and white illegitimate babies in the U.S.A., 1945–1965, *Gender and Hist.*, 4(3), 343–363.

Sollum, T. (1997) State actions in reproductive health issues in 1996, *Fam. Plann. Perspect.*, 29(1), 35–40.

Spielvogel, A.M. and Hohenor, H.C. (1995) Denial of pregnancy: a review and case reports, *Birth*, 22(4), 220–226.

State v. Buffin, 511 So. 2d LA Ct. App. (1987).

State v. Doyle, 287 NW 2nd NE (1978).

State v. Hopfer, 679 NE 2d, 328 OH Ct. App. (1996).

State v. Maurico, Supreme Ct. AL 523 So. 2d 87 (1987).

State v McGuire, 200 W. VA 823; 490 SE 2d 912 (1997).

State v. McKown, 475 NW 2d 63 (MN 1991). (See *Juvenile and Fam. Law Dig.*, February 1992, 79–80.)

Stevens-Simon, C. and Kaplan, D. (1998) Teen childbearing trends: which tide turned when and why?, *Pediatrics,* 102, 1205–1207.

Stevens-Simon, C. and McAnarney, E.R. (1994) Childhood victimization: relationship to adolescent pregnancy outcome, *Child Abuse and Neglect,* 18, 569–575.

Stinson, R. and Stinson, P. (1981) On the death of a baby, *J. of Med. Ethics,* 8, 5–18.

Stoiber, K.C., Anderson, A.J., and Schowalter, D.S. (1998) Group prevention and intervention with pregnant and parenting adolescents, in *Handbook of Group Intervention for Children and Families*, Stoiber, K.C. and Kratochwill, T.R., Eds., Allyn and Bacon, Boston, 280–306.

Stout, J.W. and Rivara, F.P. (1989) Schools and education: does it work?, *Pediatrics,* 83, 375–379.

Straight, S. (January 25, 1998) Very first person: the secret of motherhood: birth may come naturally, sometimes unexpectedly, but nurturing must be learned, *Los Angeles Times*, p. 14.

Sunstein, C.R. (1992) Neutrality in Constitutional law (with special reference to pornography, abortion, and surrogacy), *Columbia Law Rev.,* 92, 1–52.

Sussman, G.D. (1975) Wet-nursing business in the nineteenth century, *Fr. Hist. Stud.,* 9(2), 304–328.

Symonds, D.A. (1997) *Weep Not for Me. Women and Ballads and Infanticide in Early Modern Scotland*, Pennsylvania State University Press, University Park, PA.

Taylor, T.S. (April 7, 1998) Woman with disorder gets probation in infant's death, *Chicago Tribune*, p. 1.

Thane, P. (1979) Women and the poor Law in Victorian and Edwardian England, *Hist. Workshop J.,* 6, 29–51.

Thomas, J. (December 4, 1998) Man accused of injecting HIV in son, *The New York Times*, p. A18.

Thompson, K.R. (1998) Comment: the putative father's right to notice of adoption proceedings: has Georgia finally solved the adoption equation?, *Emory Law J.,* 47, 1475–1509.

Tilly, L.A., Scott, J.W., and Cohen, M. (1976) Women's work and European fertility patterns, *J. of Interdisciplinary Hist.,* 6(3), 447–476.

Tobin, E. (1993) Law and literature: imagining the mother's text: Toni Morrison's *Beloved* and contemporary law, *Harvard Women's Law J.,* 16, 233–273.

Toufexis, A. (April 11, 1994) When is crib death a cover for murder?, *Time,* 143(15), 63–64.

Trachtenberg, J. (1943) *The Devil and the Jews: The Medieval Conception of the Jew and Its Relation to Modern Anti-Semitism*, Yale University Press, New Haven.

Trexler, R. (1973) The foundlings of Florence 1395–1455, *Hist. of Childhood Q.*, 1(4), 259–275.

Tribe, L. (1990) *Abortion: The Clash of Absolutes*, W. W. Norton, New York.

U.S. v. Washington, ex Rel. Jones v. Washington, 836 F. Supp. 502 (ND IL 1993).

U.S. v. Welch. U.S. App. (1994).

Valverde, L. (1994) Illegitimacy and the abandonment of children in the Basque country, 1550–1800, in *Poor Women and Children in the European Past,* Henderson, J. and Wall, R., Eds., Routledge, London, 51–64.

Van Biema, D. (August 31, 1998) Faith or healing? Why the law can't do a thing about the infant-mortality rate of an Oregon sect, *Time*, pp. 68–69.

Vance, P.C. (1985) Love and sex: can we talk about that in school?, *Childhood Educ.*, 61, 272–276.

Vasillopoulos, C. (1994) *Medea* and the transformation of the tragic polis, *Soc. Sci. J.*, 31(4), 435–461.

Ventura, S.J. (1984) Trends in teenage childbearing, United States, 1970–81. *Vital and Health Stat.*, Series 21, No. 41, DHHS Pub. No. (PHS) 84-1919, Public Health Service, U.S. Government Printing Office, Washington, D.C.

Ventura, S.J., Martin, J.A., Curtin, S.C., and Mathews, T.J. (1999a) Births: final data for 1997, *Nat. Vital Stat. Rep.*, National Center for Health Statistics, Hyattsville, MD, 47(18).

Ventura, S.J., Mathews, T.J., and Curtin, S.C. (1999b) Declines in teenage birth rates, 1991–98: update of national and State trends, *Nat. Vital Stat. Rep.*, National Center for Health Statistics, Hyattsville, MD, 47(26).

Waggoner, M. (October 22, 1999) Good child care pays years later, study says, *The Philadelphia Inquirer*, p. A3.

Waldron, K. (1990) Postpartum psychosis as an insanity defense: underneath a controversial defense lies a garden variety insanity defense complicated by unique circumstances for recognizing culpability in causing, *Rutgers Law J.*, 21, 669–697.

Waltner, A. (1995) Infanticide and dowry in Ming and Early Qing China, in *Chinese Views of Childhood*, Kinney, A.B., Ed., University of Hawai'i Press, Honolulu, 193–219.

Ward, L.M. (1995) Talking about sex: common themes about sexuality in the prime-time television programs children and adolescents view most, *J. of Youth and Adolescence*, 24, 595–615.

Weaver, P. (June 10, 1998) Suspect in toddler's death "snapped" over dirty diaper, *Tulsa World*, p. 12.

Weaver v. State, 24 AL App. 20B; 120 So. 706 (1931).

Weber, D.W. and Bosworth, C. (1991) *Precious Victims*, Signet Books, New York.

Webster v. Reproductive Health Services, 109 S. Ct. 3040 (1989).

Weckerle, C. and Wolfe, D.A. (1998) Windows for preventing child and partner abuse: early childhood and adolescence, in *Violence Against Children in the Family and the Community*, Trickett, P.K. and Schellenbach, C.J., Eds., American Psychological Association, Washington, D.C., 339–369.

Weisenburger, S. (1998) *Modern Medea. A Family History of Slavery and Child Murder from the Old South,* Hill and Wang, New York.

Werblowsky, R.J.Z. and Wigoder, G., Eds. (1965) *The Encyclopedia of the Jewish Religion,* Holt, Rinehart, and Winston, New York.

Werner, O.H. (1917; reprint, 1960) *The Unmarried Mother in German Literature with Special Reference to the period 1770–1800,* AMS Press, New York.

Wexler, D.B. (1997) Therapeutic jurisprudence in a comparative law context, *Behav. Sci. and the Law,* 15, 233–246.

Wexler, D.B. and Winick, B.J. (1991) Therapeutic jurisprudence as a new approach to mental health law policy analysis and research, *Univ. of Miami Law Rev.,* 45, 979–1004.

Wheeler, K.H. (1997) Infanticide in nineteenth-century Ohio, *J. of Soc. Hist.,* 31(2), 407–418.

Wheelwright, J. (July 28, 1998) Women: a life given … and taken. How can a woman manage to conceal her pregnancy for nine long months, then kill her newborn baby?, Julie Wheelwright reports, *The Manchester Guardian,* p. T4.

Whitner v. State of South Carolina, Opinion No. 24468 (1997).

Wilczynski, A. (1991) Images of women who kill their infants: the mad and the bad, *Women and Criminal Justice,* 2(2), 71–88.

Wilczynski, A. (1997a) *Child Homicide,* Greenwich Medical Media Ltd., London.

Wilczynski, A. (1997b) Mad or bad?, *The Br. J. of Criminology,* 37, 417–436.

Wilczynski, A. and Morris, A. (1993) Parents who kill their children, *Criminal Law Rev.,* 31–36.

Wiley, C. (1990) Staging infanticide: the refusal of representation in Elizabeth Robin's *Alan's Wife, Theatre J.,* 42(4), 432–446.

Wilkey, I., Pearn, J., Petrie, G., and Nixon, J. (1982) Neonaticide, infanticide, and child homicide, *Med., Sci., and the Law,* 22, 31–34.

Williams, B.J. (1981) A critical review of models in sociology, *Annu. Rev. of Anthropol.,* 10, 163–192.

Williams, G. (1978) The legal evaluation of infanticide, in *Infanticide and the Values of Life,* Kohl, M., Ed., Prometheus Books, Buffalo, NY, 115–130.

Williamson, G.L. (1993) Postpartum depression syndrome as a defense to criminal behavior, *J. of Fam. Violence,* 8, 151–165.

Williamson, L. (1978) Infanticide: an anthropological analysis, in *Infanticide and the Value of Life,* Kohl, M., Ed., Prometheus Books, Buffalo, NY, 61–73.

Wilson, E.O. (1980) *Sociobiology* (abridged ed.), Belnap Press of Harvard University Press, Cambridge, MA.

Wilson, E.O. (1990) Biology and the social sciences, *Zygon,* 25(3), 245–262.

Wilson, E.O. (1998) *Consilience: The Unity of Knowledge,* Knopf, New York

Wilson, J.Q. (1994) On abortion, *Commentary,* 97(1), 21–37.

Wilson, S. (1988) Infanticide, child abandonment, and female honour in nineteenth-century Corsica, *Comparative Stud. in Soc. and Hist.,* 30(4), 762–783.

Winick, B.J. (1997) The jurisprudence of therapeutic jurisprudence, *Psychol., Public Policy, and Law,* 3, 184–206.

Winpisinger, K.A., Hopkins, R.S., Indian, R.W., and Hostetler, J.R. (1991) Risk factors for childhood homicides in Ohio: a birth certificate-based case-control study, *Am. J. of Public Health,* 81, 1052–1054.

Wissow, L.S. (1998) Editorial: infanticide, *New England J. of Med.,* 339(17), 1239.

Wolman, B.B., Ed. (1965) *Handbook of Clinical Psychology,* McGraw-Hill, New York.

Wright, R. (1994) *The Moral Animal: Evolutionary Psychology and Everyday Life,* Pantheon Books, New York.

Wrightsman, L.S., Nietzel, M.T., and Fortune, W.H. (1998) *Psychology and the Legal System,* 4th ed., Brooks/Cole, Pacific Grove, CA.

Wrightson, K. (1982) Infanticide in European history, *Criminal Justice Hist.,* 3, 1–20.

Wurf, M.K. (Summer 1997) Welfare Reform Bill tackles teen pregnancy, *Girls Ink,* p. 3.

Yorker, B.C. (1995) Current topics in biomedical ethics: covert video surveillance of Munchausen Syndrome by Proxy: the exigent circumstances exception, *Health Matrix: J. of Law — Med.,* 5, 325.

Zajac, B.M. (1989) Legal issues in neonatal intensive care. *Hosp. and Health Sci. Adm.,* 34(4), 578–587.

Zibart, E. (1996, August) The *Medea* syndrome: women who murder their young, *Cosmopolitan,* 176–179.

Zimmer, C. (1996) First, kill the babies: evolutionary explanations for infanticide, *Discover,* 17(9), 72–81.

Zingraff, M. and Thomson, R. (1984) Differential sentencing of women and men in the U.S.A., *Int. J. of the Sociol. of Law,* 12, 401–413.

Zitella, J.J. (1996) Note: protecting our children: a call to reform state policies to hold pregnant drug addicts accountable, *John Marshall Law Rev.,* 29, 765–798.

Zurzola, A. (June 10, 1998) Dad weeps for mom who vanished, left baby in toilet, *The Bergen County Record (New Jersey),* p. a3.

Index

A

Abandonment, 32, 70, 75
  concealment of, 74
  in France, 34
Abortion(s), 23, 49, 119, 123
  as alternative to neonaticide, 32
  case involving religion and, 62
  contemplation of, 61
  controversy, 120
  on demand, 63, 121
  in later trimesters, 124
  partial, 122
  reasoning to permit, 121
  women enduring, 2
Abstinence
  education, 139, 140
  -only philosophy, 141
  prolonged, 23
Abuse of corpse, 112
Adam Bede, 12, 13
Adolescent fathers, 66
Adolescent mother groups, program for, 148
Adoption, 31, 49, 58
  as historic alternative, 149
  place for, 67
  as response to unwed pregnancy, 69
Adultery, 27
AIDS, 94, 138, 140, 149
Alan's Wife, 15
Amenorrhea, 50
American law, 85
American stereotype, 77
Amniocentesis, 120
Ancient cultures, legacies of, 4
Anger, 101
Anglo-American laws, 83
Animal rights, 132

Anthropologists, 19
Anxieties, chronic, 134
Arson, 54
Asian cultures, 26

B

Baby Doe case, 131
Babysitting, 95
Basque country, 34
Bavaria, study of neonaticide, 29
Beatings, 52, 98
Beloved, 14
Biosocial illness, 105
Birth control, 129, 144
Blood, HIV-tainted, 93
Blue-collar workers, 99
Breastfeeding regulations, 68
Brief Psychotic Disorder, 106
Britain
  law in, 84
  national mortality rate for infants, 34

C

Canon Law, of Catholic and Protestant
      churches, 5
Caretaker, children's, 96
Catholic church
  Canon Law of, 5
  perception of life by, 120
Centers for Disease Control and Prevention,
      41
Charges, variations in, 79
Child
  abuse, 98